PRAISE FOR

SPECTACULAR IN A LOSING EFFORT

"*In Spectacular in a Losing Effort*, author Jerry F. Pillarelli takes the reader along for the ride in such a descriptive manner that you will think that you were actually there. Reflecting on the remarkable highs and lows of his life, Pillarelli's journey takes you to every corner of the nation, world, and even up to the stars. This book is 'spectacular' in every way!

— MARCUS HEERDT, AUTHOR AND TRAVEL WRITER

"A travel memoir that grabs the reader's attention from the opening scene and doesn't let go until the last line. If you're ready for a ride on the truly wild side, read this funny, moving, and occasionally revelatory memoir. It's the journey, not the destination, Pillarelli reminds us, and when we have the courage to follow our dreams, the trip will be spectacular."

— KELLY J. BEARD, AWARD-WINNING AUTHOR OF
THE MEMOIR, *AN IMPERFECT RAPTURE*

"Did the fire department come or not?" I asked myself this question at the end of page four of *Spectacular in a Losing Effort*. I received the answer many exciting and entertaining pages later, in which Jerry gives deep insights into his life and his thoughts. He tells the story of his life to date, starting with his travels in his early youth, his time in the military and his professional life up to the present day, with a great deal of humor, lively and vividly - at times I had the feeling that I was right in the middle of the action. In his stories, he skillfully combines his travel reports with information that can be helpful for your own travel planning, this also applies to his photo tips. You can really lose track of time when reading his adventures - at least that's how I felt. And did the fire department come? Well, read for yourself!

Spectacular
IN A
LOSING EFFORT

A TRAVEL MEMOIR

JERRY F. PILLARELLI

For information about this title or to order other books and/or
electronic media, contact the publisher:
Jerry F. Pillarelli
Tucson, AZ

All photos including cover photo by Jerry F. Pillarelli

Cover and interior design by The Book Cover Whisperer:
OpenBookDesign.biz

Publisher's Cataloging-in-Publication data
Names: Pillarelli, Jerry F., author.
Title: Spectacular in a losing effort : a travel memoir / Jerry F. Pillarelli.
Description: Tucson, AZ: Jerry F. Pillarelli, 2024.
Identifiers: ISBN: 979-8-9892224-0-7 (paperback) | 979-8-9892224-1-4 (ebook)
Subjects: LCSH Pillarelli, Jerry F.--Travel. | Retirees--Travel--Anecdotes. |
Photographers--Biography. | National parks and reserves--United States. | United
States--Description and travel. |
Recreational vehicle living--United States. | BISAC BIOGRAPHY &
AUTOBIOGRAPHY / Personal Memoirs | TRAVEL / Parks & Campgrounds
Classification: LCC E160 .P55 2024 | DDC 917.3/04/92--dc23

Library of Congress Control Number: 2023923620

979-8-9892224-0-7 Paperback
979-8-9892224-1-4 eBook

Printed in the United States of America

FIRST EDITION

CONTENTS

Acknowledgments

A SPECIAL THANKS TO my editor, Julie Brock Reeves, for expertly refining the end product and for not charging me by the comma. To Susan Grattino for her marketing expertise. To Vicky Buckner for helping me navigate the social media world. To Dave Mason for building my book/author website, and to everyone who participated in my focus group review process. They all helped prove that it takes a village to make me an author as well as a viable member of society.

FIRE!

Beeeeeeeeep Beeeeeeeeep Beeeeeeeeep…

Jarred from a deep sleep I sat up in bed… "What the hell!" I bolted toward the ear-piercing sound and stood looking toward the front of my RV. Still muddled from being asleep, I tried to comprehend what I was seeing. "What is going on…what is going on?" Puffy, wispy strands of serene ashen smoke floated in the air in front of my refrigerator.

Beeeeeeeeep Beeeeeeeeep Beeeeeeeeep…

I grabbed my glasses and took several steps until I was surrounded by the smoke. I checked the refrigerator settings display but it was blank. I dove to the floor at the base of my bed and pulled the cover off of the circuit breaker panel. The refrigerator breaker had tripped. It was off.

Now what? My mind raced as I tried to produce an answer.

I threw on a pair of shorts and the long-sleeved pullover I had worn the night before. Grabbed my keys, opened the linen cabinet, snatched my flashlight, and ran through the delicate bands of smoke toward the front of the RV. There I unlocked and threw open the door and bounded down the steps, running around the front of the vehicle to where the refrigerator vent was. I paused trying to comprehend the meaning of the smoke streaming upward from the vent.

"NO!"

I ran back inside through the still peacefully floating smoke and into my bedroom. Cell phone. I froze. Where is it? I looked around until my brain caught up with me. Plugged in next to the bed. I ripped the phone from the charger.

Shoes. I stuffed the phone in my pocket and grabbed my shoes and the socks I took off before I went to bed.

What else? I yanked open the drawer and snatched my emergency "go bag" as I headed back through the smoke to get the fire extinguisher near the front door.

I hit the steps and threw my shoes, socks, flashlight and go bag out the door and was about to grab the extinguisher when I remembered my laptop. Normally it would be open on top of my desk but I was planning to leave early in the morning for my next destination, so instead it was secured in the top drawer. I stumbled back into the cabin where the peaceful wispy smoke was turning into a thick dirty soul-crushing veil of soot. I fumbled with the latch of the strap that holds the desk drawers in place while the RV is moving. I ripped open the drawer, grabbed my laptop, and headed back toward the door. This time I took the fire extinguisher with me as I ran outside to where my go bag had landed and, as gently as possible, laid my laptop on it.

I sprinted around the vehicle to where I saw the smoke before…and now there was fire!

"NO!"

I pulled my phone from my pocket and punched in 6-1-1…damn…9-1-1.

I pulled the pin on the fire extinguisher.

"9-1-1 what is your emergency?"

"My RV is on fire!"

"What is your location?"

"I'm in the RV park…in La Grande."

"Which RV park are you in?"

"I don't remember the name; outside of La Grande…Hot…Lake…"

"Hot Springs. I am dispatching help now. Is everyone out of the vehicle?"

"Yes, please hurry!"

"What space are you parked in?"

"I don't know…" I remember thinking I was pretty sure they would be able to tell when they got here…

She started to say something else, but I put the phone down on the nearby electrical box and turned my full attention to the fire creeping upwards from the refrigerator vent on the side of my motor home…on the side of my *home*!

I trained the fire extinguisher on the expanding blaze and pressed the trigger.

"HELP…HELP!" I roared. For some reason I never yelled "FIRE!"

White powder sprayed from the nozzle onto the flames shooting from a spot a full four feet above me.

I yelled out again, "HELP…HELP!"

The spray fanned out from the tip of the extinguisher and there was a flicker as the powder hit its mark.

A man came up to me from the back of the RV.

"Is everyone out?"

"Yes."

"Have you called the fire department?"

"Yes."

He ran off toward the front of the vehicle just as the extinguisher spurted out its last gasp of fire-retardant powder.

I yelled, "NOOOO!" and slammed the extinguisher to the ground at my feet.

The fire had grown and was now leaping into the night sky above the roof of the RV! I froze for a split second trying to figure out what to do next. Water! I ran to the fresh water hose connected to the RV, locked behind a compartment door about ten feet from the rear of the vehicle. I reached into my pocked for my key chain and rummaged through the janitor-like collection of keys until I found the right one and opened the compartment door. I grabbed the hose and began to twist it off the RV connection, water spraying from it with each turn, until it was disconnected. I pointed the hose toward the fire with my thumb intensifying and focusing the stream of water. Unfortunately, the hose was connected to a water filter and a water regulator, so the effort produced little more than a misty haze.

Something in me still believed I could put out the fire until I glanced into the kitchen window and saw flames rolling across the ceiling, rolling like something you would see in a movie. I knew then I had lost the battle.

"NO…NO!" I violently threw the still sputtering hose to the ground and stood glaring at the intensifying flames.

At that moment I went from active participant to spectator, watching everything I owned burn.

Two

Start Your Engines

For as long as I can remember, every year around Easter, my parents packed up the car and headed out on the road to visit my grandparents in Arizona. It was something I always looked forward to and appreciated even more as I got older. Not only would we be spending time with Grandma and Grandpa Pillarelli, but we would also be heading to warmer weather and seeing the sights along the way.

Starting out just south of Chicago in our hometown of Dolton, we would trek westward. In the early days we followed a path along old Route 66 through places like Rolla, Missouri; Tulsa, Oklahoma; Amarillo, Texas; and our jumping off spot of Santa Rosa, New Mexico, where we started heading south.

There were the milestones along the way I always looked forward to. One of the first big ones was crossing the great Mississippi River. It was always interesting, going over the big steel bridge and pressing up against the window to try to look straight down at the expansive river. I can remember seeing it at flood stage when we crossed in Davenport, Iowa, one year. I was amazed to see the river overflowing the railroad bridge and rising within feet of the bridge we were driving across! And the years we crossed in St. Louis always gave us the opportunity to see the Great Gateway Arch. As we moved into Oklahoma the game was to be the first to see an oil well, but it had to be a working well to earn the twenty-five-cent prize, so we kept our eye out for that distinctive bobbing motion.

Then came one of the biggies: As we approached Tucumcari, New Mexico, we all started looking for the first mountain. It was actually a small butte, but after the flat grasslands of the Midwest and the even flatter and more desolate expanses of the Texas panhandle, the thing looked like Mount Everest and it marked our symbolic crossing into the West.

From there it was more mountains and sights that were foreign to us for all except two weeks out of the year. We would pass by White Sands National Monument and Dad would tell us about the nearby missile range where the first test atomic bomb was dropped. Shortly afterwards we would drive to Las Cruces over the San Andres Mountains where the Lost Padre Mine was said to be.

Then, once in Arizona, we would look for Texas Canyon, where boulders were stacked in odd formations and one even looks like a surfacing whale. When we saw the whale, we knew we were getting close to Tucson.

The trip took a minimum of two and a half days, but only because dad kept us moving on schedule and at a rapid pace. Up and out of the motels in the morning and on the road as soon as breakfast was done, we needed to cover a lot of territory each day.

Getting fuel was like a pit stop at the Indianapolis 500—gas and go! While the car was filling up, everyone made a trip to the restroom. If timed properly, and if everyone did their part, we would all be in the car and ready to go as the fuel bill was being paid.

One of the family's most unforgettable stories happened during one of our pit stops. This was a trip to Arizona just after my sister, Sue, was born and my mother's mom, Gramma 'Boda (kid-speak for Svaboda), from Minnesota was along for the trip. Mom and I were riding in the back with baby Sue strapped into her car seat and Gramma 'Boda up front with my dad. We pulled into the gas station and everyone swung into action. Being only about four years old, the actual details escape me, but I do remember Mom took me to the bathroom with her and when we came out, we were standing in the rain. Dad, Gramma 'Boda, baby Sue, and the Chevy were gone. (Dad was always a Chevrolet man, so even though I don't remember the car, I know it was a Chevy.) Apparently when Gramma 'Boda got into the car and shut the door, Dad thought everyone was onboard. Since the car was fueled up, it was time to get back on the road. I'm not sure how they realized we were missing, but they figured it out about a quarter mile down the road and made their way back to the service station to pick us up. I also don't remember how the conversation went once we got back in the car, or maybe I'm just blocking it out of my memory…

In the early years before sister Sue came along, I had the entire back seat to myself. As a three-year-old, I had some interest in the world as it flew by, but as you might expect when cooped up in the back of a car for 1,800 or so miles, boredom would set in. It was then I created a friend named Arnie. Arnie was actually my dad's boss' name and I heard him talking to my mom about him all the time. I don't know what the real Arnie was like, but in my make-believe and bored kid state he was a rough and tumble sort of guy. For instance, I would be sitting or lying on the back seat and Arnie would push me onto the floor. This happened all the time and more when my mom started turning around to ask me what happened. "Arnie did it! He pushed me!" I would reply. I'm pretty sure my parents were amused by Arnie and my make-believe back seat world, at least for the first few hundred miles…

Once Sister Sue grew older, the whole back seat dynamic shifted dramatically, and not to my liking! Sharing is not one of my strong points as many who know me will tell you, and I'm sure the episodes in the back seat on our trips are one of the reasons why. Or at least it's my assessment of the situation and how it plays into my personality to this day. And since Sue always blames my alleged torturing of her through the years for any

problem she might have, this seems to be a good place for me to make up…
ah, I mean, reveal to all how her invasion of my space affected me over time.

Obviously, when you stick a little sister into an enclosed area with the
kid who owns the aforementioned area, you're going to have problems.
And it doesn't help when said little sister makes up things to get her older
brother into trouble. If she sees this differently, she can write her own book!
Anyway, the trouble, no matter how it came about, led to the infamous back
seat line. It went right down the middle including the hump on the floor!
Now, to be fair I will admit to violating the back seat demilitarized zone
once or twice in an attempt to judge how strict the oversight was. In a space
as small as the interior of a car, it was pretty much as I expected—strict.
My mother acted to stem any advances in a swift manner, usually with
just a glance over her shoulder. All it took was the squeaky voice of my
little sister saying, "Mom, Jerry touched my side!" and I'd get The Look.
There was no due process, no hearings, just prairie-style justice as Mom
was judge, jury, and executioner with Dad waiting in the wings listening
in case he had to take extra measures once the car came to a stop for the
night. Lucky for me I don't remember any escalation ever needing to happen.

Generally, even after Sue came along and took over half of my…I
mean…our back seat, things ran pretty smoothly considering we were
locked in a car for two and a half to three days at a time. After all, it was
a fun time for all, Dad getting away from work and Mom and the kids
getting out of the everyday household grind. We all enjoyed the trip as
much as the destination.

But there was one thing no one enjoyed, no one looked forward to, no
one cared to discuss: the coffee can! I don't believe my parents are responsible for the discovery of this use of a coffee can, and although our prefer-
ence was Folgers, I'm quite sure many other brands would be acceptable,
but as a kid I didn't want to think about it. In case you haven't figured it
out yet let me spell it out for you. The coffee can, the large one-gallon size

with plastic lid, was used by us kids to go potty while in motion. Little bladders were not designed to hold liquids for long, so something had to be done to keep the trip on schedule. We had less than three days to get to our destination and we only stopped for fuel to keep the car running. The coffee can process wasn't so bad when I was the only back seat occupant, but things got a little more involved once Sister Sue invaded my space…I mean…took over half of my area…I mean…you know what I mean! At any rate, this wasn't such a tough process for me, but was quite a bit more difficult for Sue. To be honest, I don't remember this happening too much, so either the rules were relaxed after Sue came along or I was damaged by the whole thing and I'm blocking it out of my memory. And one other thing I can't quite remember is that my parents must have been dumping the can and washing it out at each stop, so it couldn't have been a favorite thing of theirs either. I wonder if they took turns or went all "rock, paper, scissors" to see who had coffee can duty?

Our family trips were pretty constant through the years: two weeks at Easter, Dolton to Tucson and back. Then there was the year that stood out as a sort of aberration, an extended trip that turned out to be my true introduction to the national parks.

It happened because my dad needed hernia surgery. He worked all his life as an appliance service repairman and at the time he was with a company based out of Gary, Indiana. Somewhere along the line, or maybe it was a progressive thing, he developed a hernia that needed to be repaired. All the lifting and moving of heavy appliances had caught up with him. He worked out a plan with his boss, Arnie, yes, the namesake of my back-seat character, which called for one month off for recovery time. I'm not sure this would be the case today, but this was the mid-60s when recovery time dictated longer rest periods for healing. He had the surgery followed by a short recuperation period at home, followed by what would become our grand tour of the west.

The ultimate destination, as always, was Tucson and Grandma and Grandpa Pillarelli, but with the extra time we could add a few more stops to the itinerary. Both Sue and I were now old enough to better appreciate what we were going to see along the way, and although I don't remember there being any back seat issues, that doesn't mean there weren't any. I can only guess our now advanced age meant we had settled down a little and the skirmishes were fewer and farther between. Then again, I'm not consulting my parents at the time I am writing this, so they may have a different view of the situation and the maturity level of those two kids in the back seat at the time. I'm going to say we were near angelic and leave it at that; they can also write their own book if they want to refute my version of the facts.

One other thing had changed, or in this case was missing altogether—the coffee can. I can only imagine it was gone because of several key factors, not the least of which was we had more time on this trip. Stops could be longer and more relaxed, and if need be, more frequent. In addition, we tended to spend more time in one place as we were actually visiting areas rather than just passing through them. Then there was the kid factor and presumably we were older, more mature and generally more in control of our bladders. But I don't want to bury the headline here. The coffee can was gone!

The first major stop was in Meadowlands, Minnesota, to visit my Gramma 'Boda. Meadowlands is approximately 45 miles northwest of Duluth and where my grandparents acquired 80 acres in the early 1930s, clearing the wilderness and farming the land to survive. My Grandfather Frank initially built a log cabin which my mother lived in for several years. This fact provided Sue and me with all the information we needed to give my mom a hard time. "Mom, did you know Abraham Lincoln?" we would ask when we wanted to get under her skin. This was usually met with The Look, a subtle way of telling us not to push any further.

Gramma 'Boda worked at the local school as a cook for most of her life because in 1948 Grandpa Frank, who was a County Commissioner at the time, was gunned down by a man who had been refused a local liquor license by the commissioners. After being rejected he returned with a gun and opened fire, killing my grandfather and two other board members. He then retreated into the woods and committed suicide. With kids to feed, Gramma's work at the local school cafeteria became the family's primary income. Although I never met my Grandpa Frank, we may have had a shared appreciation of travel and exploration because in 1928, he and a few of his buddies bought a Ford Model T in Mount Olive, Illinois, and took off on a cross-country road trip to California. Of course, calling it a road trip is somewhat a misnomer as there were no great cross-country interstates at the time. Instead, I'm sure it was a true adventure and they had to blaze a lot of their own trails as they went along!

After our visit with Gramma 'Boda we went west into South Dakota where we visited Badlands National Park and Mount Rushmore, and then on to Montana to see the Little Bighorn. I really don't remember much about any of them, and although they are incredible places to visit, nothing much stood out for me. You would think, for a kid my age at least, the site of four gigantic heads carved into rock on the side of a mountain would make some sort of impact, but for some reason it did not. I have no explanation. It must be a kid thing!

On the other hand, I do have vivid memories about our next two stops, Yellowstone and Grand Teton National Parks. Yellowstone made a clear impression on me because I remember some of the boiling hot pools and the sight of Old Faithful spewing forth in all its glory. And I remember that the mountains in Grand Teton on a cool overcast day looked massive from our view across Jackson Lake. I also remember the mosquitos there. They were huge and they were everywhere, so the stop by the side of the lake was a rather short one.

A more pleasant memory happened as we were driving through Yellowstone. Suddenly traffic ground to a halt and about ten cars ahead of us we could see the reason—BEARS…and not just bears, but a bear and her two cubs! This was exciting! I'd never seen real bears before. Oh sure, I had seen them once on a field trip to the Brookfield Zoo in Chicago, but they were behind glass and bars. These were REAL bears in a national park…in the wild! I remember not being happy they were so far away but as one car after the other drove past them we got closer to the wild bears. It was obvious what the draw was for the bears, as we watched people throwing food out their car windows and the bears going to retrieve and eat the food.

Now, even I knew you weren't supposed to feed wild animals and there were signs posted everywhere saying so, but that didn't stop anybody. Quite frankly that was none of my business right now, I was just thrilled to see the bears and they were getting closer by the minute! Finally, it was our turn! Dad rolled up slowly behind the only car between us and the small bear family. Mother bear was dealing with food being thrown from the car ahead of us and as we watched her, one of her yearling cubs strolled toward us on all fours. Now it was right alongside of us. My nose was glued to the back seat window as I watched this cub rise up on its hind legs and walk over to Dad's window! This cub wanted food and we all knew it. Dad frantically rolled up his window. There were no push button windows in those days, so he applied a lot of elbow grease instead. As the window closed the cub latched onto the car with his claws in the track between the glass and the door. I think Mom was yelling, "Go Jer, go!" and Dad slowly eased the car forward, leaving the cub standing there on his two hind legs looking like a little traffic cop as the other cars slowly passed by. What a thrill! You don't see anything like that in Dolton, Illinois!

Clearly, the bears were the highlight of the entire trip, and although we still had to make it down to Tucson, I don't really remember anything as spectacular as our wild bear encounter.

I do remember my parents having a brief discussion about stopping to see the Grand Canyon, but for some reason they decided against it. It was probably Sue's fault. We should have fed her to the bears! No matter, that national park place was cool!

Three

Development Years

Our yearly excursions from Illinois to Arizona continued through the 1960s but changes were looming. Not only had my second sister, Vicky, come along in August of 1969, but I was starting eighth grade a month later. Events like these within a middle-class family in a quiet suburb of Chicago were considered normal and hardly interesting or worthy of much discussion beyond welcoming the new baby, and commenting on how big I had gotten and how exciting it was that in a year I would graduate to high school. Unfortunately, it was the subject of graduating to high school that was the topic of the day, not only in our household but throughout the nation. As the end of the decade approached, the country boiled over with controversy and rage; the Vietnam War, racism, hippies, and politics all slamming together to the point where even the quiet suburbs were affected. For us, the primary issue was bussing. Instead of going to the nearby, nearly all-white Thornridge High School, the plan was for me to instead be bussed to Thornton High School, a nearly all-Black school in Harvey. The two schools are only a few miles apart but might as well have been on different planets. Irrational fear would dictate the next steps and the decision was made to move to Arizona.

Dad and I drove out to Tucson first, leaving Mom with baby sister Vicky and middle child Sue. The trip was like all of our trips out West, no messing around just driving. As always, we arrived at our destination in two and a half days. There were a few key differences, however, the first one being that this time we were pulling a small U-Haul trailer with the majority of the family's belongings, everything else was either sold in garage sales or given away to local relatives. Second, I was riding up front for the first time. It's a completely different experience when you're riding shotgun! So, when we hit the heat of the desert and the weight of the trailer started to overheat the engine, I was right in the middle of things as Dad took action to rectify the situation. The air conditioning went off, the windows went down, and the heater went on. He explained to me that running the heater would help cool the engine, but we definitely paid the price as we were scorched by the combination of the sun and the blasting heater. The extreme measures saved the day and allowed us to reach our destination without skipping a beat.

Once in Tucson we took up residence in the motel my grandparents owned on South 4th Avenue, the Park Motel would be our home base while we resettled as a family. Mom and the two girls would fly out sometime later and we eventually settled in a trailer home on the west side of town. Dad purchased a dry cleaning and coin-operated laundromat with a friend who also moved to Tucson from Chicago, and I would eventually get enrolled in my new high school to mark the completion of the moving process.

Looking back, I'm not sure things were any better than they would have been had we just stayed in Dolton and did the whole bussing thing. Cholla High School was a new school but because of overcrowding we were divided into shifts, morning and afternoon. For me that meant an early morning bus ride to school, large chaotic classes, and what seemed like an exceptional amount of homework. All that could be overcome, but it was the makeup of the school itself which made the whole move seem unnecessary. Cholla was predominantly Latino with white and black students as the minorities. There was even a whole new group I never dreamed I would be dealing with, the cowboys. These were individuals which could be better characterized as rednecks, and although not all were bad some of the more prominent cowboys were definitely troublemakers. How did one know who a cowboy was? Well, they wore the big cowboy hats and cowboy boots. It was not hard to distinguish them from the rest of the student population. In my first week at the school, I had heard there was trouble between some cowboys and Black kids and I saw several cowboys carrying around pieces of wood with nails stuck in them. I never saw or heard of any incidents, so someone obviously dealt with the matter quickly, but it was disconcerting all the same.

A year later we moved once again, this time just over the Tucson Mountains to a five-acre plot of land west of town that my grandparents had purchased after selling the Park Motel. This was their retirement landing spot, and we would be living out there with them. It was both interesting and isolating to live so far out of town and a world away from our suburban Chicago home. I'd always found the desert fascinating and now we were living in the desolate middle of it— saguaro cacti, palo verde trees, scorpions, snakes, and all! We were still in the same school district and Cholla would remain my high school, but now my bus ride was almost an hour each way. In addition, all the friends I had made in the trailer park were now too far away to keep in touch with except when I saw them at school. I lived on the family compound with little access to the outside world until my senior year when I was finally able to purchase my own car.

The rule in the Pillarelli household, decreed for me since I was the oldest, stated that before one could drive, one would have to be able to pay for their own portion of the insurance. Not particularly easy for a seventeen-year-old male in high school, especially one living in the middle of nowhere! I mean, if you had no transportation, how were you going to get a job to make the money you needed to pay for insurance so you could drive to a job? The ole catch-22. Early on there was an older woman down the street who paid me to water her plants several times a week and this made me a few dollars, but it was hardly going to provide me with enough money to pay for my insurance premiums. One day while riding my bike to my plant watering gig, a different lady stopped me to ask if I might be interested in another job. She lived a little farther down the road and was running a canary farm with about twenty pens that she could use help cleaning each week. Sure, I said, how hard could that be? So, on the following Saturday I rode over to her place. As I got closer, the squealing grew louder and louder until I could see the source—a building about one hundred feet long, undoubtedly filled with canaries. The tour of the facility was unlike anything I could have ever imagined. This was a full-time business geared toward shipping canaries to pet shops throughout the United States. There were twenty pens, each approximately six feet wide by eight feet long, housing one hundred birds per pen. My job, if I chose to accept it, would be to clean all the seed chaff and bird crap off of the floor and haul it outside to be discarded. Twenty pens, once a week for twenty dollars. This was big money compared to my plant watering job. I'm in! I would soon find out the pay was good for a reason. You see, to clean the pens, you would have to actually work under all those birds. No matter how hot it was, a long-sleeved shirt, hat, and facemask were required because while you were in there you were getting shit on by one hundred squealing birds! Sorry about the language here, but it can't be described any other way. If there was a television program in 1972 called "Dirty Jobs," this job would have easily qualified to be on it. But no matter, the object was to make some money, and out here in the desert this was as good as it got!

My two jobs paid off when I got my driver's license and was able to kick in for car insurance. This enabled me to drive the family car, a 1970 Chevrolet Impala with a 350 cubic inch V8 engine. These were, after all, pre-gas shortage days! I didn't get to use it much because it was our only car, but when I did, I enjoyed my independence to the fullest. Once, while coming back from taking the SAT for college with a carload of my fellow "scholars," I was hauling down a dirt road showing off my driving skills when one of the guys said, "You might want to slow down, there's a curve up ahead." Unfortunately, I was just topping a rise in the road, so by the time I saw the curve I was already in it, and it was actually an S-curve. I cranked it hard left into the turn and then back right and then left again and before I knew it, we had spun around and were pointing toward the direction we had just come from. Luckily, we stayed on the road and didn't hit anything. I turned to look at my friends and they were all just sitting silently with their mouths open. To this day I still insist it was this incident that taught me what not to do when a car started to spin. My story is that I'm a better driver having gone through this experience. Needless to say, my parents didn't hear about this event until I was around fifty years old—way too old to be punished!

Halfway through my senior year of high school I had saved about two grand above and beyond what I would need to continue paying for my auto insurance, and it was time to get my own car so I could be even more independent. Dad would help with the search, which was primarily undertaken by digging through the want ads in the local papers. I don't remember how long we searched, only that one day we saw an ad for a 1970 Chevrolet Camaro for 2,000 dollars and I wanted it. I almost expected my folks to veto the choice outright, but there was absolutely no pushback and Dad took me across town to check out the car. It was awesome! White with blue interior, 307 cubic-inch V8 engine producing 200 horsepower and virtually spotless. This model, also known as the 1970 and a half, was the first of the second-generation Camaro and it was a sports car. Done deal. I bought it.

Now we were talking. No more school buses and I could get out with my friends and more importantly get a job in Tucson. I had a friend working as a busboy at the Tucson Racquet and Swim Club on the north side of town, quite a drive but there was money to be made there and the hours would permit me to work after school. The job also meant I could use the club on my time off, and since I had recently learned to play tennis, getting to use the courts would be a nice bonus.

I became a busboy extraordinaire, working not only the main dining room but also events in the upstairs bar and periodic Western cookouts for the week-long tennis camps held during winter months when the weather was beautiful, especially compared to the rest of the nation. During the school year I primarily worked weekends so as not to affect my schoolwork. It was only after I graduated that I took on the 3 to 11 p.m. shift, and without school hanging over me I was able to have a little more fun. Once our shifts ended, my friends and I would hang around the club, maybe take a swim, and then take off for an early morning snack at Denny's. A few times we even gambled everything and raced our cars down the empty streets. How we never got caught is a mystery and looking back, how we never wrecked is just dumb luck. During this period, I would often get home around four or five in the morning, sleep until 1 p.m., and then head back to work. I rarely saw my family and when I did it was just in passing as I went out the door.

A few notable events took place while I worked at the club, which provided me with a taste of the larger world around me. In 1974 the site was host to the American Airlines Tennis Tournament and I was thrilled to meet and get Arthur Ashe's autograph. I did the same with some of the great Hollywood actors of the day including Michael Landon, Lloyd Bridges, and James Franciscus. And in 1976, Jimmy Connors headlined the U.S. Davis Cup team in an early round sweep over Venezuela.

In addition, NFL quarterback Jim Plunkett was staying at the resort on the day in 1975 when he was traded from the New England Patriots to the San Francisco 49ers. That was particularly interesting considering

I knew of the trade before the rest of the world and even picked up the telegram sent to Plunkett confirming the deal.

But these all pale in comparison next to having served Moses! Charlton Heston, the legend from the movie *The Ten Commandments* in the flesh, stayed in the resort casitas for about a week while on business in Tucson and each evening came in for a quiet dinner. I couldn't have been more ecstatic if it had actually been Moses!

Since we left Chicago there had been no extended vacations. The best my family could muster was our yearly Labor Day trip up to the Kitt Peak Observatory picnic grounds about an hour from our home. We would pack up the family, including Grandma and Grandpa Pillarelli, wrap up a lunch of some kind, and head down the road, arriving around noon. At approximately 6,800 feet, the mountain was much cooler than the desert this time of year, where the temperatures could still reach 100 degrees even in September. Once we found the perfect picnic site, we would unload everything and everybody and commence picnicking. We'd chow down on sandwiches and potato salad or maybe chicken and coleslaw. Lunch was over in about an hour, and we would immediately begin to pack everything and everybody back into the car and head home. The entire outing took, maybe four hours door to door! These events were legendary and are still talked about at almost every family gathering to this day!

Obviously, I was craving some adventure and the Kitt Peak jaunts just didn't cut it. So immediately after graduation in 1975 I took off with friend and fellow graduate Russ to the San Francisco area. Russ had family in the area so we would have a place to crash for at least part of the trip. The plan was to tour some of the city and take in a few baseball games as my team, the Chicago Cubs, were scheduled to play the Giants at Candlestick Park during the week we were there.

We left Tucson and drove straight through to the Bay Area, arriving late at night. Russ didn't want to go to his family's place so late because he didn't want to wake them. I could understand his reasoning, but we were working on a tight budget and getting into a hotel would drain our cash levels and leave us with less "walkin' around money." Russ came up with the idea to find a place to park and just spend the night in the car and I agreed. After driving around for a while, we finally settled on a well-lit parking lot. I took the back seat and Russ took the front and we drifted off to sleep, waking up the next morning when the sun flooded the car through the partially open windows. We were so exhausted from the drive that both of us seemed to get a good night's sleep with the only disturbance being sirens blaring sometime around 1 or 2 a.m.

We drove to a nearby Denny's we saw the night before so we could fully wake up and grab some breakfast before heading to meet up with Russ's family. It was there we learned the sirens we heard were because of a double homicide less than two blocks from where we slept. Thinking about how vulnerable we were sleeping in an empty parking lot definitely woke us up.

We spent the next several days traipsing around San Francisco, in particular the wharf area and around the Presidio where we had a view of the Golden Gate Bridge. The skies were as clear and as blue as could be and I snapped a picture of the bridge with an Instamatic camera I brought along on the trip. We also took a ride across the San Francisco-Oakland Bay Bridge, where we were surprised to see the parking lot filled with cars at the Oakland Coliseum, home of the Oakland Athletics. Russ is a big Athletics fan, so he worried he'd misread the schedule because he was sure the team was supposed to be playing on the road this week. Not knowing what could be going on we decided to swing around and find our way back to the stadium. If there was indeed a game today, we wanted to attend. The place was packed, and when we got to the entrance we realized why. Billy Graham, the evangelical Christian preacher, was holding one of his "crusades" at the stadium. No need for us to stick around, so we headed on our way.

A few days later we had tickets for an actual baseball game. The Cubs were playing the Giants in a night game. Even during the warmest summers Candlestick Park would be cool to cold at night because it sat right on the bay and tonight would be no exception. There was a definite chill in the air, but along with it came the unmistakable smell of roasted peanuts, popcorn, and hot dogs.

Because neither the Cubs nor the Giants were any good that year, we were able to snag some field level seats behind home plate. The actual baseball game hardly even mattered. It was the atmosphere of a live Major League Baseball game that made this special.

Russ and I had taken in several of the local minor league Tucson Toros games, most notably the night the Toros were down 8–0 in the bottom of the ninth inning and roared back to win 9–8. Counting Russ and me, there were only twenty-five fans in the seats at the end. It was a memorable experience, but it was still the minor leagues.

I'd been to only a few Major League ballparks prior to this, once to Comiskey Park in 1968 to see the Detroit Tigers play the White Sox on a night where eventual thirty-one game winner Denny McLain beat the Sox. Then I went to Wrigley Field in 1971 where I got to see the Pittsburgh Pirates Roberto Clemente in a 12-inning game that ended when the Cubs Joe Pepitone hit a home run to deep right-center field.

Tonight's game would in no way rival either of those experiences. In fact, by the fifth inning we were bored, and Russ suggested we go take a walk to check out the game from the upper deck. No one was up there, but we figured that was just because the game wasn't sold out. We set out to find our way around the ballpark and to the upper deck in center field. It was an interesting view but the winds whipping through the park were even colder way up there, so we decided to return to our field level seats.

We headed into the upper deck concourse and were working our way to the ramp down to the lower level when a police officer called out to us. He yelled something like, "What are you guys doing up here?"

Russ replied with something to the effect of "What's it to ya'?"

I knew I would have to take charge of this situation and told Russ to shut up as I moved forward to talk to the cop. Apparently, there was some sort of city ordinance decreeing the upper deck off limits to all fans when no upper deck tickets were sold, so technically, we were trespassing. As Russ stood quietly mumbling to himself, I explained to the officer we were from out of town and just wanted to explore the ballpark, not having any idea it was a problem to be up here. He seemed to understand what we were up to and finally told us to head back down to the lower deck, which we did, and he followed us the whole way just to be sure.

IN THE FALL I enrolled at the University of Arizona as an astronomy major. The truth be told, I was unsure of both decisions. On the one hand, going to college just seemed like the thing to do, the next step after high school. I honestly didn't have any direction or a goal to work toward, so I was hoping something might come to me as I moved through the process. As for choosing astronomy as my major, well, when I first came to Tucson, I was amazed at what I saw in the night sky. The darkness, helped by strict city light ordinances, was filled with stars like I had never seen before. Planets, nebulas, and even the Andromeda Galaxy were visible with the naked eye, and one could identify the outline of our own galaxy of stars as well. I asked Santa for a telescope my first Christmas in Tucson and began exploring the universe, documenting the things I saw in a notebook. I would get up early in the morning to view meteor showers or lunar eclipses and dreamed of discovering something never before seen by human eyes. It only seemed natural to take something I was so interested in and try to turn it into a lifelong career.

Along with all the mandatory core freshman classes including English, history, and psychology, I also enrolled in the undergraduate courses for students in my major. This meant I would be taking an advanced derivatives class as well as Astronomy 101 for majors.

The first day in the astronomy course was classic. I sat down in an auditorium with over 200 other students and watched as the professor strolled in below me. The huge blackboard and the slope of the room made him look like he was at the bottom of a canyon. He threw his books onto the table and immediately announced the class name, just in case someone was here mistakenly, and then paused looking up at his crop of prospective astronomers.

"Everyone look to your right and to your left. Two of the three of you will make it through undergraduate astronomy courses. One of those two will make it to graduate school, and that person may end up with a job." He emphasized the word "may."

Of course, as with everyone else in that auditorium, I thought that person would be me. It wouldn't take long to understand how wrong I was, and the eye-opener would be the derivatives class. I didn't like math anyway, and in the back of my mind I knew in order to be an astronomer I would have to excel in advanced mathematics. It wasn't until I sat staring blindly at a blackboard full of equations, all of which somehow are used "to show the amount by which a function is changing at one given point or the slope of the tangent line at a point on a graph often written using dy over dx…" that I realized I might not be the one guy who may get a job in astronomy.

Going forward, things fell apart rather rapidly.

I was still living at home, twenty miles or so from the university, and still working at the racquet club at least five days a week to earn enough money to pay for gas and other essentials. Work, travel time, and a growing disinterest in school took its toll, and after two semesters of lackluster grades and dropped or incomplete classes, the writing was on the wall, at least for me.

So, when I sat down with my dad to let him know I was going to be dropping out of school, I thought I had figured out what my next steps would be.

"Things aren't going well in school, and I've decided not to go back next year."

"So, what are you going to do next?"

"I'm going to work full-time at the racquet club."

"Do you plan to be a busboy the rest of your life?"

"No, I want to be a waiter someday." I heard it as soon as it came out of my mouth. My plan sucked!

His eyes drilled right through me for what seemed like an hour or two, after which he noted I had a friend who had just enlisted in the Army and maybe I should look into the military too, you know, rather than simply aspiring to be a waiter.

I didn't have to think about it long and set out to see what my options would be. I visited a US Army recruiter who, after giving me the basic rundown on serving, set me up to take their aptitude test, which would then be used to determine what military jobs I might be qualified to get into. The results came back positive, and I was told I could do almost any-thing from being a boots-on-the-ground soldier to a whole list of technical positions that would require advanced training courses. I gravitated to a list of aviation-related positions and finally settled on the 35 Kilo MOS (Military Occupation Code), Avionics Technician. The position entailed working with the communications and navigations electronic equipment on fixed wing aircraft and helicopters. It could turn into a career, and if not, I would still be working with military aircraft, which seemed exciting.

With that, the only thing left to do before signing the enlistment papers was to determine where I would initially be stationed. It was important to me to know every possible detail of this before I made this crucial life pivot. The recruiter shuffled through a stack of papers and pulled out two possibilities based on the MOS I had chosen and the date of enlistment.

"The 35 Kilo school would be starting in January of 77. You would enter the service and boot camp in October of this year and based on those factors you could be stationed in Fort Campbell, Kentucky, or in the Second Infantry Division in South Korea."

I selected South Korea. If I'm going to do this, I'm going all the way!

Four

Traveling Army Style

After a two-day stay in Fort Jackson, South Carolina, just long enough to collect a duffle bag of Army issue clothes, boots, and supplies, I was ordered onto the third of five buses full of fellow enlistees bound for Fort Gordon, Georgia, where we would all begin to experience the true Army lifestyle in boot camp. In less than two hours all of our lives would change radically. Uneasiness hung in the air; we knew what was coming but had no idea how we would react to it or if we were truly tough enough to survive it.

We rolled through the main gate at Fort Gordon and pulled up to a set of old white two-story wooden buildings. Standing in a row were five men easily identifiable as Drill Sergeants because of the impeccably starched uniforms and distinctive olive drab wide-brimmed hat they each wore. Everyone watched as the five men marched to one of the stopped buses. Bus number one was boarded first and after no more than a minute recruits started running out of the bus down the street in front of the white wooden buildings, where they immediately fell into formation, five rows of six soldiers each, and stood at attention. Our bus filled with nervous murmurs as we watched the situation unfold knowing our time was coming. Bus two was next as the scene was repeated…now the door to our bus was flung open and a large Latino man entered and stood before us.

"I am Staff Sergeant Del Basque. You will call me Drill Sergeant. Is that understood?"

"Yes Drill Sergeant!" we responded in unison.

"I can't hear you!" he roared.

"Yes Drill Sergeant!" this time yelling at the top of our lungs.

"You are the Third Platoon and you will fall out in front of building three, is that understood?"

"Yes Drill Sergeant!"

"Fall out," he yelled as he exited the bus and we all jumped to our feet in unison and row by row departed in rapid succession. Like the two platoons before us, we had been taught at Fort Jackson how to fall into a formation and our fear of making a bad initial impression on our Drill Sergeant worked well for us as we executed the task at hand. I found myself in the middle of the fourth row, or squad, eyes forward, waiting for the next command. Drill Sergeant Del Basque informed us the Corporal standing next to him would now call out the roll and when we heard our name we would reply with "present."

As roll call began, the Drill Sergeant, reviewed his troops, stopping periodically to comment or yell into the face of one of my fellow platoon members. We all stood locked at attention, eyes forward, hoping not to draw the attention of our new leader. He finished the review of the first squad, moved through the second and the third, and rounded the corner to begin looking over my squad. As far as I could tell there was no discernable pattern that would indicate which unlucky soul would draw his attention next.

And now he was walking up to me; he turned and faced me, repeatedly poked his index finger into my chest and with his face just inches from mine said, "You're not going to make it, you puny punk!" Not exactly the glowing chamber of commerce kind of welcome I would have hoped for, but in an instant, it was over, and he moved on to his next victim.

The next eight weeks were spent either locked in our Korean War-era barracks or drilling to become soldiers. Marching, cleaning, and firing our weapons, pitching tents, going on grueling forced hikes with full backpacks and gear. The only break I got was the day I had KP—Kitchen Patrol—and missed the trip through the gas chamber. Instead of getting to experience what it felt like to inhale tear gas, I was peeling potatoes and stirring large pots of food for lunch. I knew I was fortunate, but it was obvious just how lucky I was when the company returned from their gas chamber excursion, eyes red and watering, not a smiling face in the crowd.

My first extended time alone away from home was certainly extraordinary as one might expect under the circumstances. Understanding what it meant to be a soldier and learning to work as one with the other soldiers helped me move through boot camp quite efficiently. Sergeant Del Basque's first impression of me, whether he meant it or not, would be wrong. Not only did I make it, but I became a squad leader and qualified as expert with the M-16 Assault Rifle, expert with grenades, and graduated at the top of my platoon with a promotion to Private, E2.

BOOT CAMP ENDED IN mid-December, and I found myself back home for the Christmas and New Year holidays. It would be January before I would have to return to Army life and this break allowed me to "detox" and begin to feel a little like my pre-boot camp self. Only it wasn't quite that easy. The eight weeks of military indoctrination was actually pretty effective in changing the way I thought and behaved. Obviously, the Army knew what they were doing and how to do it as they've had 200-plus years to refine the process.

My physical appearance had changed. Eight weeks of intensive workouts had turned me into a leaner version of my pre-Army self, and my hair was now just stubble as they kept us totally shaved during our training. But other things changed that were much more understated. I was more direct in addressing people. I stood straighter. And though I had always been a well-ordered individual, now I was keeping my things impeccably regimented—clothes hung facing the same way and spaced equally throughout the closet, t-shirts, underwear, and socks folded, shoes neatly in a row, and most importantly, bed always made with perfect hospital corners and tight enough to bounce a quarter off of it.

Everyone noticed and accepted the changes and understood it was still me with the added military programming layered on top. However, there was one modification people thought to be odd if not a bit troubling. I could eat any meal in fewer than twelve minutes, and often more quickly.

In boot camp there were five platoons of thirty soldiers for a total of 150 men in our company. The mess hall was a small wooden building much like our barracks, which would accommodate one platoon at a time; therefore, only thirty soldiers could be seated for any one meal. If each platoon were allowed an hour to eat it would take five hours to feed the company. If they were allowed thirty minutes each it would take two and a half hours to feed the company. You can see where this is going. Our Drill Sergeant's goal was to feed the entire company of 150 men in one hour. That's twelve minutes per platoon! And that's not sitting and eating time, the clock was started when the first member of a platoon walked in the door! It went something like this for each platoon: The clock would start and one man after the other entered the dining hall, each picking up a tray, fork, knife, spoon, and plate as he entered. As soon as the servers put food on your plate you began to eat it. As you might expect, there were no choices to be made, you simply ate what they gave you. As you exited the serving line you grabbed a plastic cup filled with either water, juice, or a soft drink (at least there was a choice to be made here) and headed for a table and sat down. At this point, depending whether you were at the front of the platoon or the rear, you had anywhere from ten to six or seven minutes to devour your meal and be out of the mess hall—not just finishing your meal, but having already eaten and deposited your dirty dishes, silverware, cup, and tray in the proper receptacles and be standing outside in twelve minutes flat. By then the next platoon was already hitting the service line to enjoy their twelve minutes of fine Army dining.

Now our leaders weren't barbarians. There were some Sunday dinners where they allowed us fifteen minutes per platoon and since we were in training on Thanksgiving Day, each was permitted to take up to twenty minutes.

With that as a backdrop, you could see why my family and friends were a bit concerned when I wolfed down food placed before me in record setting times. In fact, my mother had to tell me several times during Christmas dinner to slow down. To this day I still at times find myself shoveling meals into my mouth with reckless abandon. It is a remnant of my boot camp experience.

THE MILITARY CALLED ME back again in January, this time to begin my specialty training in avionics—the repair and replacement of aviation electronics. As it was, I was going back to Fort Gordon Georgia, site of my all-too-recent basic training. However, this time things would be different, still a heavy dose of military discipline but a lot more relaxed. We had barracks with four-person rooms rather than open rows of bunk beds; we had weekends off and were allowed to go anywhere on or off the base instead of being restricted to the boot camp compound; and most importantly, the large mess hall accommodated several hundred soldiers at a time and one could show up at any time during a two-hour period and sit down for as long as you liked to eat a meal as opposed to…well, see above.

When avionics school started, because I had already been promoted to Private, I was the ranking member of our twelve-person training class and would therefore be the squad leader.

Over the next fourteen weeks we would learn the ins-and-outs of working around military aircraft, primarily the Bell UH-1H Iroquois "Huey" helicopter and the Bell AH-1 Cobra gunship attack helicopter. Both models were present in our hanger workspace where we trained replacing "black box" electronic components for communications and navigations systems and learned to troubleshoot aircraft wiring issues.

While in training, life was campus-like, and even though there was little time for extracurricular activities during the week, I frequently went out with classmates for dinners and happy hours on the weekends. Since we were in the Deep South, two things drew my attention: golf, as the Masters would be played in April just down the road in Augusta, Georgia, and NASCAR (National Association for Stock Car Auto Racing).

My interest in NASCAR had been fueled back in Arizona when I watched the live broadcast of the end of the 1976 Daytona 500 where David Pearson and Richard Petty, battling for the lead, collided and spun each other coming out of turn four as they headed for the checkered flag. Both cars wrecked into the infield grass, but it was Pearson who was able to restart his car and crawl over the finish line to win the race, with Petty finishing second. The final laps of the race were amazing to watch and the combination of my interest in cars, speed, and the strategy of racing made me an instant fan.

Now I was living in the center of the NASCAR universe. Racetracks were all around me and I didn't want to pass up an opportunity to experience one of these spectacles. The Atlanta 500 was on the schedule for Sunday, March 20, now all I needed was a plan. I didn't have a car so I would have to catch a bus to and from the track in Hampton, Georgia about thirty miles south of downtown Atlanta. Greyhound had buses leaving from the fort direct to Atlanta and back, and there was a bus from Atlanta to Hampton on the morning of the race. I booked a ticket to Atlanta on Saturday, the bus to Hampton on Sunday morning, and the trip from Atlanta back to Fort Gordon for late Sunday evening. I also booked a hotel room in downtown Atlanta for Saturday night. The only hole in the plan was there were no buses leaving Hampton going to Atlanta after the race. No way I was going to let that little detail stop me, I was convinced I could hitchhike my way to the bus station…somehow. With all that in mind I purchased my ticket to the race, and I was all set to go.

I got up Saturday morning, made my way to the bus station, climbed aboard the sleek Greyhound bus and away we went. This was the only route that fit my schedule and it was a tedious one. Normal drive time from Fort Gordon to Atlanta is approximately two hours and twenty minutes, but this bus ride took six and a half hours! It was a mail stop bus, sort of like riding on the Pony Express, it stopped at every little town along the 156-mile route. We picked up people at some stops, but the real purpose was usually to grab a big white fabric bag with "U.S. Mail" emblazoned on it. Six and a half hours! That's an average of no more than twenty-four miles an hour!

We arrived in Atlanta late in the afternoon and luckily my hotel was within walking distance of the bus station. After sitting all day, it felt pretty good to get out and take a walk. It would be easy to find where I was staying since I could easily see the round glass encased Peachtree Tower, Atlanta's tallest building at seventy-three stories, and it was a beautiful sight! My hotel was directly behind it. An older brick building, maybe twenty stories, it was nothing special but would serve the purpose. I got into my plain drab room and hunkered down for the night in preparation for the big day, race day.

I was up early on Sunday morning to catch the bus to Hampton. The race would start at 1:00 p.m. The bus ride went smoothly, but the bus station was still several miles from the track, so I headed for the main road and stuck my thumb out looking for someone who might be headed to the race and willing to pick up a respectable looking clean-cut guy. I caught a ride with a family of four who were going to the race and in minutes we were in sight of Atlanta Motor Speedway. After being dropped off I found my way to the will call window and picked up my ticket so I could get inside and start looking around.

It was quite a sight: A one-and-a-half-mile oval track with twenty-four-degree banking in the turns. The only thing that could be cooler would be to watch the cars race on it.

The 500-mile race took three and a half hours to complete, was won by Richard Petty, and I enjoyed every lap. Next came the fun part, getting back to Atlanta.

There were 50,000 fans in the stands this day, so when the race ended, the roads around the track became a parking lot. I got back out to the main road to look for a ride, but everything was at a standstill, so I just started walking. It was now about 6:00 p.m., so I had roughly three hours to travel the thirty miles to downtown Atlanta. That was doable. I kept walking, not even trying to get a ride because I was moving faster than the traffic. Hampton was a one-horse town and the track had only two-lane roads radiating from it, so this was going to take a while to break up. I was beginning to worry about catching my bus, but I did remember there was another bus to the fort scheduled to depart sometime later. No doubt it was to catch stragglers returning to the base from wild weekends in Atlanta, or maybe a crazy race fan or two.

I was only a few miles from the track when traffic started to break up a little and it was already almost 8:00 p.m. It was looking more likely I was going to miss those buses. I was supposed to be in morning calisthenics formation at 6:30 a.m. sharp, and the Army frowns on soldiers being late to anything, let alone not showing up at all. So as the cars began to move at a brisker pace, I stuck my thumb out to see if I could get a ride. The cars roared by me without so much as a glance my way. I'm sure most people were frustrated by all the traffic and since they now had their foot on the accelerator, they weren't going to let off. Finally, an old beat-up Ford van pulled off the road and a young woman leaned out of the passenger window and asked me where I was going.

"Downtown Atlanta" I replied.

"We're not going that far but we can drop you near the airport."

"Perfect." It wasn't, but it was my best bet right now.

"Get in back," she responded.

The back door swung open to reveal a guy and a passed-out girl on an old mattress. I climbed in. I had no choice. They asked me what was going on and I explained my situation to them. The passed-out girl woke up and mumbled something, the guy sitting next to her laughed and shrugged his shoulders as if to indicate he had no idea what she said, and shortly thereafter we stopped so I could get out to continue my journey.

The new plan was to get myself to the airport where I could catch a cab to the bus station downtown. I hated to spend the extra money, but time was running out and I was almost certainly going to miss my first bus.

I was now on the entrance road to the airport, so I put my thumb out again and started walking. It took a while, but I finally got a ride from an older couple who dropped me at one of the concourses. From there I caught my cab.

By the time I arrived at the bus station it was after 9:00 p.m. I had missed my scheduled departure and would now have to hope I could get a seat on the next bus to Fort Gordon. Luckily, there was a midnight departure scheduled with seats available and the trip would only take about four and a half hours, not as many stops on the red eye back to the fort. At least I would get back in time for the morning formation and avoid the wrath of the U.S. Army.

By the time I arrived at my barracks it was roughly 5:00 a.m. so I had just enough time to clean up and get dressed for calisthenics. Somehow, I'd made it, and after this experience I was confident I could make it through just about anything.

AVIONICS TRAINING CAME TO an end in late April. I graduated at the top of my class and received a double promotion through Private First Class (E-3) to E-4, Specialist 4, which is the technical grade comparable to a Corporal in the infantry. Now I would head home to Tucson for a few weeks of leave before making the biggest move of my life to South Korea for a year of duty, just south of the thirty-eighth parallel and the demilitarized zone between North and South Korea.

Five

South Korea

THIS WAS TRAVEL ON A SCALE I NEVER COULD HAVE IMAGINED. I took a commercial flight to San Francisco and after a short layover boarded a military charter, all soldiers, for the flight over the Pacific to Seoul. With a short stopover just south of Tokyo, the entire trip was close to thirty hours long, and since we were flying west, I lost an entire day of my life crossing the International Date Line. It was exhausting, and even though we were on a commercial plane, this was still a military flight, so our meals were all box lunch style. The one high point of the trip was flying over Mount Fuji and its snow-capped peak. That was a beautiful sight I'll never forget.

Once in South Korea I was shuttled north to Camp Gary Owen, less than fourteen miles from Panmunjom, the Joint Security Area that straddles the North and South Korean border and lies in the Korean Demilitarized Zone (DMZ). My dad had fought in this region during the Korean War in the early 1950s, so this could be considered a kind of Pillarelli family homecoming. The present was absolutely nothing like what he had to endure, but it wasn't normal either.

Camp Gary Owen was part of the Second Infantry Division, and it was in a highly militarized area. Although soldiers were allowed to walk the streets in civilian clothing, there was a midnight to 6:00 a.m. shoot-to-kill curfew in place, which included the local population as well. The only thing that moved during those hours were the Military Police patrols. Anybody else was automatically deemed a security threat.

When I arrived, I was assigned to the Fourth Squadron, Seventh Cavalry and would eventually be moved several miles away to Camp Stanton Army Airfield; however, they didn't have room for me at the time so I would have to stay at Gary Owen for two months. For now, they would have to find a place for me to stay and something for me to do. Welcome to South Korea!

My guide took me back down toward the main gate and pointed out some of the things I would need to know about the camp, including the camp post office, affectionately known as Custer's Last Stamp Stand, a reference to the fact the Seventh Cavalry was once commanded at the battle of the Little Bighorn by General George Armstrong Custer, and it was one of the last U.S. post offices as you head north into the DMZ.

I would be bunking in a half empty Quonset hut, basically the only open area they could find, where they dragged in a bed and locker and told me to make myself at home. On the one hand it was like having a private room, while on the other hand, I was stuck alone in a foreign country without so much as a fellow soldier to talk to like I would have if I were in the barracks with the rest of the company. To top it all off, my interim job would be in the Unit Police squad taking shifts as a camp gate guard. As before, my rank meant I would be a squad leader, but the work entailed checking vehicles into the camp and dealing with soldiers with passes to leave the compound. Not a problem when they were leaving, but they were often combative and contentious when they returned late or drunk or both. Then we had to write them up and report them to their commander. More than once I had a guy take a swing at me because he objected to the process.

When my two months in the Unit Police were up, I was moved a few miles down the road to Camp Stanton Army Airfield where I would finally get my chance to do what I was trained to do, work on helicopters.

Tucson to South Korea was over 6,300 miles of travel, but the most exciting flying I would do would be with the squad I was now joining. It was the unit commander's team consisting of four Huey helicopters. This group was accountable for getting the colonel wherever he needed to go, and our responsibility was to have the aircraft ready at all times.

The team was made up of four crew chiefs, one for each helicopter, several aircraft mechanics, various support personnel, and of course me, the avionics specialist. The pilots were attached to the company and were scheduled as needed. These pilots also used our helicopters for training exercises and check rides along the thirty-eighth parallel, allowing them to get acquainted with the procedures for flying in the DMZ where a mistake could get you shot down by the North Koreans.

Every helicopter going up always had a pilot, co-pilot, crew chief, and because they were flying in a highly militarized area, there was always a fourth person on board, a door gunner. This was necessary because the aircraft always flew with two M60 machine guns mounted on each side just outside the rear compartment. It was as much a show of force kind of thing as it was for readiness as we normally never flew with ammunition.

Door gunner is not a team position but instead a voluntary or secondary job taken on by individuals in the squad. Needless to say, I volunteered. How could anyone pass up an opportunity to get flight time and be trained on firing up to 200 7.62 mm caliber belt-fed rounds per minute from a helicopter!

I had fired the M60 in basic training, so I was familiar with the weapon. Now all I needed was to understand the intricacies of firing it from the air. Of course, this would mean live fire training on the munitions range. We landed at the range where our guns were fitted with the standard 200 round ammunition can, and the munitions belt was fed into the weapon via the flexible feed chute. The crew was given instructions and we were cleared to take off and make our approach to the firing range.

I was ready. As a door gunner I wore, in addition to my flight suit and helmet, a full body harness which was attached to a "monkey strap" connected to the aircraft. This was necessary when flying with the doors open to prevent a crew member from falling out of the helicopter when he was seated in the door gunner position.

The radio cracked to life with instructions informing us we were clear to fly through the range and open fire when ready. The pilot responded to the range tower and then squawked over the intercom, "Here we go, gunner fire when ready." The helicopter began to move forward from our hovering position. Before me at varying distances were several old Jeeps, trucks, and tanks. They were my targets. I began firing four to six-round bursts from my machine gun. Aiming a weapon from a helicopter can be difficult for two reasons: First, you generally don't use a conventional sight. Instead, every fourth round is a tracer round, which you follow to home in on your target. Second, the rounds are affected by the rotor wash, which pushes the projectile down as it leaves the barrel. As I got used to the trajectory of my rounds, I could see them hitting the mark. My confidence grew and I fired more rapidly. The helicopter picked up speed and I became John Wayne in the movie *The Green Berets*, swinging the machine gun forward and aft, strafing one target after the other. And then it was over. Two hundred rounds do not go far when you're in rapid fire mode, but it was the thrill of a lifetime.

My other experiences were not quite as exciting, but I did get plenty of flight time and saw a lot of South Korea, and a little of North Korea too. The pilot check rides in the DMZ ran along the fortified border between the two countries. We flew over Freedom Bridge and could see Panmunjom and the Joint Security Area just to the north, but it was after we left the no-fly zone when we found ourselves flying right next to the border looking directly into North Korea. We could actually see the anti-aircraft guns in the distance following us as we passed their positions.

On one memorable check ride the pilot being tested was asked what his next course correction would be, and when he answered it was clear from the reaction of the instructor his choice was not correct. The instructor told him what heading to take and informed him if he would have proceeded on his selected path we would have strayed into North Korea.

Some months later the entire company was put on alert early one morning. Usually, we did this sort of thing every few weeks to test our readiness, but when I got to my aircraft and helped load the M60 guns, I was surprised to see the munitions vehicle pull up and issue us several 500 round ammunition cans. Readiness alerts never involved live ammo. Something was going down. It turned out another company's Chinook helicopter took a wrong flight path and drifted into North Korea, where it was immediately engaged by anti-aircraft fire and shot down. Three crewmen were killed and the fourth was wounded and being held prisoner. The entire Korean peninsula was on edge as the two sides negotiated a resolution. We sat on the tarmac in our fully loaded, fully armed helicopter for the better part of the day before we were told to stand down as an agreement was reached to return the U.S. soldier to the south. It was the closest I would ever come to combat and the closest I would ever want to.

ONE OF THE BENEFITS to being in the Far East was electronics. Everyone I talked to who had been stationed in Asia said a person was crazy if they didn't take advantage of the available deals on stereo equipment and cameras. I was not generally a huge audiophile, but I did like music and I wasn't going to pass up an opportunity to get some cool electronics. I bought all the necessary components: Receiver, dual tape deck for making recordings, turntable, and a set of Bose 301 speakers. This was not by any stretch of the imagination a show-stopping system, but it was a substantial setup, and the cost was markedly less than what I would have had to pay stateside. And I could have it all shipped directly to Tucson so it was there when I got home.

Almost as an afterthought I also decided to buy a camera. Why not, they were cheap. I ended up getting a Canon AE-1 single-lens reflex (SLR) camera with a power winder attachment and two lenses, a 50 mm and a 100 to 200 mm zoom. It would take a few years, but this purchase would take me down a path I would follow for the rest of my life.

North Carolina

Heading back to the states allowed me to get back the day I had lost almost exactly a year earlier. This time I left Seoul and arrived in San Francisco half an hour before I'd left South Korea, the magic of the International Date Line.

It was nice getting back to "civilization," and once again I would have the opportunity to spend some time with family and friends before moving on to my next assignment. The new toys I had purchased before leaving South Korea stayed in the boxes so they could be shipped directly to my next stop, North Carolina. Truthfully, I didn't even care about those things right now because I was excited about another item I had ordered before I left the Far East, a new car. Here too, I had the benefit of shopping using an Army program that offered purchase assistance and deep fleet discounts. It was sitting at a local dealership waiting for me—a brand new 1978 Chevrolet Camaro.

It stayed new for less than thirty-six hours. I went out to a bar with my friend Dave the evening after I picked it up, and when we came back out to the parking lot, I was shocked to find someone had slammed into my right rear quarter panel. Not just a scratch or a little dent, the whole panel was smashed inward. And of course, no note, the culprit had just hit it and run.

Damaged quarter panel and all, I loaded up the Camaro and drove across the country to Fort Bragg, North Carolina. I was now attached to the 72nd Aviation Unit supporting the 82nd Airborne Division. Our company deployed and operated self-contained tactical air traffic control units to support Army and Air Force field operations. The avionics equipment in those rigs were now my responsibility.

Although there would be no more open-door helicopter flights in my future, it was the "tactical" in our company's mission statement that provided me with my next opportunities for exotic travel. Whenever the paratroopers of the 82nd went anywhere for training, we went along to support them. So, just months apart, we would deploy to Alaska and Panama. Unfortunately, we would go to Alaska in January and Panama in May.

All our trips required us to pack up our gear, all the electronics and tools we might need, the tactical air traffic control units, and the vehicles they were mounted on. To get all this to the deployment site, we called on the assistance of the U.S. Air Force, who loaded us, equipment, troops, and all, onto a C-141 transport airplane. There's nothing like lifting off while sitting in a canvas jump seat with a two-ton truck sitting directly in front of you. After takeoff and prior to landing we were able to get up and move around the cabin…I mean fuselage…and even find ourselves a place to lay down and catch a nap, no matter if it was the hood of a vehicle or in the bed of a truck.

The Alaska trip took us from Pope Air Force Base, adjacent to Fort Bragg, to a base in Washington state for refueling and then on to Eielson Air Force Base near Fairbanks. From there we unloaded and deployed our rig to our assigned site. Lucky for our unit, unlike the paratroopers and infantrymen we were supporting, we were bunking in a barracks with all the comforts of home. This was key, because things don't get much stranger than Alaska in the winter. The sun rises at 10:30 a.m. and sets at 3:00 p.m., and the temperatures routinely hit fifty degrees below zero during our two-week stay. We had arctic parkas and boots using pressurized air as insulation to keep us from freezing, but we still had to take shifts when working outside, spending no more than ten minutes at a time in the bitter cold.

As challenging as the conditions were, we still found a little time to get out and explore. On one particularly warm day, I think it was about ten degrees below zero, a few of us took a truck and went for a drive. Upon finding the Trans-Alaska Pipeline we hurriedly got out and climbed up on it to get a quick picture. Somehow, I feel like if we had gotten caught standing on the pipeline there might have been trouble, but thankfully, we didn't find out.

A second excursion was a bit more bizarre, even if it was sanctioned and attended by our commanding officer. As a reward for our hard work, he wanted to take us out for a beer. He borrowed a van, and we went in search of a bar. Fifteen soldiers jammed into a Ford Econoline van driving in what became a dense fog with blowing snow. Visibility was no more than ten or twenty feet and there were not many establishments in the area that looked like they served beer. We settled on a place called the Topless Hamburger, a local strip club half buried in the snow, distinguishable only because of the large neon sign with a woman's figure on it. This place looked pretty good to a van full of soldiers. Beer and girls in the cold of Alaska, what more could you ask for? Inside it was a different story as the dancers were seriously long past their prime any way you wanted to measure them, so we threw down a few beers and returned to the van for the trip back to the base.

LESS THAN FOUR MONTHS later I found myself on another transport plane heading toward the equator. Having just been to Alaska at the worst time of the year, it could easily be argued going to Panama in May wasn't a great deal either. Temperatures were in the mid to high nineties with the humidity in the oppressive range virtually every day. Our accommodations were not as comfortable as in Alaska. This time we found ourselves in bunk beds set up in an aircraft hangar without air conditioning, just large commercial fans to circulate the air. Each day we would get shuttled to our unit deployment site on the top of a jungle-covered hill overlooking the Panama Canal. You could hear strange animal noises in the surrounding area, monkeys and birds of all kinds, nothing like I had ever heard before, and the jungle was so thick you could easily get lost stepping only ten feet off of the road.

On an evening excursion away from our barracks/hanger to get a feel for the local surroundings, away from the usual military experience and the Canal Zone, I went with several of my fellow troops to a nearby bar. Usually not one to drink to the point of getting drunk, tonight I found myself having a few extra drinks which made me feel a bit tipsy. As several of us headed back to our base we came upon street vendors selling various kinds of food. Hungry after our night out we decided to get something to eat before turning in for the night. I was drawn to a vendor selling cubes of meat on a stick for twenty-five cents. The aroma of the juices dripping through the barbeque grate onto the coals below smelled wonderful and made my mouth water. Five cubes for only twenty-five cents, I'll take two! I was finishing my first skewer when one of the other guys came over to do what I had not done, inquire about the nature of the meat on a stick. "This monkey meat," said the vendor. I froze for a second, looked at my compadre and said, "it's really good," and then I resumed eating my snack on a stick. It didn't hit me until the next day when I put together the idea of what I had heard in the jungle along with the sizzling cubes of meat I had eaten. I ate a monkey! But it was tasty!

As unique as this place was, it was still a poor Central American country. Taking a tour of the Canal Zone, we went to the Miraflores Locks to witness the incredible architectural and technological wonder that made it possible to connect the Pacific Ocean via the Gulf of Panama with the Caribbean Sea and the Atlantic Ocean. Seeing a massive container ship in what looked like a bathtub being lowered so it could continue its trip to the west was a remarkable experience that is hard to compare to anything else if only because of the scale of the endeavor. The rest of the Canal Zone tour took us closer to Panama City and to some of the old provincial buildings erected in the early 1900s to house the administrators and staff required, not only to oversee the construction of the canal, but also to manage its use right up to the present day. Carved out of the jungle, it was a beautiful, well-kept, and impeccably landscaped area that felt like a nice city park or perhaps a college campus. Contrast this with what we saw just outside of the zone, where people were living in cardboard boxes precariously perched on plywood and two-by-four stilts in a flooded area next to the road. Panama City as a whole was just slightly more evolved, there were of course all kinds of modern structures and businesses, but the majority of the city reflected the poverty of Central America. It was on par with what I had seen in the villages in South Korea away from the city of Seoul. The reality of third-world life is one of the surprising aspects for an American traveling around the world to exotic places, yet it made one appreciate the struggle some people have to endure in their everyday existence. Everyone should have to witness something like this at least once in their lives, not from the comfort of their couch but with their own eyes. Seeing it in person makes it resonate so much more. You may not be able to change the way things are, but you won't be able to overlook it or dismiss it so readily.

BACK IN NORTH CAROLINA my military life was about to be altered dramatically, and it would change in favor of more travel and exploration. Not long after the three-month period where I found myself standing on both the Trans-Alaska Pipeline and the Panama Canal, I would find out my Fort Bragg unit was being disbanded and I would be shipped out to another organization. Where was to be determined. With only about a year and a half left in my enlistment, I had expected to live out my service right here in North Carolina. Suddenly I was facing a move and was surprised when I was asked to list my top three choices for relocation. Knowing full well the military would most likely put me wherever they wanted me to be I made out my list: Europe, Hawaii, Colorado. Who wouldn't want to go to Europe or Hawaii? And I just added Colorado because I could not think of any other place I wanted to be located. In fact, in my weak moments, I thought about reenlisting in the Army for the opportunity to be stationed in Europe so I could travel and see the sights. Imagine my surprise when my orders came down stating I would be relocating to Stuttgart, Germany! Little did the Army know their chances of getting me to reenlist just went to zero.

Seven

Germany

My new home would be the Stuttgart International Airport at a U.S. military compound directly across from the civilian concourse buildings. The barracks, the mess hall, and our aircraft hangers were all just a few hundred yards from the main runway, giving us all a unique view of the operations of a major airport. Our proximity to the runway was dictated by our need to have access for the planes we flew, the OV-1 Mohawk. Primarily an observation and battlefield surveillance aircraft, the twin engine, tri-tailed, bug-eyed OV-1 was a strange looking bird that reminded some of a grasshopper. We actually had one in our Georgia avionics training hanger and were required to understand its systems in order to graduate from the school, so all I would need was a refresher course to get back up to speed. The specific mission for our aircraft was to support Army operations throughout Germany and to keep an eye on the East – West German border, the Iron Curtain. Several times during my stay the unit was scrambled in the middle of the night to get the Mohawks into the air because the combined forces of the Soviet Union and East German armies had activated their tanks and made an all-out run at the border. They would line up and aggressively charge west to see just how the NATO (North Atlantic Treaty Organization) forces would react. Of course, they always stopped short of breaking any treaties, but their movements would activate every military compound in West Germany. They would get their answers but, with the help of our OV-1 surveillance aircraft, we would also gather important tactical information ranging from troop strength to the number of tanks and their origin. It was a dangerous game played out regularly between the two forces dividing Europe and the world.

GERMANY, AND TO A greater extent Europe, was a wonderland to me. Everything about this region I had read in books, learned in school, or seen on television was now available to me. It was all within my reach. Paris, Vienna, Rome, London—if I didn't get out to see these places there would be no one else to blame but myself.

The USO (United Service Organizations) would set up one-day and multi-day trips where soldiers and their families could sign up and visit cities and historical sites throughout Europe. I took advantage of several opportunities to get out of the barracks and tour the region. The clock workshops of the Black Forest and the Neuschwanstein Castle, the structure the Disney castle was designed after; Vienna, Austria, along the Danube River; and München, Germany, to visit the Glockenspiel in the Marienplatz, or central square, along with the site of the 1972 Olympics. On my own I would also go to visit high school friends who were now in the Air Force and stationed in Trier, Germany. Together we went to Cologne to see the sights and climb the 533-step spiral staircase, a 330-foot vertical rise, to the top of the Cologne Cathedral to see the world's largest free-swinging bell.

Closer to home in Stuttgart, I visited the Porsche factory and museum, vowing to someday have a Porsche of my own, and attended the Cannstatter Volksfest, the city's own version of the München Octoberfest, a multi-week celebration reveling in everything Bavarian including beer, brats, and oompah bands.

Unless you have attended an Octoberfest in Germany it is hard to understand the scale of the event. There are rides, like the Ferris wheel and roller coaster, and trader booths selling anything from clothes and traditional Tyrolean Alpine hats to herbs and spices. Then there are seven to ten beer garden tents, most of which are named after the brewery sponsor. Take for instance the Schwaben Brau tent, where you will find row upon row of picnic tables and benches, enough to seat over 5,000 people. The colorful tent is resplendent with streamers and twinkling lights and seems to go on forever. On the opposite end from the entrance is a stage with a large oompah band playing traditional Bavarian songs and a crowd of revelers swinging side to side in unison with the music.

One side of the tent has a long line of multi-skewer roasting cabinets with five to six whole chickens rotating on a single long spit. Nearby there are other German favorites like schnitzel and bratwurst being fried and grilled in huge numbers.

The beer is poured on the other side of the tent, where waitresses dressed in the traditional dirndl carry ten to twelve one-liter beer mugs at a time across the floor.

The dirndl is the folk costume of the region; if you have ever seen a St. Pauli Girl beer label you know what a dirndl looks like.

The aroma of the foods and the sound of the music and singing hit you as soon as you enter the tent. It is almost overwhelming. Your first task is to weave your way through the pulsating crowd and find a place to sit. Next you wait for your waitress, place your order and then just enjoy the atmosphere until your food and drink arrive. In such a large crowd it is incredible how efficiently this process works.

I went with the whole chicken—one cannot help but be swayed by the visual of a wall of roasting birds— and a dark beer. Orders are taken by the table so everyone gets served all at once. When everything is ready, the first waitress arrives carrying ten heavy glasses filled with beer and gently sets them down at the head of the table. Everyone helps distribute the beer.

Then the food arrives in the same manner. The chicken, torn from the bones by hand, was delicious, but the spectacle of the event was amazing. Even as we ate, we swayed to the music and periodically everyone would raise their mugs in unison and sing out "PROST," German for cheers, and then guzzle some beer. As always, it gets more interesting the more you drink, nothing unusual there.

I had come to the festival with friends and as with most attendees our objective was to visit at least three or four of the beer tents. This was particularly important, as we planned to collect several of the brewery emblazoned liter mugs for our collections. We made it to three, and I'm not going to pretend I actually drank three liters of beer, but I did get the mugs. Still, after acquiring the third mug I found myself stumbling alone through the festival grounds still sipping that last beer and thinking out loud, "Wow, I'm in Germany!" Somehow, I'm not sure how in this pre-cell phone era, we all came together and got back to the base, three mugs richer than we were earlier in the day.

⟶

ANOTHER MEMORABLE TRIP TOOK me on a four-day weekend USO bus tour to Paris. Once in the city we were dropped off at the hotel that would be our home base for touring on our own. Several of us, noting we were all pretty much interested in seeing the same things, banded together and came up with a plan of attack for seeing the sites. Over the next few days, we wandered around the city visiting the Arc de Triomphe, the Notre Dame Cathedral, the Palace of Versailles, Napoleon's tomb, the Eiffel Tower, and walked through the Louvre Museum.

Less than four days later, I had seen Paris from the top of the Eiffel Tower, viewed the beauty of Notre Dame from within, and gazed into the eyes of the Mona Lisa, but there was one other activity I wanted to experience while in the "City of Light." I wanted to attend a show at the Folies Bergère.

I talked two of my fellow soldiers into going to the show and we set out on foot through the 9th District in Paris. I don't remember how far it was or how long it took, but it was late afternoon, so the shadows were long as the sun set behind the buildings of the city. We arrived at our destination with time to spare, and having already purchased our tickets at the hotel earlier in the day, entered the cabaret so we could have a look around before the show began.

The Follies Bergère, which opened in 1869, is one of the most famous cabaret music halls in the world, hosting stars like Josephine Baker, Charlie Chaplin, Maurice Chevalier, and even Elton John.

After an agent at the door took our tickets, we entered the Grand Foyer resplendent in blue and gold with a large chandelier centered above and several electric candelabras, both freestanding and attached to pillars, scattered throughout. To the right and the left of the entrance, and running the length of the hall, were several bars. Each matched the décor and included a large mirror, in front of which the liquor was displayed.

We walked around the foyer for a while before finally entering the theater. Once inside, the area opened up into a large horseshoe-shaped auditorium with a balcony above. Our tickets were in the back under the balcony, which meant our view would be slightly obstructed by pillars supporting the upper tier. Unlike the foyer, the theater with its tones of red and gold, seemed to have a certain antiquity to it, which added to the appeal of the moment. Not necessarily adding to the charm were our seats, which were akin to an old lightly padded straight-backed dining room chair. One could almost imagine what it would be like to see a show here around the turn of the century just based on the way the interior was decorated.

The show itself was like nothing I had ever seen before. A bawdy burlesque dance and music review with topless showgirls in ornate flashy costumes as the centerpiece of the production. Not to be outdone, the sets were just as spectacular. At one point there was a black wall with a grand piano painted at the center and a performer suspended at the keyboard. Around the piano were doors in the wall that opened so a singer or dancer could lean out and perform as part of the musical number. I'm not much of a musical theater fan, but I enjoyed the show for its entertainment value as much as for the historical relevance of the theater itself.

Once the show ended, we worked our way outside to the street where we attempted to get our bearings so we could get back to the hotel. Since it was now dark, things looked very different. After only a few blocks we questioned whether we were heading in the right direction. The one easily recognizable landmark was the brightly lit white domed Basilica of the Sacre-Coeur on the summit of Montmartre. On our way to the follies, it was always on our left, so as long as we kept it in sight to our right on the way back, we should be heading in the right direction. Of course, it wasn't an exact science and soon we found ourselves in a bar district that none of us remembered passing through earlier in the day. This was an unusual area, brightly lit with an almost carnival atmosphere. The old buildings came to life with pictures of the entertainment offered inside stuck to boards behind glass and a barker at the entrance to each establishment. The fact that we probably looked lost, and we most definitely did not look French, was certainly obvious to some of the guys trying to attract patrons to their businesses. They quickly switched from speaking French to English as we approached. "Come inside, see the show, beautiful girls for you." It was a stretch of strip clubs, interesting but all kinds of shady looking. One of my compadres, a short stocky guy from New Jersey, was unquestionably interested. The other guy from Minnesota and I thought it would be better to pass by and head on down the street. "I give you a free beer, just come in, won't you," one man said in a heavy French accent. With that, our New Jersey friend was already moving through the door with the barker to get his beer. We followed. "Leave no man behind" meant anywhere, whether on the battlefield or a questionable street in Paris.

As I stepped through the door, I knew immediately we were in over our heads. This was a strange place. We walked through a short hallway into a dark room, maybe ten by twelve feet, with a well-worn couch along the side wall and a loveseat on another at a ninety-degree angle. There was a black curtain directly in front of the couch. Jersey sat down on the loveseat as Minnesota and I sat on the couch. There was a beer in each of our hands as soon as we sat down, and shortly thereafter two girls came out from behind the curtain, one sitting with Jersey and the other sitting between Minnesota and me. The only light in the room was a single lamp above the couch, which gave off just enough light to make it feel like you were in a police interrogation room. It was, however, enough light to see that the scantily clad women sitting with us were very attractive, and who could resist a woman with a French accent? I was still skeptical even as the woman next to me whispered basic conversation starting phrases into my ear: "Where are you from?"

"Why do you visit?"

"You are very handsome."

On and on, but as I said, the allure of the moment was amplified by her soft French accent. My guard was down until a man appeared with a bottle of champagne on ice and placed it in front of Jersey and his now topless girl. I immediately snapped out of my French girl-induced stupor and leaned forward to address Jersey. "What are you doing? Do you know how much that is?" His reply gave me no confidence he knew what he was doing. "No, but I got this." I sat back. No lilting French words spoken by a beautiful French girl could stop me from being on edge now. The girl next to me had turned her attention to Minnesota, who was also resisting her advances. Both of us watched as Jersey and his girl guzzled their champagne.

"Dude, we need to get out of here. Pay for that and let's go," I said to Jersey.

He signaled for the man who delivered the champagne, and I watched as they conversed. Jersey reached for his wallet, shrugged his shoulders, and shook his head as the man grabbed his shirt, pulled him forward and said something into his ear.

"What's going on?" I called out to Jersey.

The man now turned his attention to me and said, "Your friend doesn't have enough money to pay for his champagne."

"How much does he owe?"

"Four hundred francs." I knew the exchange rate was four to one, so the bill was 100 U.S. dollars.

I looked angrily at Jersey. "You don't have enough? How much do you have?"

"About twenty-five dollars," he said.

I rolled my eyes at Jersey and took out my wallet, where I had about twenty dollars. Now, I had put 100 dollars in my shoe before we left the hotel, emergency money just in case, but I wasn't going to go there if I didn't have to. I pulled what I had out of my wallet and showed it to the man. Minnesota did the same. Between the three of us we had about sixty dollars.

"Not enough, pay now."

"We don't have enough," I said.

The man moved to stand over me. "What do we do about that?"

His demeaner went to the next level as he scowled at me.

"We're Americans. We want to talk to the American Embassy." Even as I said it, I knew it was not going to make things better.

The man crouched down to me and said, "How about I just take half your mustache?" as he grabbed my upper lip.

"Okay, I got the money." He called my bluff and I promptly folded.

He let go of me and stood back up and watched as I pulled the cash from my shoe.

After settling the bill and escaping to the safety of the dark unknown streets of Paris, I told Jersey how stupid he was ordering champagne with only twenty some odd dollars in his pocket. He tried to give me his watch to settle up with me, but I refused and said I wanted the cash when we got back to Germany. He shipped out to a new assignment a little over a month later without paying me back. I should've taken the watch.

Eight

Backpacking Europe

ONE OF THE REASONS I WAS SO EXCITED ABOUT LIVING IN EUROPE was that the 1980 Olympics would be held in Moscow, in what was then the Soviet Union. The plan was to take time off and travel to see the Olympics, something I always wanted to do, as well as act on a unique opportunity to get into the Soviet Union — a place few people from the West had visited. I knew access would be limited, especially for U.S. military personnel, but being in Germany would make the process easier and less expensive.

Unfortunately, the Soviets invaded Afghanistan in December 1979, and the following January, President Jimmy Carter demanded Moscow pull its troops out of the country within the next month or the United States would boycott the games of the XXII Olympiad. The Soviets refused, and sixty-five nations ended up joining the U.S. in the largest Olympic boycott in the history of the games. Just like that, my unique opportunity evaporated in the midst of a superpower standoff.

Not to be deterred, after all I was still in Europe, I came up with a new grand plan for my remaining leave time and the money, which was supposed to be used in Moscow, burning a hole in my pocket. I would take a train tour of all the great countries and cities on the continent.

I began to plan. I had already explored Germany, Austria, and Switzerland on short weekend trips, so I would not spend my time going to any of those. Any country behind the Iron Curtain was off limits, so those could be written off. That left the countries I believed were comfortably within my range: Italy, Greece, Spain, France, Luxembourg, Belgium, the Netherlands, Great Britain, and Denmark.

I would take thirty-one days of leave, get a first-class Eurail Pass entitling me to travel on any train in Europe at any time, and with a backpack and my camera, explore all the historic sites within my grasp. On the itinerary would be the Acropolis, the Vatican and the ruins in Rome, the French Riviera, Barcelona, Luxembourg City, a trip across the English Channel to visit my cousin outside of London, Paris (again), Brussels, Amsterdam, and Copenhagen. It would be an aggressive endeavor, but one I was optimistic I could achieve.

As I put together my trip and shared my ideas with other individuals in my company, I found plenty of people who were interested in my travel plans, but one person was more than just interested. I met Curt through one of my team members when he joined us for lunch at the mess hall one day. He had heard about my trip and was curious about where I was going and how I planned to get there. Over the next week or so we had several conversations and eventually he asked if he could tag along. We seemed to have some of the same interests in common and although I felt comfortable doing the trip on my own, I figured having someone to travel with might make things a little easier and provide the proverbial "safety in numbers."

We left on a train out of Stuttgart bound for a connection in Innsbruck, Austria, on June 3, 1980, traveling down the eastern coast of Italy to the port city of Brindisi. There, we boarded a boat to Greece, spending several days in Athens and Olympia. Later, in Italy, we toured Rome including, among other places, the Colosseum, the Roman Forums, and the Vatican. It was surreal to stand in the middle of the Sistine Chapel looking up at the ceiling and Michelangelo's *Creation of Adam* fresco.

Back on the train, we stopped for a three-hour tour from the Pisa train station to the Leaning Tower of Pisa and back again, a quick trip to be sure but well worth the effort.

Next, we headed for the French Riviera and the beaches of Cannes and the glamor and glitz of Monte Carlo in the Principality of Monaco. The ride along the coast was spectacular and I was amazed at all the tunnels we passed through along the way. We arrived in Cannes at 11:30 p.m. and were unable to find a place to stay, so we doubled back to Nice and were promptly chased out of the station as it was closing. It was so late and we had no place to go, so we threw our packs down in front of the station and just camped out. We were stuck in Nice. The station opened back up at 6:30 a.m., at which time we made our way inside and slept on benches until the money exchange office opened and we were able to get some French francs. After downing a few pastries, we got on a train and headed back to Cannes, where we followed our "Low-Cost Europe" guide to a place called the Mimont and checked in. For seventy francs a night, just under eighteen dollars, we got a room with a single and a double bed and a shower stall tucked in the corner with a curtain for privacy. The bathroom was down the hall. Changing into our swimsuits, we immediately headed out to experience the world-famous French Riviera beaches. It was stunning: Fine, silky sand tailing off into the most beautiful aqua blue water, surrounded by glamorous hotels along the shore in the Bay of Cannes. And for two Americans traveling abroad, there was one other rare sight we were here to see—topless women frolicking and basking in the warm sun. It was truly an eyepopping experience to say the least and a testament to how open-minded people are in Europe about all things sexual. For instance, everywhere you go in Germany there are "sex shoppes." They are on the streets, in train and bus stations, and the advertisements for them appear on television, billboards and on the sides of city buses. It's like any other commodity, shoes, cars, or groceries, a normal part of daily life. Maybe instead of showing how open-minded Europeans are it actually shows how prudish Americans can be. And, of course, Curt and I drooled over what we were witnessing, perpetuating the "ugly American" stereotype.

We took in the "sights" at the beach for about ninety minutes, which turned out to be about sixty minutes too long for me. Although I had covered myself with suntan lotion, I had neglected to put any on my sand covered ankles and feet, and now they were burned. I gingerly went back to the room to get some rest and fell asleep until about 6:30 p.m.

The plan for the night was to take the train to Monte Carlo to do some evening sightseeing. As I got ready it was obvious that I had really overdone it that day. My feet were just slightly toasted as they remained in the sand most of the time, but my ankles were purple. Purple! Pain-wise that's beyond bright red! It hurt to put on socks.

We made our way to the train and once we pulled into Monte Carlo, we took off up the rocky hill to the Principality of Monaco and strolled around through the narrow streets taking in the ambiance of the city and the beautiful views of the sea and Monte Carlo below. Our walk took us to the front of the castle, and we were surprised when the large wooden doors swung open and a bronze chauffeur-driven Rolls Royce appeared with Prince Rainier in the back. Princess Grace was not with him. No doubt he was on the way to some glitzy state event. We, on the other hand, had to make our way back down the hillside on foot, which for me was a painful process. Every step aggravated my well-done ankles.

Night had fallen and the lights of the swanky city of Monte Carlo were blazing, particularly around the famous casino. We walked along the rows of upscale hotels and along the boardwalk by the bay. It was getting late, so we caught the train back toward Cannes, but when we pulled into the station in Nice, everything shut down and we were asked to disembark. After inquiring further, we discovered there wasn't another train sched-uled to go to Cannes until 6:00 a.m. the next morning. What? It was only 11:30 p.m.! We were stuck in Nice again, two nights in a row! We stormed around for a few minutes pledging if we ever got rich, we would pay to have the city of Nice destroyed. After calming down, we made our way out to the taxi stand to see how much the trip to Cannes would cost. As luck would have it, there was a couple from Sweden who were also trying to get back to Cannes, so we teamed up and split the 180 franc-fare for the thirty-minute ride. Curt and I each shelled out about twelve dollars, which was twelve dollars more than we had expected to spend on transportation tonight. The cab dropped us at the chic Martinez Hotel right on the beach, where the Swedish couple was staying. It was quite a thrill to drive up in a Mercedes and have the doorman open the car door for us, only to watch us disappear around the corner as we headed for our low-cost hotel two blocks from the beach.

Sleep did not come easy as my tender ankles caused me to wake up whenever I moved a muscle. The next day we were scheduled to be true tourists and we set out, cameras in hand, to visit all the places we had already been, except this time during daylight. Our prime objectives were going to be back in Monaco and Monte Carlo, but the ugly Americans in us decided to head back to the beach first to see if we could get a picture or two of some lovely French girls bathing topless on the beach. Our reasoning was we needed something to show the guys back home. And yes, we did feel like dirty old men, however, not only did no one seem to mind but we also weren't the only ones out there with cameras shooting the wonders of the French Riviera.

After accomplishing our first goal of the day, it was back on the train to Monte Carlo, where we methodically went from place to place getting all the photos we wanted to get. Being a big auto racing fan, I was particularly interested in walking some of the Circuit de Monaco, the road course for the world's most prestigious and glamorous Formula One automobile race, the Monaco Grand Prix. We scrambled to the Grand Hotel Hairpin and through the Tunnel ending up at the Nouvelle Chicane where, in a nearby parking lot, we watched the Second Annual Grand Prix for Radio Controlled Cars. Not exactly the prestige and glamor of the real thing but interesting and exciting, nonetheless.

We ended the day early as my ankles were screaming at me, boarding a train back to Cannes, this time early enough that there wasn't even a stop in Nice. We weren't going to get fooled three days in a row, no way!

The adventure continued as we rolled into Barcelona, Spain, for a few days and then took a bullet train to Paris for a connection to Brussels, Belgium, and Luxemburg for a day each. Then it was on to Amsterdam.

Getting off the train in the Netherlands' largest and most famous city, we first found our way to the information desk where we picked up maps and fliers, exchanged our money for Dutch guilder, and made a reservation at the King Hotel.

This was undoubtedly the nicest place we had stayed in during the entire trip and the 62.50 guilder (approximately thirty dollars) included an all-you-can-eat-and–drink-breakfast, and we're talking real food, not continental breakfast stuff! After getting ourselves checked in, we went to dinner at the China Garden, which came highly recommended by the hotel staff. I devoured a plate of sweet and sour pork, which was excellent, made even better by how reasonably priced it was.

After filling our bellies, we hit the pavement to partake of the many charms of Amsterdam. To get an idea of what to see within walking distance, we had inquired at the hotel as well as at the restaurant and there were two unanimous recommendations: walk along the canals to see how beautifully they were lit up at night and go to the Red Light District. Easy, this place was "overflowing" with canals and we'd do whatever was necessary to find the Red Light District.

The Red Light District, known as De wallen, was only about fifteen minutes away and had us crossing no fewer than five canals, not counting the one guiding us to our destination. All along the way the place was lit up like Christmas with twinkling white lights outlining every bridge and walkway entrance, not to mention all the eating and drinking establishments. The city was stunningly beautiful with the lighted canals stamping their unique appeal on this old-world city.

Finally, we reached the physical point of our curiosity—the approximately five-block area which was the Red Light District. Amsterdam is famously tolerant with a very liberal attitude. Virtually nothing related to basic human nature has been criminalized. Instead, it is encouraged and completely out in the open. Sex shops, peep shows, strip clubs, and sex theaters line the cobblestone streets, and even the coffee shops sell marijuana. One shop had a sign advertising its services above the door in bright red neon lights: "Fucking Good Fucking Show." This district has existed and operated, except for the neon, in much the same way since the 14th century. And its most famous legacy is prostitution in a form which is as unique as its canals. You see, the sale of sexual favors is legal here, but not on the streets. There were no streetwalkers. Instead, the ladies of the night rented their own rooms, complete with a bed, where they stood or lounged in various stages of undress behind a large picture window lit by a red light. This was the male version of a shopping mall... only infinitely better!

This is how it worked: As a gentleman walked down the street looking in the windows, browsing, if you will, the ladies would pose suggestively, but always in a classy way not wanting to reveal anything to those who were just looking. A more aggressive woman might tap on her window or take off some of her lingerie to try to draw a potential client into her lair. The man, seeking a woman to tickle his fancy, would walk around to an adjacent door and enter the room, upon which time, the fair maiden would draw the curtains on her window and well, the rest was history.

And before you have to ask, neither Curt nor I partook in any of the delights behind the glass. We were most definitely window shoppers. I think this was because we were young and afraid of the trouble we could potentially get into; after all, we were on a budget and also unsure if any of the ladies would take Travelers Cheques. But we did have a blast going up and down the streets checking out all the very attractive women, always disappointed whenever we came to a window where the shades were drawn. My joke was that but for the fact she was busy, she could've been the next Mrs. Pillarelli!

The place was crawling with visitors from all over Europe and the world, and there were police officers everywhere. In fact, we were surprised to see there was a police station right in the middle of the district. No one ever had to worry about how safe the area was, and it behooved the city of Amsterdam to keep it crime free as there was a lot of tourist money to be made here. But there were seedier side streets, a bit darker and less visited. We ventured into one out of pure curiosity and found it to be made up of Dutch doors, imagine that, where a lady of the evening would close the top when she was busy with a patron. No brightly lit windows here, this place was all business. We assumed this was the "lower rent" ward, and after being propositioned more directly by several of the working girls ("how about a blow job, boys"), we decided to get back on the main street where it was brighter and a little less "in your face," so to speak. It was an interesting detour, nonetheless.

Back to the window-shopping zone, we continued to enjoy our stroll through one of the best places on earth, appreciating the unbelievable variety of lovely ladies— blondes, brunettes, redheads, tall, short, busty, light, dark, and of diverse races and nationalities, but mostly all gorgeous. There was another interesting aspect to the level of open-mindedness in this city, the drug trade. As I said before, some of the coffee houses sold marijuana and there were also basic hookah lounges, but the real action, though technically illegal, was out on the street. During our short time in the district, we must have been approached at least thirty times by guys who wanted to sell us anything from Afghan hash and psychedelic shrooms to LSD and cocaine. Although we didn't buy any of their wares, we did have the munchies, so we settled on a roast beef sandwich prior to heading back to the hotel at around 1:00 a.m.

For our final day in Amsterdam, we decided to take a city bus tour to see some of the sights beyond our walking distance. We saw the Dutch Royal Palace and two houses once belonging to the painter Rembrandt van Rijn, spent a half hour in the Rijksmuseum where we saw Rembrandt's famous work *Night Watch*, and took a tour of a diamond cutting and polishing exhibit. The last leg of the tour drove us through the Red Light District, which we had walked through the night before. It was much quieter, a lot less crowded, and not near as exciting. Like the diamond exhibit, there were no free samples.

After the city tour, we still had some time on our hands, so we went to a movie theater near the hotel to see Dudley Moore and Bo Derek in *10*. It was in English with Dutch subtitles and was a fun movie to sit and relax to after many days on the road. Afterwards, we again went to the China Garden for dinner before heading back to the hotel. Hard to believe we spent two days in Amsterdam and had Chinese food both days. Then again, we didn't need any more variety in our lives after all of our window shopping.

———

AN ALL-DAY TRIP BY train got us to Calais, France, for our crossing of the English Channel. We reserved seats on a hovercraft that would make the trip in less than thirty-five minutes. It was the longest thirty-five minutes of my life! Dark, cloudy skies, high winds and rough seas made the channel an ominous sight. It looked like every World War II Normandy invasion movie I had ever seen. And now we would be crossing it in a hovercraft riding on a cushion of air and bounding off of every wave. The craft bounced and rocked for the entire trip. We were sitting in airline-style seats in a compartment with about 100 passengers and it wasn't long before we started to hear a lot of moaning and groaning. People started to get sick about ten minutes into the trip, and I could feel myself spiraling out of control as well. I reclined my seat, closed my eyes, and just started counting by ones to infinity. I've found this technique not only helps me get to sleep, but it can be used to maintain control when I start feeling "poorly." And I was feeling poorly. For the record I got to 667, give or take a number or two I might have missed, but it worked, and I made it to dry land without incident.

The crossing really drained me, but we still had to go through an exhaustive Customs check before we made it to the bus that would take us to the Dover train station. In a mental fog from the crossing, it was good to be in a vehicle with four wheels on the ground. As the bus got underway, a groundswell of terror came over me. We're on the wrong side of the road! Luckily, my brain caught up to the present and realized where I was, so I only thought it and didn't say it out loud. Once on the train I could relax.

Cruising into London, it was nice to see Parliament and Big Ben all lit up. Here was another great European city to explore. Curt and I took the underground to Waterloo Station where we checked for our connection to Haselmere, which is about an hour east of London and where my cousin Tony lived. Unfortunately, there wasn't another train until 5:22 the next morning, so we took a stroll to the Thames River to see a little of the city before going back to the station where we would obviously be spending the night.

We've slept in some of the best train stations in Europe and this was one of the biggest; even better, it was open all night. Resting against our backpacks, we actually slept until it simply got too cold for us. At about 3:00 a.m. we got up to walk around to keep warm and exchanged our money so we could get some hot soup. The bathroom was heated, so we settled there until a bobby came in to shoo out a homeless guy. We left before we had to be told, relocating to the stairs to the bathroom, where at least it was warmer than inside the drafty station. The bobby approached us to ask if we had tickets and where we were going. We let him know and he told us to follow him. If the train was in the station, he said we could sleep there. He put us on the train and walked away saying "there you go mates," in his unmistakable English accent. We slept soundly until the train got underway.

It was nice to see familiar faces from back home, Tony and Deanna and son Zach, who was shy and wouldn't come near me, made us feel right at home. They took us to see Stonehenge, which was about an hour to the east. It was the day of the summer solstice, so the fields around the monument were overflowing with tents as the Druids camped out there for their annual celebration.

The next day, Curt and I took the train into London. For me it would be a day of sightseeing, but Curt was boarding a train to Gloucester where he would be staying with friends. We were finally each going our own way for the first time since we left Stuttgart almost three weeks ago. Although we got along well, he often wanted to spend his time in pubs and bars, while I wanted to be out exploring the countryside and combing through the historic places wherever we were. It was a constant battle, but we were able to make it work—days exploring, evenings in a bar for dinner… whenever possible.

I stayed with Tony and Deanna for three more days, going into London each day to check out all the historical and tourist sights. Everywhere you turn there is something to see, and I visited most of it. I got the lay of the land by taking a city tour and then set out on my own to visit, among other things, Westminster Abby, where all coronations take place, 10 Downing Street, where the Prime Minister lives, the Changing of the Guard at Buckingham Palace and the Tower of London, where I saw the British Crown Jewels as well as the spot where Anne Boleyn was executed… among others.

I did, however, miss one thing that I regret to this day. Each morning when I took the train from Hazelmere to London, it stopped at Wimbledon Station, site of the oldest tennis tournament in the world and one of four Grand Slam events. And it was taking place while I was there. We watched the tournament on the television at Tony's place. I was a tennis player, albeit only an average one, learning in high school and playing fairly regularly when I worked at the Tucson Racquet Club, where I also attended several tournaments. So, I don't know what I was thinking. It was a lost opportunity, much like when I was in avionics training at Fort Gordon in Augusta, Georgia, as the Masters golf tournament was being played a few miles away. I'll say it again: I don't know what I was thinking.

Leaving England was a bit more enjoyable than arriving had been. First of all, the weather was more favorable and, second, my return trip across the English Channel was on a large ferry rather than a hovercraft. It took about an hour and a half longer, but it was smooth as silk, and because I was up and walking around with my eyes open, I actually got a good look at the White Cliffs of Dover, something I missed on the way in.

From Calais I was headed to Copenhagen, Denmark, but had arranged for an overnight stop in Paris to go through the Louvre Museum one more time. This would be my third trip through the "City of Light," and this time a fortunate encounter would expand my cultural world.

Having run through the Louvre several months ago, this time I decided to get myself on a tour of some of the more famous items in the museum: the French Crown Jewels, the Venus de Milo and Winged Victory statues, and paintings by Rembrandt, David, and Da Vinci, among others. On the tour I met a guy from Sydney, Australia, named James and we discussed our travels as we went from one exhibit to the next. Afterwards he suggested we visit the Musée de l'Orangerie, which houses a collection of Impressionist and post-Impressionist paintings by the likes of Manet, Cezanne, Sisley, and Renoir, to name but a few. I was mesmerized by this unique style of painting. Claude Monet's soft interpretations of differing light on objects such as water lilies, grain stacks, and the Houses of Parliament in London; Edgar Degas' pastel drawings and oil paintings of dancers, the Pointillist renderings of Georges Seurat—one experience with these artists' works left me with a lifelong love of Impressionist art.

After Paris, I spent several days in Copenhagen touring the city. There I visited Tivoli Gardens, the second oldest amusement park in the world, where you can do everything from ride a roller coaster to play the slots. It is an amazing place which, lit up at night, is beyond beautiful, particularly near the Chinese Tower and boating lake. The park sets off a spectacular firework display every night that rivals most Fourth of July celebrations back in the States.

I took the next few days to get back to Stuttgart, only stopping in Kitzingen, Germany, to visit with Penny, a friend I served with in North Carolina, so the fireworks in Tivoli Gardens symbolically marked the end of this remarkable month-long trip.

With only 109 days left before I was discharged from the Army, I was "short," a term used for those of us who were destined to go back to civilian life. In four years, I had traveled around the world and gained experiences that would not have been possible to achieve in school or from a book. Having again been promoted while in Germany to Specialist 5, E-5, I would leave the Army with an appreciation for what service meant, for what teamwork truly was, for what it took to be a leader, and for what I was capable of achieving.

Nine

Civilian Again

Back in Tucson, I had to figure out what was next. I moved back in with my parents on my grandparents' five-acre lot west of town, which as an adult felt even more isolated than it did as a high school kid. Luckily, I had kept my Camaro, so I had the transportation I needed to get around, but I also needed to be able to put gas in it, which meant getting some kind of job.

Having gained advanced training with aircraft in the Army, it was my intention to put that experience to good use and try to get a job in the aviation field. And since I had no other direction or plans, this had better work out. I applied at every business located in a hanger in the greater Tucson area and eventually got a job with a company called Acme Aviation at Ryan Field. This was perfect since they were located west of Tucson, roughly five miles from home. Acme was a small company that maintained and refurbished planes. I would not only be working on communication and navigation systems, but also doing whatever else needed to be done on the aircraft entrusted to the company.

Acme was a fly-by-night company, and from the name, you almost expected there to be some connection to the Road Runner and Wile E. Coyote from cartoon lore. We worked on a DC-3, which most of us were convinced was being used to shuttle drugs from Mexico into the U.S. At one point, Acme's owner left town with all the company's funds.

However, there was one saving grace, and it came in the form of a Hollywood movie crew that needed to film a key flight scene that required rigging and maintaining the aircraft to be used in the movie. Management signed on immediately and the next few weeks were entirely dedicated to the effort.

This would end up a B-level comedy action movie called *The Pursuit of D.B. Cooper*, about the only unsolved hijacking of a commercial jet in U.S. history and what might have happened to the perpetrator. On the other hand, the cast was A-level, beginning with Academy Award-winning actor Robert Duvall as an airline insurance investigator, and Treat Williams as the hijacker who parachuted out of the back of an airliner with $200,000 in cash and was never found.

Also working on the film was Art Scholl, a famous acrobatic pilot and aerial cameraman with stunt credits including television shows like the *Black Sheep Squadron* and *Fantasy Island*, and in later years films like *Indiana Jones and the Temple of Doom* and *The Right Stuff*. In 1985, he was killed when his plane had mechanical problems and spun into the ocean while filming *Top Gun*. One of his distinctive Super Chipmunk N13Y stunt planes now hangs in the National Air and Space Museum in Washington D.C., where I was able to view it on a visit there in 2004.

Acme Aviation's role in the movie was to prepare and maintain two identical Boeing-Steerman Model 75 biplanes, one for flight and the other for a climactic crash scene where Treat Williams, as D.B. Cooper, would steal the plane and repeatedly dive it onto a car driven by Robert Duvall, as the insurance investigator, eventually poking a hole in the top of the car with the plane's landing gear. Ultimately, the plane would drop thirty feet off the edge of a dry desert wash and Duval would crash the car down on top of it. Of course, stuntmen were used throughout the sequence and

Scholl would do all the stunt flying. There was one problem: It had to look like Williams was flying the plane while the stunts were taking place.

Enter Acme Aviation and its crack mechanics. The Steerman to be used in the flying scenes was a crop duster with a hopper in front of the cockpit that was used for dropping chemicals onto crops from the air. We came up with a plan to cut out the hopper, extend all the aircraft controls forward, and add a seat that allowed Scholl to sit up front and be just high enough to see where he was going. This way he could fly the plane and Williams could sit in the actual cockpit and act like he was the pilot doing his pilot thing.

I worked on all facets of the redesign and execution of the buildout, but my crowning achievement came when the director determined that the existing windshield in front of the cockpit was getting in the way of filming Williams when he was "flying" the plane. I was responsible for resolving the issue by cutting it down to size, so I would actually be able to see my handiwork on the silver screen when the movie eventually came out; an unsung Hollywood star was born!

Two THINGS I FOUND out about myself in the seven months I worked for Acme Aviation were that I didn't like working as a mechanic and I didn't like getting dirty. Something would have to change. I would have to come up with another career.

One benefit of being a military veteran was the GI Bill, which provided for low interest, no-money-down home loans and funds for going to school. I didn't need a home right now, but going back to college could help me figure out what to do with the rest of my life. Unlike my first attempt at higher education when I thought I wanted to be an astronomer, this time I knew I needed to be more practical. I decided to enroll in the business school and major in accounting. Not only was it practical but it was also boring. In my last year, after taking some mandatory computer classes, I decided to move in another direction, taking on the extra course load to become a Management Information Systems (MIS) major. Now, I didn't drop the accounting altogether, but decided it could be a benefit to keep on my resume as part of a double major. Of course, this meant I had to keep my grades up in a discipline I no longer cared about, and it wasn't easy. In my last semester, just as I was getting ready to graduate, I was informed by my Corporate Accounting professor I was getting a D-plus in his class. I went into his office and I was very honest, telling him, "I'm not going to be working as an accountant anywhere. I simply took this class to complete my double major, but I will be pursuing a career in computer programming where I'm doing very well. All I ask is you please raise my grade to a C-minus so I don't have anything lower than a C on my transcript."

He sat back in his seat and sighed, "Okay, just get out of here." It worked! I was on my way to graduating and entering the corporate working world, although I didn't know what or where that would be just yet.

As I WAS WORKING hard to keep my grades up there wasn't much traveling going on, but there were two trips. One influenced my life, and another just plain scared me a little.

Reasonably close to getting back into school I went with several friends on a driving trip to Grand Junction, Colorado, to see my friend Dave, who had initially taken a job with a camera store chain in Tucson and had now moved to manage the Colorado store. Dave and I had always been auto racing fans, so we talked about it a lot. Our dream was to get rich and rent out Phoenix International Raceway, buy ten to twelve identical Camaro race cars like they used in the IROC (International Race of Champions) series, and run races with all our friends. It was the getting rich part that never happened.

Consequently, one of the activities Dave planned for us was a trip to Grand Mesa for the Land's End Hill Climb, a timed contest where racers of all types, from open wheeled to sports cars, competed on the steep dirt road going from the bottom to the top of the mesa. Started in 1916, this was the third oldest race in the country behind only the Indianapolis 500 and Pikes Peak Hill Climb. Dave and I each had our cameras and we arrived early to scope out the best spot for photographing the race. We settled on a 180-degree hairpin turn near the top of the course where we could capture the race from several different angles. Once the festivities started, we were all over the place shooting the action. Eventually I locked myself down on the outside of the hairpin, so I had a straight shot of the cars coming into the turn and then sweeping to the left directly in front of me. It was incredibly exciting only it was also very dangerous. If an approaching car happened to enter the turn too fast and lose control, it could potentially slide right into the spot where I was standing. I thought about it all day, including what I might do if it happened, right up until each moment the cars approach, when I locked into the action so hard I thought about nothing else but getting the perfect image. I became blind to the danger as I concentrated on the task at hand. Nothing bad happened, and once we got back down to the city, we immediately went to the camera shop to get our rolls of film developed. As we watched the uncut images roll off the developing machine, we commented on the shots. A full frame image of a white Camaro with a maroon and blue hood, dust swirling off of the wheels, came into view; it was a perfect full frame shot. "Dude, that's a great shot," I said to Dave, immediately assuming it was his image.

He shot back, "That's not mine, that's yours. I was on the inside of the turn when that car came by." He was right, it was my shot and several more followed. I shocked myself but realized this was something I could do.

Late in my college career I moved in with Melody, a girl I had met in one of my accounting classes. We lived together for about a year until she graduated and went off to join an accounting firm in El Paso, Texas. I still had a semester to go, so we decided the best thing for us to do would be to break things off and go our separate ways. However, before she left, we took a trip into New Mexico to visit Carlsbad Caverns National Park and White Sands National Monument.

On the return trip along a desolate stretch of US 180 in Texas, our trip took a turn that could have landed us on an episode of the *Twilight Zone*.

It was the middle of the week, and we hadn't passed another car going either direction for at least an hour when all of a sudden there was a loud pop and the driver's side of the car sank. We had blown the left rear tire. I took my foot off the gas and slowly coasted to a stop on the shoulder. We were in Melody's Nissan Maxima so I asked, "Do you have a spare?" hoping the right answer was forthcoming.

"Yes, I think so," she said. We both got out to inspect the damage. The tire was shredded. We either hit something or the tire was already in bad shape and just let go, I wasn't sure which. I popped open the trunk and started to unload our mountain of luggage when we heard a rumble coming from behind us. We both froze. The rumble became louder and now we could see the shape of a motorcycle approaching in the distance. "Get in the car," I said to Melody, but she didn't move. The rumble grew louder. It was the unmistakable roar of a Harley. The bike began to slow and move to the right, coming to rest on the shoulder behind us.

The rider was straight out of Hollywood central casting: big, tall, wearing black boots, jeans, a black t-shirt covered by a black leather jacket. He wasn't wearing a helmet so you could see his weathered face. He had a thick black and gray mustache and unruly goatee and windblown hair of the same colors settling just above his shoulders. He looked rough and menacing. All I could think of was there was no one else around. He was going to kill me and rape my girlfriend, or even worse, kill my girlfriend and rape me!

"You guys look like you need some help," he said as he swung himself off of his bike.

"That's all right it's just a flat tire. I've got it," I replied tentatively.

He walked over to me and looked in Melody's direction. She was wearing jeans with a tight maroon sweater. "Hey," and he nodded to her.

"Hello," she said.

He stood next to me on the left rear side of the car. "You really did a job on that tire. You got a spare?"

"Yeah, it's buried in here somewhere," I said with a nervous chuckle, regretting I even used the word "buried."

He helped me unload the rest of the luggage by moving it off onto the side of the shoulder. That's when I saw the back of his jacket read "Hells Angels" with the unambiguous winged skull logo below it. Below that, it said only "Nomads." It doesn't get any more intimidating than this. I glanced at Melody and raised my eyebrows. She shot back the same look.

I pulled up the floor of the trunk to reveal the spare and jack and began to free them from the bolt holding it all together.

"I take the jack, you get the tire," he said as he picked up the tools and made his way to the remains of the left rear tire. "Where you guys headed?"

"Back to Tucson. We took a trip," I said. I really didn't feel like engaging in small talk.

I took the spare out of the trunk, and he already had the car on the jack and was removing the last lug nut. He passed me the flat and I rolled the spare to him, and he put it on the car as I stowed the shredded tire and covered it up so I could begin to reload the luggage.

"Done. All set," he said as he lowered the car and removed the jack. He got back up from his squat and was once again towering over me. "Where do you want this stuff?" he said, referring to the jack and tire iron.

"Thanks, just throw it on the side. I'll put it away after we get a new spare."

He helped me load the last bag and I slammed the trunk shut. "Well, that's it. Thanks for your help," I said holding out my hand to thank him.

"No problem, you have a good trip," he said as he shook my hand and then walked back to his bike.

Melody and I got back in the car as the bike roared to life and sped off down the road ahead of us.

"Can you believe we're not dead?" I said.

She cleverly replied, "He wouldn't have had to kill me!" We laughed.

I WOULD BE GRADUATING in the fall semester of 1984, which was also a presidential election year. Colleges and universities were seen as hotbeds of young voters, so it wasn't a surprise that several of the candidates showed up on campus at the University of Arizona. I was beginning to see events of all kinds as photo ops and candidate rallies were no exception.

The Gary Hart campaign came to the university and held a rally on the mall in front of the historic Old Main building, drawing a large crowd. I showed up early to stand on the front row so I would have an unobstructed view of the proceedings and I was able to get some great shots.

The appearance of the Reverend Jesse Jackson the same campaign year drew the most attention of all the candidate appearances. Jackson would be speaking inside at the main auditorium where seating was limited and by invitation only, so I had to come up with a plan if I wanted to photograph the candidate. I knew there were only a few entrances and I could rule out the front door, as the crowds there would make it hard to get him into the building. So, I waited until just before the event was scheduled to begin and I followed the press. It looked like he would be entering through the eastern side door, so I positioned myself on the south side of the door. There were police everywhere, including on the rooftops of the surrounding buildings, some with assault rifles.

Soon his white Cadillac limousine showed up with Secret Service agents running alongside. The car stopped almost directly in front of me and one of the agents opened the door to let Jackson out. I squeezed off a few pictures but unfortunately, the other agents swarmed around him and blocked my view. Then he moved toward the crowd and started shaking hands while moving toward my position. Since I had a long lens on my camera, he was actually too close to photograph; however, I stuck out my hand and he shook it before disappearing through the door to the auditorium. I had missed my shot, so I needed to move to a new location for when he came back out after his speech.

The Secret Service had repositioned the Limo so it could easily pull out of the area, so I took up a position directly across from the driver's side of the car, which was at a ninety-degree angle to the door. This spot gave me an excellent view of both the door and the limo. I stood there with the crowd for over an hour before there was a flurry of action. The press corps came to life and moved between where I was standing and the door. All of a sudden, my view was blocked by people and television cameras. There was no time to relocate as the door swung open and Jackson strode out to a point in front of the line of press and began to answer questions. I had no shot. In desperation, I focused on Jackson's arm, the only part of him I could actually see, and using a technique I had seen press photographers use in the past, I then held the camera above my head and over the line of press and hit the shutter button, ripping off several shots and hoping one of them would come out. Next, he moved toward his car and jumped up onto the running board to elevate himself so that he could wave to the crowd. He was right in front of me now and I took some more images. A cheer went up and then all hell broke loose!

There was a commotion to my left. Two Secret Service agents dove into the crowd at the spot of the disturbance and a third simultaneously grabbed Jackson, pulled him off the running board and threw him into the car, which sped away as the door was closing. In a split second the car was gone and it was all over.

Everyone was stunned.

The uproar was later revealed to be a fight that erupted when one guy accidentally hit another guy with his camera. Not knowing what was happening, the Secret Service sprang into action. It was actually amazing to watch the scene play out and see how quickly they reacted in an effort to get the candidate out of harm's way, even though the threat actually turned out to be no threat at all.

The next morning, the local newspaper ran a picture on the front page of Jesse Jackson shaking my hand. My dad, a lifelong Republican, was not amused.

THROUGHOUT THE SEMESTER, ALONG with socializing and keeping my grades up, I was interviewing with companies in hopes of being hired before I left school. I was angling for a computer programming position, and hoped to use my accounting classwork as an extra benefit for any company who brought me on board. There was no need for anyone to know about the deal I had to strike with my corporate accounting professor.

The recruiter interviews held at the university went well and I accepted invitations to visit three companies: Burroughs (now Unisys) in Escondido just north of San Diego, California, FMC in Sunnyvale, California, and Shell Oil in Houston, Texas. I also rejected visits to Hercules, a rocket propellent company in Utah, and EDS (Electronic Data Corporation) in Dallas, Texas. EDS, founded by Ross Perot was interesting in that they offered visits to anyone who qualified, but once your visit was over you had to accept or decline their offer before you left the facility. There would be no going back home to talk to family or to compare their offer to other companies. It was a little crazy and sounded a little militaristic. Having been in the military already, I had no interest in returning to that lifestyle. On the other hand, I turned down Hercules because they were in the middle of nowhere Utah and I had three other solid visits in actual populated areas.

All three of my company visits went well. Burroughs was a great company located in some beautiful rolling hills outside of the city. FMC had a nice office building just south of San Francisco, and Shell Oil had its Information Technology building right next to the Astrodome.

All made me offers, so I simply had to choose. The beautiful San Diego area with their perfect year-round weather, the exciting southern bay area with its high-tech companies, or Houston.

On the face of it anyone would choose San Diego, then San Francisco, then Houston. But they all offered me the same amount of money, $25,000 per year, plus benefits. It came down to the cost of living. In Houston, I would be living in a two-room apartment and have money to spare, as opposed to a small studio apartment anywhere in California, eating ramen noodles for dinner every night. I wanted to live in California, but I knew I would live better in Texas.

Houston would be my new home and Shell Oil Company would have me as their newest computer programmer.

Ten

Houston

In Arizona it may be 110 degrees, but the joke is at least it's a dry heat. Houston was the opposite. The first thing you notice is the humidity. The air is thick and it doesn't matter what time of year it is. In the summer it's hot and sticky, in the winter it's cold and damp. I had experienced this kind of humidity in Panama, but I was only there for a few weeks; now I was going to be living in it.

I was totally unprepared. Coming from Arizona I was used to the heat. My Camaro didn't even have air conditioning, you just rolled down the windows to cool off. Don't get me wrong, it's not ideal to get into a car that has been sitting in the Arizona sun. It's so hot you can't touch the steering wheel, but once you got moving the air made it tolerable.

In Houston, as soon as you stepped outside, you were dripping wet.

Now I understand people living here would surely have the opposite view if they were to find themselves in Tucson, particularly in the summer months, but let's be honest, no one talks about wintering in Houston because of the weather. And therein lies the difference—Arizona weather can be perfect in the winter months.

Of course, this is neither here nor there; now I was living in Houston and I would have to adapt. Step one in this process was to slam air conditioning into the Camaro. I needed to be cool and dry when I got to work, not hot and sweaty. Since I had opted to leave off the factory air conditioning when I bought the car, saving myself about $600, my only option now was to install an under-dash unit in front of the passenger seat for approximately $900. Not only would this be a $300 loss, but friends would for years joke about it, saying the reason I wasn't successful with women was because my air conditioner chilled them down before the date even started. Nevertheless, the new air conditioner worked like a charm to keep me comfortable in all other situations.

Shell Oil Company was an ideal first corporate job. The work force was young and everyone worked together like one big family. In fact, this was one of the things the recruiters stressed when I was interviewing for the position. If you did your job and worked well with others, Shell was the kind of place that would keep you around for your entire career. You would be encouraged to retire with the company.

I came into the company on my first day with a collection of new recruits who completely represented this ideal, and as I moved to different work groups, I found friends along the way. There was an employee association that sponsored activities such as happy hours, softball and bowling leagues, golf outings, and nights out to go to the games of the local professional sports teams.

As for work itself, I learned quite a bit, starting out designing proprietary systems in a development group and eventually moving to a support organization. One of the things I learned was I didn't like the support function. These were the firemen and women of the computer trade. When something went wrong or failed, they were the ones who had to respond to track down the issue and fix it as soon as possible at any hour of the day or night and usually under duress. You had to have a particular mindset and skill to enjoy being in a support organization.

It was not for me; I liked building things, meticulously discovering the intricacies of a process and mapping out the flow so it could be turned into a computerized system. I found gratification knowing I developed a program that made people's jobs easier or gave them the information they needed to do their job better. A constructor rather than a repairer. As an aside, the people I worked with were much happier to be talking with me as a developer because I was building them a new system, as opposed to talking with a support programmer who was there to fix something broken. Makes perfect sense—you're always happy when you buy a new car, but not so much when it breaks down and you need to get it repaired.

Another substantial event that happened in Houston was when I got married. In addition to making friends among my fellow employees, I also met the woman I would wed, and together we would take the biggest trip from my time in Houston, when we traveled to a Sandals Resort in Montego Bay, Jamaica, for our honeymoon.

MOST OF MY OTHER trips during this time period were much shorter and also much closer. I took a trip to New Orleans for the Jazz Festival and several years earlier in 1985 went with friend and fellow Shell employee Kay to College Station to see her alma mater Texas A & M play Arkansas, followed by a run up to Dallas to see my beloved Chicago Bears destroy the Dallas Cowboys 44 to 0 in the Bears Super Bowl season. Of course, I took my trusty camera and got some pictures, but we were in the upper deck, so they looked like something you would see from the Goodyear Blimp.

I had better luck at other sporting events in Houston and there were a lot of them. I had football season tickets with my wife to the Houston Oilers and shared basketball season tickets with friends to the Houston Rockets.

The Rockets organization had a policy whereby if the floor seats were not filled after the first quarter, season ticket holders could come down and sit in the lower level. I took advantage of this rule several times, including once when I sat for three quarters in a courtside seat. It was there that

Rockets big man and future Hall of Famer Hakeem Olajuwon blocked a ball into my hands. I regret not standing up and sinking a three, but more importantly, it was unfortunate that I didn't have my camera with me, because you don't often get as close to the court and the action as I did that night.

However, there were other outstanding events where I did have my camera. Two were in the Astrodome, the first domed sports arena in the world, where I attended the 1986 Major League Baseball (MLB) All-Star Game, and in 1989 when I went to the National Basketball Association (NBA) All-Star Game.

I loved shooting sporting events. Capturing the action was almost as exciting as the game itself. But as I looked down from my seat, I realized I would most likely never experience shooting from on the field. Those positions were reserved for professionals associated with newspapers and magazines like *Sports Illustrated*. Maybe there was an opportunity in this. Could I develop my photography skills and then pass what I learned on to others just like me so they could benefit from my experiences? I started to play with the idea and began to take notes on how I approached the games I was attending. How to do the best one could from the seats they were in; it wasn't always possible to get field-level or courtside seats for most people simply because of the cost, so how did I deal with this? How to deal with the lighting; how to deal with having spectators in front of you; how to follow the action in different sports, and even how to check ahead to see if the stadium or arena would even allow you to have a camera in their facility.

I knew I would also have to include some images to illustrate my tips and procedures, and they would be the toughest to collect because they needed to be quality images. As I gathered the information and outlined my thoughts it came to me, I would call my book "From the Stands."

AFTER ALMOST SEVEN YEARS with the Shell Oil Company and as the bottom dropped out of the oil industry, my wife and I were laid off with numerous other employees on one fateful day. Everyone knew things were not good, but we all held onto the dream of this being a family where if we did well, we would retire from this company someday. In the end, it was money over "family" and corporate America would never be the same.

We were in shock. When we got back to our apartment, we both just fell on the floor and cried. What would we do now? How would we make ends meet with both of us out of work?

We each received a package with several months of pay, but we knew we had to come up with a plan pretty fast. Since we had the time and agreed that we would like to live somewhere else, we mapped out a strategy to visit several different areas of the country to see if we could land somewhere we liked better. We narrowed our list down to Sacramento, California; Denver, Colorado; and Atlanta, Georgia. After taking several trips, we settled on Atlanta. My wife's parents lived there, but more important to me was that it would be home to the 1996 Summer Olympics.

Eleven

Home Park

During my time in Houston, I would for the first time in my life, visit my home in Tucson as a vacationer. The main reason was to visit family and friends. However, I missed the desert and the higher elevations since Houston was so flat that overpasses were exciting. It was always good to get back home and see mountains and the towering saguaro cacti. We actually have them in our yard. When we first moved out to our five-acre plot of land in the desert, my grandfather Tony would drag me along when he went on his "hunting" trips. He was looking for small saguaros to dig up and bring back to replant on our land. I believe if we had been caught there would've been trouble, as it is illegal to dig up saguaro cacti in the state of Arizona. Fortunately, there was no one else out here to see us on our covert raids. Today, our little plot of land has twenty-five to thirty large mature saguaros while the surrounding area is sorely lacking.

Accordingly, one of my destinations when I was in town was to take a drive through Saguaro National Park, just ten miles from home. It is the land of towering saguaros, rugged mountains, and stunning sunsets. I love exploring here; the desert is fascinating to me. Most people think of the desert as dry and lifeless, but it is actually alive in ways most people cannot imagine. The cacti are either using or conserving water depending on the season. Animals are either hibernating in the winter or active at night during the summer in order to stay out of the blazing sun. And the months of April and May are a particularly good time to visit since many of the plants, including the saguaro, are in full bloom. It's hard to imagine the carpet of color as the wildflowers blossom under the cacti and trees, which are also in bloom. The desert puts on a spectacular show during this time.

EVERYONE IS USED TO seeing the summer thunderstorms, the monsoon, which sweeps over the landscape with a short but powerful burst filling the dry washes with raging water. Just as fast as the washes fill, they are empty again. I can remember as a teenager watching the normally dry Santa Cruz River, which runs just west of downtown and is over thirty feet deep and approximately 100 yards across, fill to the brim with runoff from a thunderstorm as water roared down from the mountains to collect in this channel. It was an awesome sight and a formidable power.

Every year several people in this area get caught up in a flash flood by driving into water deep enough to sweep their car away, or in some cases the wash was dry when they entered it and the water appeared out of nowhere.

On one occasion I was in the park hiking on a bright sunny morning with only scattered clouds above when a thunderstorm developed in the distance. I could track it as it moved across the landscape, the cloud initially standing out on its own with sunlight surrounding it, seeming to dump rain like it was spilling over the edge of a large waterfall. Slowly it moved in my direction, growing and merging with other clouds until there was no more sunlight, just ominous darkness. I hurried back to the car as the rain began to come down, marveling at how quickly things had changed. As I got in the car, the skies opened up. The dry ground soaked up what it could and then the excess water began to run off into the gullies and washes, the smaller tributaries fed the larger ones, which poured into even larger ones until there was water running everywhere. I made it off of the dirt loop drive to the paved park road but could only go so far as I came to a wash, dry just a few hours ago, that was now completely filled with water and looked like a class-five rapid. Large branches swept by me in a flash, and it was easy to see I would be here for a while. My ride had higher clearance than most standard cars, but I would need an amphibious vehicle to get through what I was seeing in front of me. I was joined by others who were now also stranded. Some turned around to see if they could find another way out, but I knew the area well enough to know there were not a lot of options and I was sure they all looked exactly the same.

As the storm waned and the sun peaked out through the clouds some grew impatient. A large pickup jacked up several feet made the crossing through the raging torrent. He made it look easy, but his clearance was probably four times mine; I stayed put.

Almost as fast as the water filled the dry wash, it began to subside. I could now see a small sandbar across the road and channels of water still cutting a path through it. A guy on the other side of the wash got out to take a closer look, and then got back in his Toyota and began to move forward. I readied my camera. This car was lower than mine. He might get through or he could stall or wash away. Either way, I would get a picture and a better idea of how treacherous the water was. He charged forward, waves of water looking like wings being expelled from under the car on both sides. He wavered but got through to the other side, where his engine started to sputter and cough. He pumped the accelerator to give it more gas, and eventually the car responded so he could drive off. If he could make it then I definitely could. I looked at the guy next to me who was in a small pickup, raised my hand and shrugged my shoulders as if to say, "Why not?" and drove toward the now only slightly raging water. The pickup followed. I gunned it and drove along the same path I witnessed the car take only moments ago. Water sprayed everywhere and my Subaru swayed and bounced from side to side as I hit the sand accumulated on the pavement under the water. I came through without any problems and stopped to watch the pickup to make sure he also made it across, and he did.

I drove on knowing full well this wasn't over. Having driven this road many times, I knew there were at least twenty to thirty more "dry wash" crossings ahead of me, most of them smaller but a few wider and deeper. However, it had stopped raining so I knew their flow should also be slowing down.

I made crossing after crossing without any trouble until I was out of the park, when I came to a long line of traffic in a construction zone, the middle of which had been washed out by the storm. About an hour later I was able to cross, but I came upon several still-running washes less than a mile from my home that had also backed up traffic. In all, the normal thirty-minute trip took over two hours to complete. And after another two hours, less than four hours after the first raindrops started to fall, all the washes were dry again.

⟶

FLASH FLOODS ARE A normal occurrence in the Sonoran Desert, which ranges from southern Arizona into northern Mexico. What is rare in this area, at least in the desert, is snow. It happens in varying degrees from time to time, usually just a dusting, which melts when it hits the warmer than air desert floor.

On one occasion, I awoke to large flakes floating down from above and covering everything in sight; a blanket of the white stuff where the desert once was. Having spent my early years living in Chicago and forced to deal with the stuff every winter, I'm not a fan. I don't like the cold, and snow is the visual representation of being cold, feeling cold, dampness and desolation, the lack of warmth. In Tucson we like to say, "If we want to see snow, we go to it, it doesn't come to us!" Yet there it was.

This happens here just enough to remind the transplants from the north and east of what they were escaping. They often laugh at the chaos created by a dusting like this and remind everyone this amount of snow doesn't even slow people down where they come from, whereas here, it tends to clog traffic and sometimes shuts down schools and banks.

As I said, I wasn't happy at first, and then I realized this might well be an opportunity to photograph the desert in a way which it is not often seen. So, I headed off into the park where I found an interesting landscape being transformed into a desert winter wonderland by the rapidly accumulating cold, damp white stuff. Time is always of the essence since snow doesn't last long here. Luckily, it was early on a Saturday morning and traffic in the park was almost non-existent. In fact, the only people on the roads were doing exactly what I was doing, looking for photo ops.

There's nothing like seeing the normally dry landscape draped in white; the prickly cacti capped with puffy white snow. I snapped away as the unusual was everywhere I turned. But like the flash flood, in a few hours it was all gone.

—➤

THERE WERE SO MANY different things to see here. I tended to spend a lot of time hiking the trails and, of course, taking photographs. However, like a snowflake, it's never the same as there are so many different types of unique plants and cacti in this area, the most unique being the park's namesake, the saguaro.

Living over 150 years and growing up to 50 feet tall, the mighty saguaro is the symbol of the Old West, standing tall over the other residents of the Sonoran Desert. Visitors to the park marvel at these unique inhabitants of the southwest; they are the celebrities everyone who visits here comes to see.

What most don't see, or photograph, is how the "Sentinel of the Sonoran Desert" is just as majestic in death as it is in life, as the saguaro's wooden framework continues to stand tall in its skeletal form long after its biological existence has ended.

Along with admiring the mighty living saguaro standing tall under the

Arizona sun, I've found it is just as important to recognize the significance of the still upright and felled saguaros in death, as they represent the equally important end of the cycle of life in the Sonoran Desert.

Twelve

Coming to Atlanta

The decision to move to Atlanta forced another decision—what we were going to do for jobs. My wife landed a position at a company called SSI or Stockholder Systems Incorporated (which later became Servantes, which later became Checkfree), while I decided to move into a completely different direction and became a stockbroker.

I signed on with Raymond James Financial and spent several weeks in Tampa taking courses designed to familiarize myself with the industry and prepare me for the goal of passing the General Securities Representative Exam and the Securities Agent State Law Exam, both of which I needed in order to obtain a securities license. I accomplished both once I returned to Atlanta and became a full-fledged stockbroker. In name only. What I quickly realized was the job was ninety percent sales and ten percent knowledge. Sell at all costs, don't lie but if you leave certain negative information out of a conversation with a client, well, you didn't actually lie. You needed to be able to sell your grandmother without feeling a tinge of guilt or remorse. I couldn't do it; I was honest and told everyone everything, which gave them pause about buying from me. I lasted one year.

It would be back to a computer-related job for me, and with help from my wife, I was able to get on at SSI and became a quality assurance (QA) engineer, testing applications before they were rolled out to clients.

With our newfound financial stability, we were able to purchase a house in the northern Atlanta suburb of Alpharetta. We even started a family when we bought a miniature pinscher I insisted on naming Killer. He lived up to his name, the little guy, only about twelve pounds fully grown; he was loaded with personality and would challenge anybody or anything. He used to sit in the bay window, where he would bake himself in the sun, and whenever the UPS truck drove by, he would go crazy barking until it came back by on the way out of the subdivision. I often thought we should shop the situation to FedEx for a commercial.

Alas, having a home and a dog to keep us together was not enough, and divorce was imminent. After much deliberation we worked out a deal whereby I kept the house and got custody of Killer.

I was able to stay single for several years until I met Vicky, a contractor at SSI. Once I finally convinced her to go out with me, we became inseparable. She was everything my ex-wife was not: vibrant, exciting, and a little wild. She was exactly what I liked and wanted in a woman.

IN THE SUMMER OF 1996, the XXVI Olympiad came to Atlanta, and I was thrilled to be going to this iconic spectacle I had dreamed of attending for as long as I could remember. As soon as I was able to, I applied to get the booklet of events along with the ticket information and application. I studied the event schedules and filled out my ticket request in hopes of getting to at least a few of the big venues and medal finals. Except for a few events, I applied for a single seat hoping it would increase my chances of attending the games. Most people would want two or more tickets together and I hoped this would create single-seat availability for me to take advantage of. I scored! I received tickets to track and field, USA men's basketball, wrestling, boxing, weightlifting, water polo and women's gymnastics.

All the sports were amazing to witness, and I had my camera every moment along the way, but the two most interesting and dramatic events were wrestling and track and field.

I was lucky enough to get tickets to the gold medal freestyle wrestling session, where all weight categories were decided, but the match of the day, the heavyweight class, provided everything and anything you could ever ask a sport to deliver. The match pitted Kurt Angle of the United States against Abbas Jadidi of Iran. Of course, the arena was mostly pro-USA, but there was also a large contingent of very vocal Iranian fans. It was all tied one to one at the end of regulation and went into overtime where no points were scored and the match decision went to the judges. The arena erupted in chaos as both wrestlers' contingents shouted and chanted. After much deliberation, the referee took the gladiators to the center of the mat to declare a winner. There was a pause and it appeared the Iranian attempted to raise his own arm in victory before the referee took control and raised Angle's arm. Snap, I got the picture. Pandemonium broke loose. Most of the crowd was cheering; the Iranians were booing. Angle fell to his knees and clasped his hands together as if to pray as Jadidi and his coach confronted an official in protest. Snap, I got the picture. The roar was deafening and seemed to go on without weakening. Angle was crying. Jadidi was on his knees in frustration. It was as intense a moment as I have ever witnessed and it continued into the medals ceremony as the Iranian initially refused to go to the medals stand. Ultimately, he was coaxed into position and the medals were handed out, but as the U.S. national anthem began to play, Jadidi looked away from the flags and stared at Angle. Snap, I got the picture.

Track and field was calmer but no less dramatic. My ticket strategy had landed me on the second row on the backstretch of the oval track and right across from the long jump pit, where I saw Carl Lewis give a gold-medal performance. During the session, Michael Johnson of the United States won gold in the 400-meter race, and I captured my own prize as I caught a picture of Johnson in full stride, both feet off the ground, with his famous gold track shoes glistening under the lights. Several days later I was also at the track when he won the 200-meter race, thus completing the coveted "double."

As the games wound down, I was getting all my film developed. I had shot fourteen rolls, which cost me a pretty penny to process. On the other hand, I was quite proud of my work and put the best of the best of the images, about one hundred, into a small album and took it to work to show off to my coworkers. People were impressed and began asking me to sell them reprints, several wanting eight-by-tens. I began taking orders, and when the dust cleared, I had made enough money to pay for all my photo processing plus a little for the effort. Not bad for an amateur shooting from the stands.

——→

VICKY AND I HAD a great time no matter what we did, and we were married in 1997. We honeymooned at the Sandals in Negril, Jamaica; I had learned just how nice the all-you-can-eat-and-drink accommodations were and had no problem hanging out at their resorts once again.

Vicky also had two children, about 8 and 11 years old when we first met. This I was totally unprepared for, and I was so clueless I didn't know how unprepared I was. Our relationship was strong but as time went on, the divide over the kids and their upbringing continued to widen.

We all took a driving trip out West (Vicky was from the Phoenix area and had family there) to visit our families and to show the kids the sights. I had developed an itinerary, which Vicky signed off on, but the kids were too young to care, and the trip became a sequence of stops so they could play in a river or go to a roadside tourist trap. My frustration boiled over at Four Corners. While the kids were maneuvering themselves to be in all four states at one time, Vicky and I had a fight resulting in her jumping out of the car and me flinging the car keys at the windshield creating a large crack that expanded as we continued the trip. It was a rental, and when we got to Phoenix the company replaced it without asking any questions and I did not provide any details; I guess I did learn something useful in my stockbroker gig.

Things only got worse when Vicky came down with the flu while we visited my family in Tucson and after she got better, I came down with it as we got back on the road to head back east. The rest of the trip was a blur and I think we were all glad when it was over.

In late fall I went to Toronto on a business trip with four coworkers to meet with one of our client groups at the Royal Bank of Canada (RBC). We ended up spending several days there, and after the first long day of work our Canadian host offered to take us out for dinner and an "imported" beer. This sounded like a treat until the waiter dropped four Budweisers in front of us. Our host got quite a kick out of it as he told us he had been waiting all day to pull off this joke. We all had a laugh and were rewarded for being good sports with some authentically Canadian Molson beers.

As we talked, I mentioned I had always wanted to see Niagara Falls, and an RBC manager excitedly suggested we go the next evening. He would even rent us a car so we could make the one-and-a-half-hour trip. We were all in and I was thrilled.

The next day was another grueling work session and we knocked off a little later than expected. One after another my coworkers backed out of the trip saying they were too tired to go. It was down to just two of us, me and Tara, a petite, shapely, buxom, dirty blonde who was friendly and outgoing, and someone I had never even met before this trip. I didn't think twice since my sole focus was getting to see Niagara Falls.

I drove and we talked about everything you could imagine, including my wife and Tara's boyfriend. It was a pleasant trip; We spent about an hour walking through Queen Victoria Park viewing the falls from every angle on the Canadian side.

The falls were absolutely incredible, but it was getting late, and we had a long trip ahead of us. As we headed back to the car Tara, suggested we get something to eat before we left and I agreed. We decided we might as well go someplace where we would have a view of the falls as we ate, so we went to the Table Rock House Restaurant overlooking the thundering edge of Horseshoe Falls. We had a table right next to the window and the view was spectacular.

My phone rang as we were eating and it was Vicky. We talked and she asked me what I was doing, and I told her several of us had gone to see the falls and were now grabbing a bite to eat before we drove back to Toronto. I felt it was best to leave out any details; again, I guess I learned more than I thought I did during my year as a stockbroker. The trip back to Toronto was uneventful and Tara slept most of the way.

Months later, my wife and I were at the company Christmas party enjoying a few drinks after dinner when Tara and her boyfriend walked up to our table.

"Hey, travelin' buddy, how's it going?" Tara was dressed in a red, low-cut gown revealing her most prominent physical attributes, so to speak.

"Hi, fine. I want you to meet my wife Vicky," I said trying desperately to head off a possibly disastrous situation. Tara and Vicky shook hands.

"Oh, your wife. Well then, I guess we shouldn't talk about our romantic dinner at Niagara Falls," Tara said as she playfully thrust her hip into my shoulder.

Vicky turned as red as Tara's dress and there was steam coming out of her ears. I sensed the evening was coming to an end.

Tara left even before introducing her date, and without saying a word, Vicky got up and walked out of the ballroom. I followed knowing full well I was marching off to my demise, figuratively, I hoped.

I explained Tara was joking and yes, it was just the two of us and yes, we did have dinner and yes, dinner was overlooking the falls and I didn't mention all this when you called because I thought it would be…awkward.

The party was over, and the ride home was long. On the positive side, at least I had an opportunity to see Niagara Falls.

⟶

CHECKFREE SOLD THE LEASING application I was working on to a small Chicago company called Summit National, and the deal included separating the employees from Checkfree to encourage them to make the move to the new company. We basically didn't have a choice; it was either go with Summit National or you were out on the street.

I went along and since our group was staying in Georgia, I volunteered to run the office as no one else wanted the job. It was soon clear Summit was a bit disorganized and the owner was a micromanager who rarely listened to advice from anyone, so I polished up my resume and started searching for a new job.

After only a few interviews I took a QA team lead position at Southern Company Energy Marketing, which shortly thereafter separated from its parent company to go public as Mirant Corporation. It was a vibrant, upwardly mobile company that produced and sold energy, developed primarily using coal plants, on the open market exchanges.

About the time the company moved into its newly constructed twelve-story corporate headquarters adjacent to a five-hundred-seat trading floor, I was promoted to QA manager. The launch was so heralded CNBC hosted their opening bell business program from the trade floor on the first day of operations.

As 1999 came to a close, our company, like all others around the world, were preparing for what might happen when the clocks struck midnight and the new century dawned. The fear was all the programs and applications might fail because they were programed without considering the changeover from the 1900s to the 2000s. Two digits, 19, had been assumed when the code was written, in some cases thirty to forty years ago, and now the code needed to be fixed to accept "20" at just the right moment. We diligently worked to modify all our applications, but the fear was we might have missed something and so everyone was on alert as New Year's Eve approached.

At home, issues surrounding the kids had increased the divide between Vicky and me over the last year, and by the end of 1999 we had decided to divorce. Rather than spend New Year's Eve at home I volunteered to work and help make sure everything went well on the Y2K front. I had not yet announced our decision to my coworkers so at midnight I symbolically removed my wedding ring and slipped it onto my keychain. I was ready to move forward.

Thirteen

Single and Back on the Road

Divorce is never easy, but I was now experienced in the art of putting space between myself and a prospective ex-wife. Not something to brag about, but if one finds themselves in the situation it's a good skill to possess. Once again, I managed to keep the house. Last time I had to pay $5,000 for the privilege, this time it was $10,000. Another marriage resulting in divorce, and it would surely be $20,000; ergo, no more wedding bells for me! I was also able to keep Killer, my buddy, my pal, the only living thing on the planet I could trust to be there for me no matter what. Killer was there to stay, after all he had outlasted two wives.

—→

While my second marriage had ended in failure, my career at Mirant was thriving. I was receiving accolades for my organizational skills as well as the development of the QA/Documentation group. I was also enjoying my job and the team I worked with. Mirant had grown to be number fifty-one on the Fortune 500 list of top companies. It was smooth sailing.

Obviously, that meant things would have to change.

Deb, an Information Technology director and the woman who initially hired me, called me into her office and sat me down. She wanted to give me a heads up, the Infrastructure Client Support and Help Desk Group was failing badly and in a last-ditch effort to avoid outsourcing the group's functions the directors wanted me to take over and to try to reorganize it. I trusted Deb and so I had questions; I wanted to talk it out with her. Was this a good idea for me? I had no experience in what the group did. What if I didn't take the job?

In the end we agreed it would be a bad decision not to take the job even though, as she put it, this was probably a no-win situation for me.

I worked tirelessly for weeks analyzing my new team and their functions and put together a fifty-page document outlining the changes I would make. It sat on my managers desk for a week and with my existing order to refrain from making changes until given the go ahead, I became frustrated. Then I caught the Chief Technology Officer (CTO) going into my director's office and I knew I had to shake things up. The door was open so I walked in, excused my abrupt entry, and expressed to them I was ready to get moving. I said something like, "I'm sure you've read my document by now; I really need to start executing some of my plans or nothing is going to change, and this will have all been a waste of time." I had the element of surprise on my side, and it worked for me. The CTO gave me the green light right then and there.

None of the proposals in my document were based on rocket science; most were straight out of an "Organization 101" class, basic low-hanging fruit. It was beyond me how most of these things hadn't already been done.

The best example of this was with the Help Desk team. The current process was, a call would come into the Help Desk requesting service, the help desk would call one of our infrastructure engineers to tell them about the request and…that was it. Then if the requesting individual called back to find out what was going on, no one had any idea.

Enter process. Now the caller would be issued a reference number that was recorded in a spreadsheet along with the caller's name and phone number, type of request, the issue to be resolved and the name of the technician the issue was assigned to. Next, we would send the caller an email with all this information along with the reference number in case they called back wanting to know the issue status. Simple. And before anyone calls this process antiquated, this is just how things were handled until we stood up an actual Help Desk application.

It didn't actually strike me how easy it would be to please upper management with our group's progress until the next Information Technology quarterly meeting, when the CTO, having previously called the Help Desk to request assistance, put up on the big screen a copy of the email we sent him after the call, listing his reference number and all pertinent information. He proceeded to gush about our progress and then called on me and the rest of the Client Support team to stand so we could receive an ovation. If he thought that was impressive then this was going to be like shooting fish in a barrel!

I continued to move forward and in less than three months the team and I had completely turned things around. We were all getting praise for our service where once there was nothing but complaints. I was named the top IT performer of the year, which meant a raise and a large bonus. Mirant was rolling and the cash was flowing.

I WAS A MARKED man, and it was a good thing. I was the guy who could fix anything in the organization with a little process and procedure magic. Time to reap a little of the rewards.

Back in 1997 I had turned in my 1988 Mazda RX-7 and bought a Mazda Miata. At the time, the Miata was one of the only sporty convertibles on the market and the pricing made it easy to justify without straining my budget. I loved driving with the top down and the Miata, with its low center of gravity, was very nimble and handled the road remarkably well under all conditions.

With things going well at work it was time to take a much-needed road trip, so I headed north to Raleigh, North Carolina, and then east as far as

I could go until I hit the Outer Banks. This is an area I had always been curious about and what better place to take a convertible than to the beach!

From US 64, the Cape Hatteras National Seashore runs south for just over seventy-five miles all the way down the Outer Banks to the little town of Ocracoke. Along the way the beauty of the sun, sand, and ocean air made one simply want to meander as much as humanly possible.

I was looking forward to seeing the lighthouses; these historical, romanticized structures were the perfect subjects to photograph, and there were several in my sights. First was the Bodie Island lighthouse, just south of where I entered the barrier islands. I learned right away that each lighthouse had its own distinguishing markings. Of course, I had seen lighthouses before, and this was an "aha!" moment; what I thought was simply decoration actually had a very important purpose to uniquely identify each individual tower. In the case of Bodie, it was two thick black parallel bands.

A little more than halfway along the road was the most famous of the area lighthouses, Cape Hatteras. It is marked with a black band that spirals around the tower. Interestingly enough, Hatteras had to be moved further inland in 1999 to protect it from the sea eroding the sand around its base.

Farther south I had to drive the Miata onto a ferry so I could get to Ocracoke to catch an even bigger ferry that would take me back to the mainland. Ocracoke was pretty much just a strip of buildings along the road leading to the older part of town where the docks were located. And yes, there was a lighthouse there too. Much smaller than the other two, this one was all white.

The ferry to Cedar Island took two-and-a-half –hours, after which I drove south. After seeing a sign for the Cape Lookout Lighthouse, I couldn't resist taking a detour to see what I could, and of course capture another lighthouse image. Unfortunately, the tower was on the South Core Banks and was barely visible from the visitor center. If I wanted to get close, I would have to wait an hour or so to take a passenger ferry out there to see it. Not a problem, I was on vacation. The ferry took only twenty minutes to get to the cape, and along the way we were treated to a sighting of a small herd of wild horses. I spent about an hour at the lighthouse before returning to my car via the ferry. By the way just to close the loop on lighthouse markings, Cape Lookout had diamond shapes going from top to bottom.

The rest of the trip was land-based all the way home to Atlanta.

THE TRIP TO THE Outer Banks had stirred my interest in road trips. I not only enjoyed my destinations but all the stuff along the way too. It's the things you don't get to see when you fly into a place and then back out.

At work I had been moved into a new position as manager of the Data Services team. These were the Database and Data Warehouse Administrators; I thought I was lacking in knowledge with the Client Support team, but these people were at a whole other level. The only reason I was here was because Kris, the most knowledgeable person on the team, didn't want the job and everyone else was either too junior or not qualified to take it on. I had been friends with Kris virtually my whole time at Mirant and I knew he could handle the job because in my opinion he was one of the rare IT professionals who had both a high level of technical and people skills. Normally a person who was highly technical was not who you wanted to put in charge of others, or in some extreme cases you didn't even want them to talk to others; those people you would tend to isolate and just turn them loose to crank out code. However, being a family man, Kris felt taking the management position would open him up to future layoffs if problems ever beset the company. I told him straight up that I didn't think it would be an issue for him because around here he was so valuable he would probably be the one locking the doors on the way out. No matter, I was now his "boss" and would rely on him constantly for technical advice. I could hold my own in the management space.

With a new position and the company still sailing along on smooth and prosperous waters, I decided to spend some of the bonus money I had been awarded year after year on my fantasy car. Four years after my second divorce I was pretty sure I was going to remain single. In fact, I would tell anyone who would listen, "I've been married twice, the first time and the last time!" So, now it was time for me, all me! My self-centeredness, which I was not only aware of but also embraced, led to me purchasing a new 2004 Porsche Boxster. A bit of a step up from the Miata, it was still a two-seater and still a convertible. It was larger but much more agile and technically advanced. Its internal systems were built for racing, which meant you could expect Porsche-level performance as well as Porsche-level maintenance costs. No problem there since this was something I really wanted. Some questioned whether I was going through a midlife crisis, but I would tell them honestly that I had dreamed of owning a car like this all my life. Most boys, teenagers, and men do, but most can never afford one, certainly not as a kid. Now I had the money to get the ride I'd been dreaming about since I was a boy, so I was doing it! And just to make my married guy friends a little extra jealous I would point out "when I got divorced, I lost 115 pounds (of wife) and gained a Porsche." From where I was sitting, it was an incredibly good deal.

WITH A TRUE SPORTS car now in the picture, it's a good time to lay out my philosophy of driving. First of all, full disclosure, I've always had a lead foot. The only times I've ever gotten into trouble with the police were because of said foot. Now, don't get me wrong, I'm not a reckless, daredevil kind of driver weaving in and out of traffic. I'm a stay-in-the-left-lane-and-put-the-peddle-down sort of driver. And therein lies the rub. The left lane is not for slow traffic.

In Europe, the lanes are marked for ranges of speed. On a three-lane highway, for instance, the right lane would be the slow lane where you would drive forty-five to fifty-five miles per hour, the middle lane would be for driving fifty-five to sixty-five, and the left lane would be for anyone going over sixty-five. And if someone behind you in the left lane were going faster than you, you would move over and let them pass. It's called being considerate. Even though I'm usually one of the faster drivers on the road, I'm honestly always checking my rearview mirror to make sure I'm not impeding someone else, and if I am I move over and let them go by. What's so difficult about that?

The Europeans are more considerate than Americans on the road, partially due to their rules of driving and partially because they are less self-centered. Drivers should always live by this rule: If you look through your windshield and there are no cars in front of you and then you look in your rearview mirror and there are cars stacked up behind you, then YOU are the problem! Drive faster or move over and get out of the way and let people who know how to drive, and are not afraid of driving, pass you!

Regrettably, American drivers are selfish and self-absorbed. I've always said there are two types of people on the road: drivers and rolling traffic jams. Unfortunately, ninety percent of all people on the road are rolling traffic jams.

Now, WITH THE NEW car I was itching to get back out onto the road. I needed to plan a road trip to experience sights and landscapes I'd never seen before and a road to challenge the Boxster just for the fun of it.

To fit the bill, the combination of the Skyline Drive (105 miles long) and the Blue Ridge Parkway (252 miles long) would be just perfect. I had seven days for the trip.

From Atlanta I would take I-85 north to just outside of Richmond, Virginia, and from there, I-95 north into Washington, D.C., where I would spend a single day seeing some of the sights. On the drive along the interstate highways, I got to open up the Porsche and just cruise with the top down, and once I made it to D.C. I was running almost as fast to see some of the things I wanted to see. Mostly I roamed around the National Mall taking pictures of the famous buildings: the White House, Capital, Washington Monument, and Lincoln Memorial. These were the most touristy of the tourist sites, but I also ventured out to Washington Dulles International Airport where the National Air and Space Museum was located to take a quick tour of the two large hangers full of planes and space objects, including everything from the B-29 Superfortress Enola Gay, which dropped the atomic bomb on Hiroshima, to the Concord and the Space Shuttle Discovery. You can imagine how fast I had to be moving to cover all these things in one day!

But the plan is the plan for a reason, and my primary objective was to use three days driving and exploring the wilderness along Skyline Drive and the Blue Ridge Parkway. I spent the night at the northern entrance to Skyline Drive in Front Royal, Virginia, about seventy-five miles west of Washington, D.C., and early the next morning I drove off onto the peaceful roadway of Skyline Drive. As an added treat, this is also the park road for Shenandoah National Park. It's a beautiful winding ride through tree-covered hills and mountains. You could not help but feel yourself slow down with the calm world around you. And after the rush of the first few days of this trip, it sure was a welcome respite. I was easily able to cover the entire drive on the first day, and since there were very few places to eat, get fuel, or sleep, you have to exit the park road to get any needed services, so I ventured away from the quiet to get a hotel for the night.

The next day I picked up my tour on the Blue Ridge Parkway. If I thought I was able to wind down on Skyline Drive, it was even easier here as the speed limit is 25 miles per hour along the entire 252-mile road. There was no "opening up the Porsche" here, which was just fine with me. This was top-down, slow cruising at its best and the weather was cooperating all the way.

It's hard to explain how nice this trip was. Since these roads were purpose built simply for the pleasure of driving them, they don't take you to or from anything. There was hardly any traffic to be seen. I might pass a car or two every few hours, otherwise I was alone out there, and I loved it.

Like Skyline Drive, the Blue Ridge Parkway was devoid of things like shops and restaurants. These were replaced by pullouts, overlooks, and picnic areas, all surrounded by the splendor of the thick forest blanketing the Blue Ridge Mountains. I stocked up so I could pull over and eat lunch whenever and wherever I felt hungry. I stopped to sit beside places like Crabtree Falls and Linville Falls, and the tiny Abbot Lake at the Peaks of Otter, three mountain peaks that border the lake and reflect their images onto the deep blue waters. The only real civilization I came in contact with on the first day was when the road skirted Roanoke, Virginia, and then I only saw buildings from a distance through the trees.

The road itself is a wonder, and the Linn Cove Viaduct is an architectural jewel unto itself. Completed in 1983, the 1,243-foot concrete segmental bridge was designed to snake around Grandfather Mountain to protect its fragile habitat. It's a beautiful structure even though it is out of place in this stunning wilderness.

After passing by Ashville, North Carolina, I made it to Mount Pisgah, one of the only places to stay on the parkway and where I had a reservation for the night. To say I expected more than I got is an understatement. My room had a bed, bedside table, and a small bathroom and nothing more, no phone, no television, no air conditioning. Even after the last two days of peace and quiet, a wave of panic came over me. What am I going to do, how will I survive? And I'm not kidding, I felt like I had just been thrown into solitary confinement at Alcatraz! Then I took a deep breath and breathed in cool, fresh, clean air. I looked out the window at a meadow, darkening as the sun set, with deer foraging along the tree line, and the calm of this place settled upon me. Instead of panic I suddenly felt lucky to be here. I went for a walk and found a flickering firepit by the main building surrounded by chairs and travelers from all over the map. We all sat there watching the deer and talking around the fire. This place was incredible.

The next day took me to the highest point on the motor road, 6,053 feet, and then through the tunnels and along the winding roads leading into Great Smoky Mountains National Park, where the parkway came to an end. From there, I drove south into the town of Cherokee, North Carolina, where I was blasted with signs and cars and restaurants full of people. After three full days of tranquility, the sensory overload virtually knocked me to my knees. I had planned on checking out the Cherokee Casino, but I was so repulsed by what I was seeing I turned around and immediately drove out of town and headed back to Atlanta. My reemergence into the excesses of civilization triggered true panic and made me long for the serenity I'd felt just the night before.

Fourteen

Alumni Czar

While I was visiting family for Thanksgiving in 2005, my sister Vicky's husband mentioned to me one of his clients had given him some field passes to the University of Arizona football game against Washington, and he wanted to know if I was interested in going. Interested, are you kidding? My knees buckled and I almost collapsed to the floor. This was a dream scenario for me, and I spent the next several days preparing my camera equipment and thinking about how to shoot the game.

I had, of course, attended Arizona Wildcat games for years; football games are a staple of college life and fall weekends revolve around these spectacles. During my college days, my high school friend Ron, who was in his eighth year at the U of A while still trying to figure out what to do for a career, and I had season tickets at the forty-five-yard line about twenty rows up behind the Arizona sideline, perfect seats for optimal game viewing. Ron and I would always make sure to bring our friend the Captain, Captain Morgan Spiced Rum, that is. A little something to add to our Coca Colas to help us enjoy the game, particularly if the Cats were losing. Stadium security began to crack down on alcohol at games by the time I was set to graduate, so bringing in the juice became much tougher. On colder nights, and in Arizona we're talking lows in the bone-chilling fifty-degree zone, we sometimes had to get creative. Once I brought coffee to keep us warm and sunk a plastic bag filled with rum in the bottom of the Thermos, breaking the bag with a stick after we got seated. All in the name of a good time.

Now that I was stepping onto the field as a photographer it felt like a religious experience. But I couldn't think about my feelings, I had to focus; this was my big opportunity to do something I had only dreamed about, shooting an NCAA football game from the sidelines. I was all over the place. I got into position to capture our mascot, Wilbur the Wildcat, leading the team onto the field. I made sure to photograph the coach, the band, and the cheerleaders. It was still light when the game started, so I positioned myself with the sun at my back to get shots where the players were perfectly illuminated. As the sun set and the lights came on, I cranked up the ISO (digital "film" sensitivity) on the camera to allow myself to continue to shoot. I did everything right, and in the end, I got some great images. It was fun and I thought if I never did it again at least I had done it once.

$\longrightarrow$

YEARS EARLIER, WHEN I arrived I Houston after my college graduation, I immediately sought out the local chapter of the Arizona Alumni Club. It was being run by committee, which caused problems and the masses were crying out for leadership. Since no one really wanted the position, I stepped in and took things over. In those days, the main role of the club president was to make sure our games would be available on satellite at the bar we frequented. I was making those arrangements each week for either football or basketball and failure was not an option, although no one would dare challenge me on anything, fearing they would then be required to take on the task themselves. I was club president for the seven years I lived in Houston and never faced an election challenger. I was the Houston Arizona Alumni Club Czar.

When I moved to Atlanta the organization there was in flux because its current president was getting married and moving to Tennessee. Marc, the Vice President, was not interested in taking things over saying he would rather continue to hold the number two position. Not wanting to be the new guy coming in and stepping on anyone's toes, I inquired whether anybody else was interested in running the club. No one had stepped forward to fill the void and I used the opportunity to, as a polished and experienced alumni club president already, seize control. The Alumni Club Czar was once again the supreme ruler and would remain in power in Atlanta, unopposed, for twenty-two more years.

DURING MY REIGN IN Atlanta one of the most historic events was when the Arizona Basketball team captured the 1997 NCAA Basketball Championship. They were an underdog and as only a four seed, not expected to go far in the tournament. But they came from behind in the first two games to advance to the regional finals in Birmingham, Alabama, a scant two hours from Atlanta, and several of us decided to carpool over to at least see how they would do against number one Kansas. I secured a number of tickets from the Alumni Association in Tucson, and we were all set except for one problem. I was working in Toronto, Canada, with a client that week and the game was on Friday night. I tried to secure a flight directly to Birmingham but there weren't any, so I would have to fly back to Atlanta, where my girlfriend and soon-to-be-wife Vicky, would pick me up for the dash to Alabama. Everything would have to go just right in order to make this game, and of course, it didn't. Snow in Toronto delayed the flight and by the time I strode into the stadium it was halftime, but at least I was there. To my and everyone else's amazement, we beat the number one team to advance. This threw a wrench into everything since none of us expected to actually win. We all headed back to Atlanta as the next game wouldn't be until Sunday night. We got back home around midnight, and I had to drag myself out of bed for a tennis match on Saturday morning, but I was fueled by yesterday's game and I won. I spent the rest of the day preparing to go back to Birmingham on Sunday for the game against Providence, which we won in overtime, propelling us into the Final Four.

Now I had some real juggling to do as we made plans to go to Indianapolis, Indiana, to cheer the Cats on. There was no reason to think we could win this thing because we would be going up against some of the best teams in the country, but we rented a car and went anyway. First up was number one seed North Carolina, where we beat Dean Smith in his last game as the Tarheels coach. We would be playing on Monday night, the final game of the Final Four.

Number one Kentucky would be our final hurdle. They had won the tournament the previous year and were the overwhelming pick to repeat, so this would be a daunting foe to overcome. The lead would swing from team to team for the entire game; Marc was doing his best to control himself and was actually doing an admirable job considering the circumstances. I kept thinking this would be a great game to watch if I didn't have a horse in the race, but I did, and each second was excruciatingly tense. At the end, Arizona led by three when a Kentucky player buried a shot from behind the three-point line to tie the game with seconds to go, overtime. Our anxiety would continue for at least another five minutes. In the end, Arizona won and several hours later we found ourselves in a nearby hotel ballroom watching Coach Lute Olsen and the team receive the Sears National Championship Trophy, anointing them as the top college team in the nation.

We headed back to Atlanta the next day, reveling all the way in our newfound status as kings of the basketball world. Our rental car was covered in Arizona celebratory paraphernalia, and we may have actually taunted several carloads of Kentucky fans along the way, but what could they do at sixty-five miles an hour? Then just outside of Lexington, Kentucky, home of the team we had just vanquished, traffic came to a halt, road construction, how unfortunate. We were stopped and encircled by unhappy Kentucky fans just trying to get home after their defeat. We were standing still and surrounded, and a little uneasy, hoping none of the cars we had previously waved our "number one" foam fingers at were nearby. Luckily, the Kentuckians thought the situation was more amusing than anything else and as traffic began to flow again, we continued on our way just slightly more reserved from there on out.

As WITH ANY GROUP of people, there were characters in the Atlanta club. There's always the guy who drinks too much or the gal who's just there because her boyfriend brought her along; she has no interest in the game, so she talks over the announcers constantly disrupting everyone. Certain people would always show up late and, while you were trying to watch the game, wanted a detailed update about everything that happened in the first quarter.

But the real interesting faction to watch were the superstitious and negative guys. My VP, Marc, was the poster child of this party. As soon as he got to the bar he would say "I've got a bad feeling about this game," and it didn't matter whether we were playing Duke or Northern Arizona University. Marc's cohort was Jeff, a big guy with white hair, who suffered from the same affliction. No matter what, the Cats were doomed even before the game started. "Oh no, they're wearing the red uniforms, we never win in the red uniforms!" At which point I would remind them of a game where we did indeed win in the red uniforms. And the negativity would go on throughout the game and swirl over our table of alumni, infecting the weak, especially if the team was down. Then if the Wildcats actually won, well they were lucky. And if they didn't, all the superstitions were reinforced, fuel for next week's tirade.

Then came the day when Marc suddenly became an optimist. It was the 2005 NCAA regional final against Illinois and a berth in the Final

Four was on the line. The Wildcats had played well throughout the entire game and as the clock wound down to less than four minutes left in the second half, they were up by fifteen points. Suddenly overwhelmed by who knows what, Marc bought a round of celebratory shots for the alumni group. Illinois proceeded to come back and tie the game in regulation and win by one in overtime. You could bet that optimism thing would never happen again!

One of the most historic moments in my reign as Alumni Club Czar happened as we were watching our number one ranked Wildcats take on number six Kansas in Kansas' famed Allen Fieldhouse. Jeff was the ringleader for this one, but Marc was right there with him. The Cats were getting crushed in the first half, falling behind by twenty. The guys were pacing around our tables like vultures over a kill. The negativity was flowing; it was the end of the world as we knew it. Everyone was on edge and these guys were making things worse. It was time for an executive decision. I banished both of them to another room in the bar where they could watch the game. With the fog of pessimism lifted, the Cats came back in the second half to power past the Jayhawks by thirteen points. I was lifted onto the shoulders of the masses…okay, maybe not, but my bold action was hailed by several alumni. The leaders of the superstitious and negative had been vanquished, at least for one day.

Fifteen

Dream Job

One night at an alumnus gathering in 2006, during an inconsequential early season game, I struck up a conversation with Jeff that led to a game-changing revelation for me. He mentioned that he was a volunteer on the sideline at Georgia Tech football games assisting with media and crowd control. Immediately I thought I might be able to slide in and get to shoot another game if I handled things properly and I developed my pitch on the fly. I explained to Jeff my interest in shooting sports and told him I had some experience on the field as I had photographed an Arizona game just last season in Tucson. I believe he could sense my passion and agreed to talk to the powers that be in the Sports Information Office. I gave him one of my photo business cards and wrote down the link where he could find my images from the Arizona game, just in case he wanted to show his contact to reinforce my case.

A few days passed and Jeff gave me a call, the Sports Information Director had approved my request and issued me a pass for Saturday's game against Troy. I would be able to pick it up at Will Call before the game.

Lightning had struck twice; I was going to shoot another football game.

It was a beautiful September day and as I rolled up to Bobby Dodd stadium, I just couldn't believe how lucky I was to be there. I found my way to the press box where I met up with Jeff so he could give me a tour and introduce me to the Sports Information Director. I tried to remain as cool as possible. I wanted to maintain an "Oh yeah, I'm an old pro at this" kind of demeanor. I succeeded, but it was not easy. After a free lunch (man this deal was getting better all the time) Jeff took me down to the field and briefed me on the sideline rules and made it clear: I may be the Arizona Alumni Czar but here he was in charge.

Even before the game started, I was snapping away: a cheerleader getting her ankle taped before the game, players and coaches in preparation mode, fans filing into the stadium. It was all exciting and soon the real action would begin.

As the fans settled into their seats the band began to play and in no time the Ramblin' Wreck from Georgia Tech, the 1930 Ford Model A Sport Coup, which is the official mascot of the team, came barreling out of the stadium tunnel draped with cheerleaders and broke through a paper sign proclaiming their intention to destroy the visiting team, followed closely behind by the Yellow Jackets football team. This was college football pageantry at its best!

When the game finally started, I found myself running up and down the field working to get the best angles on the action. I had to be on my toes, I was a single camera guy with a 70 to 200mm lens as my longest weapon. I had to stay close to everything and got quite a workout. Late in the game I was in the back of the endzone as Tech was marching for a score. Running Back Jamaal Evans took a pitch around the right side and dove in for the touchdown right at the pilon. Jeff, who was standing nearby, yelled "Did you get that?" I looked at the screen on the back of my camera. The player was laid out parallel to the ground, the sun casting a shadow on the grass below him and the nose of the football hanging above the goal line.

I replied, "I got it!"

When it was over, I had taken more than 1,500 images and I started working on them as soon as I got home. It was a daunting task since I had no real process to fall back on. I simply started to sort through them, deleting the out-of-focus images and the ones that had no clear action or where the ball was not visible. I worked for hours just to get my keepers down to a manageable fifty images. Then I had to really go to work. Processing would take Saturday after the game and almost the entire day Sunday to complete. Cropping, sharpening, color correcting, a plethora of adjustments aimed at taking a good image and making it as close to spectacular as possible. It took almost sixteen hours of processing before I could load them onto a CD so I could FedEx them to Georgia Tech Monday morning before work. It was important they were able to see my quality images so I might be able to get out there again.

I shot one more game in 2006 and then got with Jeff at the beginning of the 2007 football season to see if there was a chance I could get on the field from the start of the campaign. I got the okay and I was off to the races. Three weeks into the season the Sports Information Director pulled me aside before the game to tell me how much they liked my work, and they were going to give me $100 per football game for my images. I was fine doing this for free, so I was pretty happy, but more importantly it signaled they wanted to keep me around for a while. From now on there would be no reason to think about making a "From the Stands" book; I was on the field!

Now I was emboldened. I had locked up my spot on the football field so the next target would be basketball. It was easier than I thought it would be. There was no convincing or negotiating to be done, I just asked, and they provided me with a pass for the year. My first two games were a women's and men's doubleheader, which I used to acquaint myself with shooting indoors under the lights. This literally was a whole new ballgame. Higher ISO settings meant there would be more noise in the images, but if you didn't go high enough the shutter speed would be too slow, causing blurred images. So, I had to learn to balance the settings out to get the optimum image quality. I was still learning as I walked into my third game, where the Yellow Jackets were squaring off to face number three ranked Kansas. This was the big time, and I was still marveling that I was there. The third ranked team in the nation was playing in front of me and my seat for the game was on the floor, and I mean "on" the floor, as in sitting along the baseline under the basket. This is the best seat in sports, hands down. Sports fans everywhere would kill for this spot. I know because I used to be one of them, but now I was the guy, and I owned the spot!

Basketball can be tougher than football to shoot, not only because of the lighting situation but also because there's less room out in front of you, and there always seems to be someone between you and the guy with the ball. Other players, the referees, all seeming to exist just to get in the way. You haven't lived until you found yourself focused in on a player going for a dunk only to have the ref jump in front of you. Nice shot of a pant leg you've got there!

But it wasn't always a bad thing to have players or referees in the way; I was learning how a clear shot of the ballhandler was not always the best shot. Having someone in the foreground could actually give a shot more depth and add drama; the defender trying to stop a guard driving to the basket or a quarterback releasing the ball just before being hit by a blitzing linebacker. Every game I shot, every image I took, showed me something new that I could apply to the next event. I felt like a baby in its formative years learning about a whole new world at warp speed.

Along with expanding on my action photography skills, I was also picking up my "around the game" game. Basketball was fast, so there wasn't a lot of time to think about shooting things other than the game itself, although that didn't stop me, but with football there's a lot of down time. The ball is placed by the referee, the teams huddle up, the teams go to the line of scrimmage, the quarterback barks out some signals, then the quarterback calls an audible to change the play and the ball is snapped.

On average the actual play lasts only five to ten seconds and then the cycle starts over again. During all the stoppage in play as a photographer, you can just stand there, or you can look for other photo opportunities. You certainly can snap a picture or two of the quarterbacks calling out their signals or a linebacker awaiting the snap, but after you've taken a shot like that once, there's no real need to shoot it again, they pretty much all look the same. So instead, I would scan the field of play around the field of play. I was looking for a reaction to the action. Coaches talking to players or signaling to the offense or defense, fans cheering, cheerleaders and dancers performing, the media patrolling the sidelines, the band playing, mascots clapping and dancing around or causing trouble with fans or cheerleaders. It was all part of the game itself and nowhere was it more interesting than in college sports.

To be honest, I sort of became famous around the athletic department for my "around the game" shots. They definitely liked my action images, and they were high quality even if I do say so myself, but I also became known for my "third column" images. Each game as I scanned for non-sporting shots, I would make sure to locate and photograph some of the coeds and sorority women in the student section. There were always women dressed to impress on game day simply because it was the place for them to be seen. I would get pictures of them and when I posted the images on my photo site, those shots would always be in the third column of each row; thus, the name. My around the game shots were the one thing that set me apart from other photographers, and when it came time to put together football or basketball yearbooks and media guides, those images showed up more often than not. Years later, when the university renovated their basketball arena, one of my images of a group of fraternity men all painted in black and yellow would show up on a wall near one of the entrances to the arena.

It was clear I had integrated myself into the Georgia Tech Athletic

Department. Along with football and basketball, I was also shooting baseball, softball, tennis, volleyball, and track and field, so now I knew I had to step up my game. In the second to the last football game of the 2007 season, I rented a 400mm lens to see if I would like it, as if I didn't know. The clarity and reach of the lens were spectacular. By the opening of the 2008 football season, I had spent $5,000 on a slightly smaller but no less spectacular version, a 300mm f2.8 Canon lens. Combined with my 1.4x extender, I now had the reach of a 420mm lens at f4. Top it off with a carbon-fiber monopod, because hand-holding a camera with a 300mm lens attached for three hours is nearly impossible to do, and I had a near professional setup.

Several games into the season I volunteered to take the bus ride to South Carolina to photograph the Jackets game at Clemson. Talk about pageantry. The Tigers have what they call "the most exciting 25 seconds in college football" as they get off their buses, rub Howard's Rock for good luck and then run down the hill into the stadium, nicknamed "Death Valley," while the band plays, flags wave and balloons are released in the sea of orange clad fans. What an amazing sight. To add to the crowd's excitement, this would be the first game for new head coach Dabo Swinney. (I wonder how he worked out?) Georgia Tech won the game, and it was there I took one of my favorite fan images of a guy who wore on his head a hollowed-out pumpkin carved to look like a football helmet. I can't imagine what it smelled like as the temperatures rose into the high eighties.

In the last game of the season, always against the arch-rival Georgia Bulldogs, I took the bus once again to shoot the game as it was being played that year in Athens, Georgia. For anyone who has gotten stuck in pregame football traffic, let me tell you, this is the only way to go. I was on board one of the six band buses and as we approached Athens, we were picked up by a police escort that cleared the way and led us directly to the stadium, leaving a trail of congestion and confusion in our wake. I've been on the other side of this equation and let me tell you this was a lot more fun.

It turned out to be a rainy November day, not the best photographic weather, although overcast is easier to shoot in than bright sunlight. I had my plastic garbage bag fixed over my camera and lens and attached using rubber bands to protect everything from the light, but constant rain. Not exactly a professional looking setup but it was very effective.

The game was close, and much to the dismay of the home crowd, the number 18 Yellow Jackets beat the number 13 Bulldogs in a close game 45 to 42. It also turned out to be one of my most productive and successful shoots to date.

As the game ended, I ran around trying to get the classic image of the Jackets players breaking off twigs from the famous Georgia Hedges as a symbol of their big victory. It was happening all over, so I got plenty of shots but nothing spectacular. Finally, as I made my way into the tunnel to head in the direction of the media room, I turned around to take one last look toward the field. Tech Defensive Tackle Darryl Richard was coming into the tunnel with a large piece of the hedges between his teeth and was pointing skyward. I raised my camera and took my last shot of the day.

I worked all day Sunday to process my images and get them posted to my website. On Monday morning, even before I could leave for work, my phone was ringing off the hook. It was the woman responsible for *The Buzz*, the Georgia Tech athletics magazine. She wanted, no, needed, the Darryl Richard image now. Immediately. She didn't want to wait for my CD to arrive at their offices; she had a deadline to meet to get the magazine out and she wanted my image on the cover. Oh, and she wanted three others for inside the magazine. To this day I'm convinced Richard was probably pointing up into the stands to tell a friend to get the keg ready because he wanted to party, but it sure did look like his arm was raised as if to say, "We're number one," and on the magazine cover it looked mighty good.

Months later I would also get a call from the *ACC Sports Journal* requesting one of my images from the Georgia game, a shot of Tech wide receiver Demaryius Thomas breaking a tackle, for the cover of their newsprint magazine. My credits were starting to be seen outside of the Georgia Tech world.

—➤

THE ARIZONA BASKETBALL TEAM had lost in the first round of the 2008 preseason NIT (National Invitational Tournament), and it gave the Atlanta Arizona Alumni Club a nice Thanksgiving treat as the team was sent to the University of Georgia to play two consolation games. About ten of us took the short drive to Athens to cheer them on and I called Nancy Yaeli, my Alumni Association contact at the U of A, to get her to hook me up with someone in the Athletic Department so I could see about getting a court pass to shoot the game for them. They were thrilled since they were only sending a skeleton crew for these games and sent the photo pass information to UGA. These games were of no consequence and being played over the Thanksgiving holiday, which didn't help attendance. In fact, there were more people on the floor than in the stands and I was the only photographer. I started talking to a newspaper reporter from the Tucson Citizen who asked me who I was shooting for, and if I would be willing to provide the paper a shot or two for pay. I wasn't going to pass on an opportunity like this and sent him some of my best shots. One made it onto the front page of the sports section and two more were published inside.

The next day before the Cats' second game, the reporter told me when his editor saw my images he was impressed and said, "This guy can shoot." The order was to get more shots from me for the second game, several of which also found their way onto the front page of the sports section.

—➤

I ALSO HAD SOFTBALL images show up on ESPN online and in the Seattle Times, but it was my trip to photograph the 2010 Orange Bowl in Miami, pitting Georgia Tech against the Iowa Hawkeyes, which would give me my widest image viewership, and it had nothing to do with any images I took at the game.

Miami in January is usually pretty moderate weather-wise, but I was "lucky" enough to be on hand for the coldest Orange Bowl on record. It was forty-nine degrees at kickoff and falling. The cold made the experience uncomfortable and Tech lost, but it was exciting to be working a major bowl game.

A few days later I turned on a FOX Sports rebroadcast of the game, just to see if I could catch a glimpse of myself on the sidelines, and I was surprised to see some of my images from earlier Georgia Tech games highlighted in the pregame show. One, with Coach Paul Johnson coming out of an artificial smoke cloud at Bobby Dodd Stadium, was a full screen shot; I had made it into the television world and the whole nation was watching.

I WAS AT THE point where I could shoot any Georgia Tech game I wanted, to include away games, and I jumped at a chance to go to Durham, North Carolina, to photograph a basketball game in Cameron Indoor Stadium, home of the Duke Blue Devils. Not only was this a venerable old arena but it was home to a storied basketball program and its Hall of Fame "Coach K," Mike Krzyzewski.

It was a thrill sitting on the baseline to photograph the game and a lot of fun to watch the rabid "Cameron Crazies" student section cheer their team on and taunt the Jackets mercilessly.

Again, nothing rivals NCAA sports for intensity and unparalleled fan support. But there's another aspect of the college game that sets it apart. It's not just the fans, not just the stadiums or arenas, but it's also the coaches. The men who spend their whole lives building a program and making it great, even though the player turnover is high. Basketball coaches like Coach K, Bill Self at Kansas, Roy Williams at North Carolina, Lute

Olson at Arizona, and football coaches like Bobby Bowden at Florida State, Frank Beamer at Virginia Tech, James Ferentz at Iowa, and Brian Kelly at Notre Dame. It was surreal sharing the field or a court with such famous coaches and to sit in the press rooms with them as they answered questions from the press; unreal.

BEYOND GEORGIA TECH ATHLETICS I had also branched out on my own to shoot other sporting events. As far back as 1982 I used my camera to capture the Coors 250, a NASCAR event in Phoenix, but until I started attending the Petit le Mans sports car endurance race in Atlanta, I really didn't shoot a lot of auto racing. The Road Atlanta course had wide open sight lines which made it easy to capture the action at radically different areas of the track: hairpin curves, s-curves, highspeed curves, and long straightaways. And the action was amplified by featuring three separate racing classes on the track at the same time.

I covered pro beach volleyball when it came to town and shot the Wednesday practice sessions at the Masters in 2005 and the 93rd PGA Championship in 2011. As a one-off, I took a trip to Lexington, Kentucky, to shoot a day of horse racing at the historic Keenland Race Course as well as a day at the La Fiesta de los Vaqueros Tucson Rodeo.

With all my experience I put together a PowerPoint presentation called "Keys to Shooting Sports/Action" for a lunch and learn where I worked. An overflow crowd of about forty people attended and it was very well received.

IN 2012 I AGAIN stepped up and supplemented my equipment with a new camera. I had been using a Canon Mark IIn, which was fast, but my new Mark IV was even faster.

With equipment of professional caliber, I continued to shoot all Georgia Tech sporting events and added the NCAA Women's Gymnastics

Championships in Duluth, Georgia to my roster. The three-day session challenged me on a whole new level as I would have to learn the movements of the competitors as they tumbled across the mat, competed on the vault, and performed dismounts from the balance beam and uneven parallel bars. I was impressed by their smooth and powerful performances, and in spite of being new to photographing this sport, I was pleased to be able to capture those characteristics in my images.

As my time at Georgia Tech eventually came to an end, I was able to take advantage of one more event on the calendar before I left Atlanta. The Jackets would be playing a football game against Notre Dame in South Bend, Indiana. Since this game was going to be played less than an hour from where I grew up in the Chicago suburb of Dolton, I gave my childhood friend David a call and proposed a sports trip like no other; we would drive from Atlanta to Dolton to check out the old neighborhood on Thursday, watch the Chicago Cubs take on the St. Louis Cardinals at Wrigley Field on Friday, drive to South Bend where I would shoot the Notre Dame Fighting Irish and Georgia Tech Yellow Jackets game on Saturday, and then drive back to Chicago to watch the Chicago Bears take on the Arizona Cardinals in Soldiers Field on Sunday.

And as if to signal the end of an era, in the closing moments of my last official Georgia Tech shoot, I ran out onto the field to get an image of the two coaches shaking hands after the game ended and was caught by the overhead SkyCam doing my job for all to see, beamed out to televisions across the nation, the perfect final image.

Over nearly ten years, I worked to hone my photographic skills in the world of sports, and I learned not only how to shoot action, but also about my equipment and how to apply that knowledge to everything else I would shoot going forward.

Jeff, my sidelines media and crowd control contact at Georgia Tech, certainly was instrumental in kickstarting my photographic journey, but years later he would only half-jokingly overstate his contribution to my success and troll for my gratitude by stating, "Without me you would be just another class picture photographer."

In response I would push back with, "Thanking you for my superb sports photography is like thanking the guy holding the ladder for Michelangelo at the Sistine Chapel!"

He had a retort, but in my estimation, it wasn't very good.

On the other hand, when all is said and done, it was my sister Vicky's then-husband taking me down on the field at Arizona, where I was able to shoot the game, that later allowed me to get my foot in the door at Georgia Tech. Ever since I've always told her, even though her marriage didn't last, it had a greater purpose, and that purpose was to provide me the opportunity to be a photographer at the NCAA level. For some reason she doesn't see it my way.

Great Roads of America

My travels had me binging on the great roads of America; the Outer Banks, the Skyline Drive, the Blue Ridge Parkway, and next up would be the Pacific Coast Highway. The PCH runs from Seattle to San Diego; it covers sixteen hundred total miles along U.S. Highway 101 into California, where you pick up California Highway 1 along the coast all the way through Los Angeles and finally onto I-5 and into San Diego. Along the way you see some of the most beautiful coastline in America.

I started out in Seattle, where I picked up a silver Chrysler Sebring convertible. I was expecting plenty of top-down time during this two-week trip. From the airport I headed south to Olympia, where I turned onto the beginning of U.S. 101 and started the first leg of my journey. The road actually goes north from Olympia into Olympic National Park, looping around its outer edge and providing views of the mountainous interior of the park. Heading west puts you on course to see the Pacific Ocean for the first time, at which point you basically turn to the south for the rest of the trip.

I battled cold, fog, and clouds through much of the park, but things cleared up a bit along the coast all the way down to Cape Disappointment and the mouth of the Columbia River. Like the East Coast, the West Coast is dotted with unique lighthouses, particularly important because of the rocky Pacific shoreline.

I would take several detours off of the PCH during this trip and the first would be to drive inland along the Columbia River, visit some of the spectacular waterfalls along the way, and then double back around Mount Hood to U.S. 101.

As I started heading inland, I began to feel bad, not terrible but enough to notice something was wrong. I tried my best to ignore it as I visited Multnomah, Horsetail, and Latourell Falls, all of which were surprisingly close to the road; so close you didn't even have to stop to see them, although I did so I could get a closer look. I stopped for the night to the east of Portland and would continue my trip through the gorge in the morning. Right now, I needed some rest, I could feel it.

Overnight things went from bad to worse; this was a full-blown cold. Anger swept over me. I was only three days into my trip and this had to happen! Damn it! In the morning I got ready and out of the hotel as soon as possible. My first priority would be to locate a pharmacy to pick up enough cold medicine to knock this thing down without putting me to sleep as I had a lot of driving ahead of me. The meds I picked up helped tamp down my cold, but they did nothing for my mental state. I was angry and feeling sorry for myself, but I knew I had to push forward, and I continued east along the gorge until I came to the turnoff for Mount Hood.

As if things weren't bad enough already, the weather was also against me. It was overcast with a light mist in the air, I'm sure the people in this area were used to this weather, but this was my vacation, and I was not happy, I was irate; and even though I was right next to the damn thing I still had not seen Mount Hood.

At this point I thought about turning back and taking the interstate back to the coast, but instead I went up toward the mountain anyway; at least I might see something new along the way even if it wasn't what I was looking for.

I was feeling lousy. The fog got thicker. I got angrier. It was all spiraling out of control. I knew I was getting close to the summit as I wound around the mountain road, but I couldn't see a thing. A ski resort sign flashed by, damn it! And then I rounded a corner and caught a flash of blue sky in front of me. Another turn and the flash of blue turned into a spot, then an opening, after which I rounded another corner, and the clouds were behind me. It was unbelievable. I was looking at the snowcapped summit of Mount Hood against a cloudless blue sky. I had to pull the car over as my eyes welled with tears. I had built up so much rage thinking that the weather and my illness were going to ruin my trip, and it was now just exploding out of me at the sight of that mountaintop. I sat there until I could compose myself and then got out of the car and took a picture.

THE OREGON COAST IS rough and rocky and dotted with sea stacks, the most famous of which is the 235-foot-tall Haystack Rock in the waters off of Canon Beach. I stopped to have a snack at a little outdoor patio restaurant and just gazed at it for a while. It's huge, and along with the other sea stacks in the area, it makes this stretch of coastline so intriguing. I made a mental note to get back here someday to explore the area further, but for now I had to move on.

Down the coast I would follow some signs to a place called Yaquina Head where there was a lighthouse, and I had heard I might get a glimpse of some sea life in the tide pools. I arrived at high tide so my timing was off, but I checked a schedule for the tides and would be able to explore at low tide if I stuck around overnight. It was getting late, so I decided to stay and then check out the pools in the morning. I'm glad I did; not only was I able to photograph the sun setting on the lighthouse, but in the morning when the tide was out, I found pools of sea stars, urchins, anemones, small crabs, fish, and snails, and I even got to see a baby sea lion on the beach while its mother watched it closely from the water. According to the park ranger, who was also standing watch, sea lions will often send their young ashore on their own to get them used to fending for themselves.

BELIEVE IT OR NOT my cold had gotten better, or maybe I was just preoccupied by all the interesting things I was coming across on this trip. Crossing into California, I got my first look at the mighty redwoods as I drove along the Avenue of the Giants, a detour off of U.S. 101 that takes you more deeply into the forest. I liked it so much I drove back through it to the north just to get another view. It also gave me some time to think about how I could photograph these giant trees in a way that would do them justice; I tried but never quite figured it out, settling on taking pictures where the road was in the frame to add perspective.

There were outcroppings of redwoods all along this road, but as I moved south toward San Francisco, an old nemesis reared its ugly head; the fog was rolling in off the coast. I was now on California Highway 1 (CA 1) and looking forward to seeing the Golden Gate Bridge. I actually thought I was going to be lucky enough to get a look at it, but when I arrived, there it was, the edge of the fogbank at the mouth of the bay obscuring the towers. I stayed overnight in the area just to try to get another look in the morning, but the weather would not cooperate. Then I made an executive decision; I was ahead of schedule, so I would go inland to Yosemite National Park, spend a day there, and then drive back to San Francisco to see the bridge, hopefully.

It was almost a five-hour drive to Yosemite, and I spent the next day racing around to try to see some of the sights. I did get to see the spectacular views from Glacier Point, but by the time I made it down into the valley the skies clouded up, muting the magnificence of the place. And by the time I got back to San Francisco the next day, nothing had changed, I still couldn't see the entire bridge.

Fog! I was getting killed by the fog. I could see there would be some amazing vistas along the coast particularly going through Monterey and now in the Big Sur area, but it was like looking through all-white stained glass. Then, out of the corner of my eye I saw these large mounds of brown moving on the beach, sea elephants! I hit the brakes, swerved into a beach parking area, swung my car into a parking spot, and grabbed my camera all in one fluid motion. I thought it was actually a thing of beauty, but the California Highway Patrolman now at my side saw it another way, and it was clear I was going to have to listen to his thoughts on the matter. As he talked all I could think of was getting out to the beach to see those spectacular mounds of blubber. It turns out he didn't even catch my gold medal performance in the parking area; he only saw me out on the road where I, as he put it, "momentarily swerved over the white line." White line! When has anyone ever been pulled over for swerving to the right on a two-lane road? I remained calm even though he was taking his time checking every paper I had and calling everything in to headquarters like he had made some huge bust. Perhaps if I was snorting a white line then things would be different, but under the circumstances this seemed excessive. As it turned out he was more interested in checking my rental car registration, after which he turned me loose saying he understood I probably swerved when I saw the sea elephants. Nice. Off I went to get my pictures.

The farther south you go on the PCH, the more people you see until you're fighting traffic instead of enjoying wildlife. Except for completing the drive into San Diego, this trip was basically over when I reached the greater Los Angeles area. Here CA 1 winds inland along city streets lined with shopping centers, various store fronts, and restaurants. The only thing good about all this was it was lunchtime and being here meant I had a lot of options. I was trying to decide between all the usual places when I spotted a local joint, an In-N-Out Burger. I had heard of these, and they were supposed to be pretty good, so I pulled in to give it a try. It wasn't even noon yet so there were no crowds, and I had a clear path to the counter where I ordered a burger, fries, and a large iced tea. I was about to pay when I noticed they were also selling some pretty cool looking In-N-Out Burger t-shirts, so I had the cashier add one to my order. I took my t-shirt and stepped aside thinking how great my timing was because people were now starting to line up for their lunch.

My number was called, and everything looked and smelled incredible. I took my tray full of food and was about to sit down when I decided it was just too nice out to sit indoors and instead went outside to sit at one of the round cement tables just beyond the side door. As I moved things around on the tray, I realized I didn't have any ketchup, so I got up, opened the door, and grabbed some ketchup packets from the counter located next to the exit. I had walked a total of about eight feet from my table, and when I turned around, ketchup in hand, I realized I had made a terrible mistake. In less than five seconds a swarm of seagulls had descended on my tray and snatched my entire lunch, and I was now watching them fly off as I walked back out the door. I was in shock; the burger was gone and all that was left was a stray French fry or two.

Just then I saw three guys walking in from the parking lot. They were laughing. "Not from around here, are you?" I just shrugged my shoulders and sat down, taking in the devastation that was once my lunch. I even contemplated eating the remaining fries but thought better of it. I could see through the window of the burger shop that there was a line of people at the counter all the way out the main door. It would take forever to get served now. I ended up going down the street to get lunch at Der Wienerschnitzel.

I had gone to an In-N-Out Burger and all I got was a lousy t-shirt! Literally!

—

When I returned to work after the trip, I spent quite a bit of time talking about the experience with anyone who would listen. People could tell there was a new passion in my voice. I had always enjoyed driving, so it often didn't matter where I was going as long as it was a road trip. This hadn't changed, but my experiences on this trip in several of the national parks made me think I wanted to explore those areas more thoroughly. Seeing the mountains and the coastlines of Olympic, the Redwoods, and the granite canyons of Yosemite showed me there was so much in each of those places and I wanted to see more; a few hours or even a day was not nearly enough. Going forward I would have to plan to spend time in the parks, and there was no need to worry about my road trip time, the two objectives were completely compatible.

—

I was now working as the Corporate Applications Support Manager for a director who was a micromanager; nothing was done unless it went through her first. Some people never learn how demotivating it is to take all decision making away from an individual, but it's done on a regular basis in corporate America, to the detriment of the team's mission.

No matter my circumstances, my team was a solid group of individuals who I had no problem empowering to do their jobs the best way they knew how; as long as I ran interference for them, the director never had to know how things were getting done. One of those individuals had just taken a trip of his own and had brought back pictures. Vinay was showing me images and telling me about his trip through Utah when I stopped him abruptly on one particular image showing a freestanding red stone arch. "Where is this?" I asked. He told me about Delicate Arch in Arches National Park. I knew I would have to go there.

MIRANT WAS NO LONGER the high-flier it had been a few short years before. Enron had tanked the energy marketing industry by collapsing under the weight of its deceptive practices and the economy was growing unstable. Layoffs ensued, and I was on the list. Resigned to leaving, I was surprised when the CTO called me in one day and asked me to stay on to take a position as the manager of the Information Resource Group. This was a team I had created for him several years earlier, so running it would not be a problem, but I was already thinking about what I was going to do with the money from my layoff package so it wasn't as easy a decision as one might think. To prod me in his direction, he assured me he would hold the promised compensation deal for me and if I still wanted to leave a year from now, he would approve the request, no questions asked. I took the deal, worked in the requested capacity for the next year, and eventually went into his office to ask to be laid off in May of 2008.

Having had a year to plan, I knew exactly what I was going to do. I would take off on a road trip of the Utah National Parks, including Arches, and then weave my way down to Tucson to spend time with family and friends, after which I would return to Atlanta to find a new job. This would be a three-month-long vacation, which I sorely needed. And I had to laugh, because as I started up my car to pull out of the parking garage on my last day, the song "Goodbye to You" by Patty Smyth of Scandal was playing on my radio.

I WOULD FLY INTO Denver and rent a car, visit some friends, and then be on my way. There was an incredible freedom to this time away from everything. With no job hanging over me, there wasn't anything to worry about or the dread of having to go back to anything.

Nonetheless, my mind was still calibrated in such a way to push me to go somewhere and then move on as fast as possible to the next place. I wasn't slowing down to really get deep into any one area. See the sights and move on, see the sights and move on.

I hiked up to Delicate Arch, the stone arch in Vinay's picture, and watched the sun set on Arches National Park. It was magnificent, and in short bursts like this, I was able to stop and really enjoy the moment.

But Canyonlands was only thirty miles away; Capital Reef less than a day away, Bryce, Zion, and then the Grand Canyon. I should have been able to slow down and enjoy these places a whole lot more.

Unfortunately, …2008. The economy was collapsing, and my three-month-long relaxing vacation of discovery became only seventeen days on the road and another several weeks in Tucson wondering what to do next.

Upon my return to Atlanta, it was clear many jobs had simply disappeared in the fallout from the global financial crisis. I had picked the worst time in modern history to walk away from a steady job to explore the world. No one was hiring, particularly when it came to middle managers. I attempted, with two other out-of-work economic victims, to build a company that could have the potential of pulling us out of our personal despair as well as give us a foundation for the future, but all it really did was give us something to do when there was no need to prepare for interviews that didn't exist.

In the end, instead of traveling and exploring the West, I exhausted my lucrative compensation package to keep up with my mortgage and bills. It would be twenty-two months before I would once again be able to rely on getting a steady paycheck.

Seventeen

Extending Limits

I was considering any and all possibilities. The job market had warmed up, but not for me. I researched developing a photography business but realized the only real way to make money in the industry was to become a wedding photographer. It would mean working the weekends, which meant not being able to shoot sporting events at Georgia Tech or going to alumni events or spending time with friends. It would mean dealing with overly sensitive brides who seriously believed the world should be revolving around them, if not stopped all together to accommodate their every wish and whim. I didn't know if making money was worth the trouble.

And in the end, I enjoyed photography so much as a hobby, making it a job could very well take away my joy for it.

In an odd twist of fate, my friend Leslie was getting married. Several times in the past she had asked me to take pictures at her wedding, but I laughed it off saying there wouldn't be enough action to keep me interested. I even told Erwin, her husband to be, I would only participate if I could orchestrate a scene where he would throw his bride off of a balcony thus allowing me to capture the action of her fall, from down below.

With all that being said, eventually I relented and took on the task. Amazing what having nothing to do and no money coming in will do to change a person's perspective on things. I would shoot all the basic wedding stuff, a picture of the cake and posed pictures to include all the family and friend group shots. None of those concerned me in the least; oddly enough, it was the "action" shots that gave me anxiety. All the things happening before, during, and after the ceremony which if missed could spell disaster. Luckily, I was able to rise to the occasion and checked all the requisite wedding photo boxes. Additionally, Leslie and Erwin were a model couple; they were laid back and just having fun, so the event didn't have the usual tenseness of a wedding. At least I didn't feel it, and I was the wedding photographer. Because of how effortlessly things went, I made a promise to myself to never shoot another wedding; there's no way things could go near as well ever again.

I MAY NOT HAVE been actively working to turn my photography into a career, but jobs were finding me anyway. I was in a workshop for unemployed people with a woman by the name of Kimma Drake, who, along with her boyfriend Paul, worked in the filmmaking industry in Atlanta. They were involved in a project where each year professional filmmakers donate their time to create a film short, for a competition called the "48-Hour Film Project." Approximately seventy teams registered for the venture, which gave each team forty-eight hours to create a film as dictated by the parameters handed down to them by the competition management. This particular year their job was to film a seven-minute "Buddy Film," with a character named Alan, a transit company worker. They must use art supplies as a prop as well as the line "I think I can do it" somewhere in the plot.

The team developed the movie short *Doommates*, about how two roommates cope with each other when one gets furloughed from his transit company job and begins spending more time at home. I donated my time to do a photo documentary of the process.

One of the actors on the *Doommates* project was Sean Maxwell, who, being a photographer himself, liked the work I had done and asked me to document a music video he was producing called "Get Away," starring local rap talent DJ Dr. Dice.

Involved as an extra on the "Get Away" video was a local singer named Trinetta Love, who was producing her own video for the song "Just for You" off of her soon-to-be released *EnFamous* album. She hired me to document that effort.

The power of networking on full display…

ANOTHER FRIEND, PATRICE, WAS involved with the Steve Harvey Foundation and would periodically take pictures for his events. On one occasion she had her hands full with the comedian, actor, and bestselling author's "Freedom Friday" charity event at the America's Mart in Atlanta, and she asked me to assist her photographing the fans and celebrity guests including NBA Legend Dr. J, Julius Erving, NBA star Kevin Willis, actor Emmanuel Lewis, and rap artist Doug E Fresh.

Subsequent to that event when Steve Harvey realized his hats no longer fit because he had started shaving his head, he decided to auction them off with proceeds going to his charity. The auction would be online, so he needed pictures of all 150 hats, and I was just the guy to take on the project. When you talk about boring projects, this one would be king, but when you're getting paid it really doesn't need to be exciting.

WITH HELP FROM DEB, my former boss at Mirant, and support from Leslie, both of whom were now employed at Fiserv, I was able to get on as the SMS Platform Manager at the company. To complete the circular effect, Fiserv was formerly Checkfree, the company I was sold away from a little over ten years earlier. I was tasked with setting up the texting function for Fiserv's mobile banking products and although I had no experience in this area, neither did anyone else, so I had to learn on the fly.

IT WAS GREAT TO be working again, or at least pulling in a paycheck; truth be told I never liked working and was fully ready and willing to retire at twenty-two years old. In fact, long ago I had designed a detailed re-envisioning of the working world whereby a person would hire on with a company out of college and get paid for the ensuing thirty years to do whatever they wanted while they were young enough to go out and explore the world, after which they would become an indentured servant until death. At least this way you could truly take advantage of the best years of your life. As of this writing I still have no takers for my plan, but you never know…

What was truly nice about being back in an office again was developing new relationships with new acquaintances. Several of these would lead me to once again, like with Leslie's wedding, get out of my photography "box."

One such acquaintance was a very attractive administrative assistant I hit it off with as soon as we met. Nsenga had a dry sense of humor and could take a jab just as easily as she could throw one; she was my kind of girl. She was also one of the oldest, young women I've ever met; single and in her late twenties, all she ever did was work in her garden and watch "Antiques Road Show" on PBS. We went out several times although the relationship never went beyond being friends, partially because of our age difference, and partially due to the fact she, as a religious woman, was looking for someone who was less of a heathen than I. Since we weren't going to actually date, I often told her I no longer had to worry about her feelings so I could say anything I wanted to her. She responded by affectionately referring to me as "jerk Jerry" while to me she was "EN," Evil Nsenga. It was the perfect modern-day relationship.

Having seen the pictures from Leslie's wedding, Nsenga inquired whether I might want to take some pictures of she and her cousin who was staying with her for a school year in Atlanta. This would be the classic, as I refer to it, "rocks and creeks" kind of stuff. It's what most people think of when they imagine the perfect portrait, sitting on a rock next to a creek.

Boring! However, again it was different, and it would give me a chance to do something I'd never attempted before. Besides, I also liked spending time with Nsenga, so I agreed. I selected a little park near where I lived that had an old, weathered building and, you guessed it, some rocks and a creek. The shoot went very well, and I was surprised to see how relaxed Nsenga could be in front of a camera.

This gave me another idea to do a photo session dedicated entirely to Nsenga. We would travel to the Chateau Elan Winery & Resort north of Atlanta and shoot her in the afternoon with a casual outfit, and then in the early evening with my Porsche in something more elegant. It would be perfect for both of us; I could play like I was some kind of fashion photographer, and she could release her inner diva.

It all went better than I could have ever expected. Nsenga had gotten her hair styled and looked amazing whether in jeans early in the day or the sexy club dress she wore as the sun went down. We used my car for a lot of the evening shots in front of the winery, which added to the scene.

Days later I emailed Nsenga to tell her I was working on the images, and they were really coming out great. She asked to see them, but I told her she would have to wait until they were done and up on my website. She didn't like my answer and demanded I send her at least one picture. So, I took an image of her standing next to my car and cropped it down so the car was in the center of the frame and all you could see of Nsenga was her right arm and leg. When she received my email and opened the picture, she thought she was having some sort of problem with her computer and was frantic because she couldn't see herself. I guess she probably had it right, I am sort of a jerk, but I still laugh out loud when I think about her getting upset seeing my cropped masterpiece for the first time.

YET ANOTHER "MODEL" PROJECT involved one more of my coworkers, a woman of Indian descent named Arti. I did a photo shoot of her that yielded many attractive and expressive images. When we'd first met, we bonded immediately as if we had been friends our entire lives, so I came up with the idea to use one of the images to create a fun faux book cover I called "7,356,977 Shades (and counting) of Arti," to represent the depth and complexity of her personality. We both still laugh to this day about another one of the images where I'd asked her to give me a sexy look while nibbling on her pearl necklace. Instead of evoking a sexy vibe it made one think, "someone give that woman a sandwich!"

—➤

I ENJOYED TRYING NEW things and working with models, but then the word "work" popped up again. I'm not crazy about setting things up; the time it takes to arrange lighting, backgrounds, and outfits. It's why I like sports so much. You just get the shot, or not, and move on to the next play. It's fast-paced. It's always something new and completely different from moment to moment; like a snowflake, no two actions in sports are exactly the same.

Eighteen

Beginning the Chase

After my 2006 Pacific Coast Highway trip out West, I had a new appreciation and awareness of the national parks, and I wanted to explore them more deeply. Before then, I would take a road trip and visit a park if it was on the way. Now my mindset had shifted, and I was going to make it a goal to visit the parks; my road trips would revolve around going from one park to the next. This new way of thinking actually had an additive effect; I would still have the excitement of the road trip and discovering things along the way, but I would now also have specific points where I could plan to see and explore these places explicitly set aside for their history and beauty.

I took short trips to visit places like Congaree National Park in South Carolina, which protects the largest contiguous area of old-growth bottomland hardwood forest remaining in the United States and Mammoth Cave National Park in Kentucky, the longest cave system in the world.

In 2008 I had attempted a multi-park tour only to have my trip cut short because of the financial crisis, but now in 2011 I was reviving the concept and reimplementing it in a big way. I would plan to visit six national parks in a loop through the northwest.

If I were an airline, Denver would be my hub. It's in the middle of everything I want to see in the West, no matter which direction I choose to go. I also have several friends there, which makes it a nice place to pass through, a place where I can feel at home with some familiar faces. One of those familiar faces is my friend Susan. We originally met in Houston while we were working with Shell Oil. She had just graduated from the University of Arizona, so we were basically related by the fact we attended the same school. Through the years we developed our friendship, bonding over discussing the poor choices we were making in our dating lives, although I will admit she had more opportunities to fail than I ever had; however, this was all in the past and she was now settled in Denver with her husband Alf and their two kids. Since I was passing through and visiting them quite often, it was debatable whether they might even be able to claim me as a dependent on their taxes. A few years earlier, they took me to visit their ranch in Basalt, about three hours west of Denver. On a trip to explore the surrounding mountains, Alf and I got out of the car to get some pictures of the snow-covered hills and Susan proceeded to honk the horn to get our attention, exhibiting a shocking disregard for the sanctity of life in an avalanche zone. This time around we simply went out to eat and I can happily report there were no incidents.

After leaving Denver I took a quick trip through Rocky Mountain National Park and then headed north into Wyoming, spending only a short amount of time passing through Grand Teton and Yellowstone National Parks.

HEADING EVEN FURTHER NORTH into Montana, I stopped for the night just outside the east entrance to Glacier National Park. I was a little worried about this park as the fifty-mile-long Going to the Sun Road was still listed as closed when I checked the status before leaving Denver. Snowplows were still working around the clock to open things up near the summit at Logan Pass. Mind you, this was on the fifteenth of July! In the morning

I crossed my fingers and headed for the east gate, where the condition of the road was my first question. Luckily, the ranger informed me the road had opened two days earlier and it was clear all the way to the west gate. My first goal was to drive the entire road and take in the beautiful vistas; from the tooth-like peaks to the large U-shaped valleys, this park is a testament to the eroding power of the glaciers that formed and transformed this area. As I drove along St. Mary's Lake, I came to the first of many mind-blowing landscapes: the view of Wild Goose Island surrounded by the reflection of the mountains on the surface of the lake.

As I continued on toward Logan Pass, it was easy to see why it took so long to clear this road as twelve- to fourteen-foot walls of snow towered over each side of the pavement. Well, where there was pavement at all. It was not unusual for the plows to destroy the road in the process of clearing it, so there were quite a few gravel sections filled with potholes to cross. The parking area at Logan Pass was surrounded by snow. It was like pulling into a black-top valley, but the views of the neighboring area were amazing.

The next day I got myself out of bed at four because I was on a mission and I would have a limited window to make it a success. I downed two small single serving boxes of Cheerios I had purchased the day before and packed up to get on the road. My objective was to go north to the Many Glacier area of the park to attempt to get a picture of Grinnell Point reflected in Swiftcurrent Lake. This area is famous, not only for the beauty, but also for the Alpine Chalet-style hotel built there in 1915. As I got closer to my target, I could tell things were going my way as the nearby mountains were reflected in the very still Lake Sherburne. I didn't want to stop for fear I might get to Swiftcurrent Lake too late to get the picture I wanted, but I couldn't help myself as what I was seeing was stunning. So, I slammed on the brakes and stopped just long enough to get a few shots and then hopped back in the car to continue down the road. There were two issues with getting this shot, stillness of the water and angle of the sun; if a breeze started rippling the water or I showed up too late, the perfect image would be impossible. I was worried about both.

I pulled into the chalet parking area and saw I had nothing to worry about. The surface of Swiftcurrent Lake was glass-like and Grinnell Point, flanked by Mount Gould and Swiftcurrent Mountain, were beautifully mirrored in the deep blue water.

AFTER GETTING THE PERFECT Glacier Park images, I made a side trip to see the Grand Coulee Dam, the largest power-producing facility in the United States, and then made my way to North Cascades National Park in northern Washington. The only access is via the North Cascade Highway, which runs through the middle of the park as ninety-four percent of the area is designated wilderness. Along the road is the beautiful Lake Diablo, where I was able to get images of Snowfield and Pyramid Peaks partially shrouded in the clouds. Sometimes a partially overcast sky can be used to your advantage to add a dramatic look to your subject, and this was definitely one of those times.

Unfortunately, not everything was as nice as could be in this area. The lake system was produced by the construction of three dams, the Gorge, Diablo, and Ross, which provide power for Seattle and the surrounding area. Not only are the dams in the park, but so are the hydroelectric power plants, which means major power lines and towers obstruct what should be some very nice views. Then again, you just have to know where to point your camera as the dramatic Picket Range can easily be viewed from the highway, and Copper Pass, Snagtooth Ridge, and the Early Winter Spires formation make for some splendid viewing on the east side of the park.

I HAD TRAVELED TO Seattle three previous times since my sister Vicky once lived there. It's a great city and you haven't lived until you've laid eyes on the Space Needle, visited Pike Place Market for all its colorful produce and goods, and witnessed the salmon toss at the fish market. My sports photography experience came in handy as I was able to capture the flying fish action.

However, one landmark had eluded me on each previous visit. I had never seen Mount Rainier. It was there of course, only it was always obscured by cloud cover. This time I was coming to the area specifically to see the mountain and I was hoping the fourth time would be a charm.

I had a feeling of doom when I arrived in Mount Rainier National Park; it was as cloudy as I had ever seen it, but the skies cleared by mid-afternoon, revealing the massive mountain and lighting up the thick old-growth forests surrounding it. Sometimes you just need to rely on luck, and I finally had my day. In fact, things cleared up so nicely I could also see Mount Adams in the distance.

—

BOTH MOUNT RAINIER AND Mount Adams are active volcanos in the Cascade Range, as is Mount St. Helens. After my trip to Mount Rainier, I thought it only right to visit Mount St. Helens National Volcanic Monument to see first-hand what these mountains were capable of when they release their full explosive potential.

It was May 18, 1980, when the mountain came to life and the full force of nature resulted in the largest landslide in recorded history. The top 1,300 feet of the mountain collapsed into the valley and the force of the blast took what was once old growth forest, much like I had seen at Mount Rainier just days before and turned it into a barren pumice plain with trees laid flat, pointing away from the blast zone. The contrast is stark and foreboding even today as plant life still struggles to re-emerge.

I hiked out on Boundary Trail #1, which travels in the direction of Spirit Lake and puts you directly across from the gaping open side of the mountain. It is an incredible view, and you can still see steam rising from under the dome inside the crater.

Unlike all the other parks I have visited, each taking millions of years to form and evolve, this remarkable place changed in an instant within my lifetime. Today not much has changed since the eruption, although I was able to see spots where plant life was returning, and the yearly bloom was taking place. It is hard to fathom what could happen if Mount Rainier, looming above the city of Seattle, were to come to life and what it would mean for the city and perhaps the entire northwest.

I HAD THREE WEEKS of vacation time each year, and I would use two of those weeks to take a national parks trip in a selected area of the country. It would start with thoroughly mapping out my route and stops before flying in and renting a car. I was seeing the things I wanted to see but still not spending the time I wanted to actually explore. Then again, there was not much I could do about it since working paid for my excursions.

Nineteen

Pacific Parks

In 2013, I would focus on the West Coast, specifically seven of the eight national parks in California. I flew into Los Angeles to start my journey, and true to form, immediately found myself stuck in traffic on Interstate 405 trying to get to U.S. Highway 101. It reminded me of the classic *Saturday Night Live* skit "The Californians."

"Stuart, take the 405 to Van Nuys and exit onto the 101…"

It was exactly what I was trying to do as I needed to get to Oxnard to catch a boat to Channel Islands National Park.

To be precise, I was headed to the island of Anacapa, which is the closest to the mainland of the five islands that make up the national park. At only twelve miles off the coast, it only takes an hour to get there; although we didn't see a lot of wildlife while on the water, we did get followed by some dolphins and checked out by a curious sea lion or two. The real fun with wildlife was to come upon reaching the island.

The ranger on board our boat explained we would encounter quite a few birds as we hiked around on the trails. Not only was Anacapa a safe haven for the brown pelican, which as late as 1970 faced extinction, but we were arriving in the middle of the seagull nesting season and there were approximately 30,000 Western Gulls on the islands, including their newly hatched chicks. The ranger explained that the birds were very defensive, often flying directly at hikers. He said pointing up directly at the birds would force them to break off their attack. These warnings seemed a bit much...until we arrived on the island and were immediately dive-bombed by the aforementioned seagull mothers; Alfred Hitchcock's horror story had nothing on this place!

Everywhere you walked, everywhere you looked, there were seagull nests with seagull eggs and tiny chirping seagull chicks; and where there are cute little baby seagulls there are protective mother seagulls. Just to put things in perspective, I was on East Anacapa, which was only a mile long, and there were 30,000 birds in nests and in the air all around me. It felt like I had stepped into a *National Geographic* documentary, and it was easy to see why this tiny island was known as the "Galapagos of the U.S."

I hiked the one-mile trail out to Inspiration Point on the western edge of the island where you get a spectacular view of the rest of the Anacapa chain with the much larger Santa Cruz Island floating immediately to the west. Did I mention there were a lot of birds? I spent the entire hike defending myself from attackers using my camera with the long lens as my "pointing" tool. By the way, it does work; the gulls would come directly at you until you pointed at them, at which time they would break off their kamikaze-style run and circle back to their nest or the chick they were protecting. And nests were everywhere, including right next to the trail. Several times I had to skirt by a squawking mother bird who would stand over her egg and nip at me as I walked past...great, now I was getting attacked by air and by land!

The way back to the boat was just as treacherous as the hike to the point. I ran across two women I had met earlier in the day, one from Sweden and the other from the Netherlands, who were traveling together and had obviously not understood the instructions given by the park ranger. As I approached, they were ducking and screaming, standing back-to-back trying to defend each other from the relentless gull assaults; they were having a tough time. I stifled my amusement at the sight of their ineffective defensive technique and gave them an in-person lesson on how to repulse the aggressive gulls. They were grateful and I watched as they walked off toward Inspiration Point holding their hands above their heads the whole way.

As for me, I survived the ordeal without any lasting psychological effects. I can only guess my past experience working at the canary farm as a teenager gave me the strength to make it through this disturbing ordeal. Either that or I was so damaged back then this couldn't possibly make things any worse.

THE COLORADO AND MOJAVE deserts converge in Joshua Tree National Park. At the lower elevations, the Colorado Desert hosts spiny plants like the ocotillo and cholla cactus, while the higher altitude Mojave Desert is home to the park's namesake, the Joshua tree. The legend goes, Mormon settlers gave the plant its name because they believed the extended arms of the tree looked like the biblical figure Joshua guiding them westward. The southern section of the park is where the tree can survive for several hundred years and grow up to fifty feet tall in forest-like quantity.

As I travel, between parks or in the parks themselves, I never turn on the stereo; no music, no talk shows, no CDs, nothing. I want to be engaged with wherever I am, and whatever I am viewing. I've always traveled this way and although some would think this odd, it is normal for me. So, as I entered this park in solitude and began to take in the scene, I was startled by a sudden blast of music, "Happy Trails to you…"

What was going on? Was this the voice of God? Was my time up? I knew the radio wasn't on. I didn't turn it on. What the hell? So, it wasn't the voice of God, it was Roy Rogers singing the song that made him famous and being unfamiliar with the workings of my rental car, I had accidentally turned the radio on with the button on the steering wheel. I could relax again knowing I wasn't going crazy, and I wasn't being "called home."

Along with the wonderous tree that is the focal point of the park, there are also many interesting rock formations, boulder stacks, and jumbles. I had seen one called Arch Rock in pictures and I wanted to see it for myself. The map indicated it was just a short hike along a nature trail from the White Tank campground. When I arrived at the camping area, I found the gate was locked, so I pulled off the road, parked, and started walking. It wasn't more than a hundred yards before I got to the first camp site so I knew I was close, and when I came upon a trail, I figured this must be my path to the arch. I walked along the flat easy path that wound around large interestingly shaped boulders, absolutely sure I was going the right way. But after 30 minutes in the 105-degree heat, I began to doubt myself; to complicate things, I was running out of water since I had left the car with only a half-filled bottle. Where was this thing? It was supposed to be close by. I wandered on through the jumble of rocks. I really could have used Joshua to guide me right then, although seeing him at this moment might have been symptomatic of a host of other issues or might indicate my impending doom. And I'd already been visited by the ghost of Roy Rogers today, so I didn't need any other dead people revealing themselves just then. I was lost, had just a sip of water left, and was getting baked by the sun; was this it, was this the end?

Then, a miracle. I rounded a corner and there it was, Arch Rock, the very formation I was pursuing. It actually looked like an elephant extending its trunk to me, but what do I know? Maybe they just didn't think Elephant Rock was appropriate out here in the desert. Then again, I might just be delirious. I took some pictures and continued down the trail hoping it would lead me back to my car. Less than ten minutes later I was back at the campground where I walked up to the back of a sign. As I passed it, I saw it read "Arch Rock - 0.5 miles." I must've done at least two miles getting to this point. No matter, I was just concerned about making it the last hundred yards back to my car so I could get some water!

DEATH VALLEY. THE NAME of this park brings to mind stark imagery that is contrary to its real beauty. Stunning vistas, rugged mountains, and colorful foothills surround the valley, which boasts the record for the hottest temperature on earth, 134 degrees on July 10, 1913.

So, let's get this out of the way. It was a little warm in Death Valley National Park during my two-day visit. Officially it was 125 degrees on the first day and 129 degrees the second; however, on day one my car registered 136 degrees on the road between Furnace Creek and where I was staying, Stovepipe Wells!

High summer temperatures are nothing new here, but this was special. In fact, as the weather service warned of possible record highs, the media drew attention to the possibility of breaking the official record. As soon as I got out of bed on my second day in the park, I turned on "Good Morning America" only to see the ABC News Chief Meteorologist Ginger Zee reporting from just down the road at the Furnace Creek Ranger Station. I jumped up to head over there before I realized what I was watching had been taped earlier in the morning.

My first day in the park had already been memorable. In my hotel room at Stovepipe Wells, the air conditioning had to run constantly at full blast, day and night, to keep the room cool enough to be tolerable; I never even had to turn on the hot water in the shower because the cold water was already hot. Later, after visiting the tortured valley floor at the Devils Golf Course, my rental car began to overheat. Remembering what I learned from my dad dealing with the problem many years ago, I shut down the air conditioning, rolled down the windows, and turned on the heat to cool the engine. It worked but I was thoroughly cooked.

For lunch I decided to cool things down a bit and head up to Dantes

View. At 5,436 feet above sea level, this mountaintop overlooks the entire valley. I found myself a nice shelf of rock to sit on and leaned back to eat my sandwich; it was like my own little throne high above it all. After a scorching morning, it was a "pleasant" ninety-nine degrees here in the shadow of Coffin Peak.

The main draw of this park is that it boasts the lowest point in the Western Hemisphere at 282 feet below sea level. The Badwater Basin is a sprawling salt flat that stretches across this foreboding valley, and the heat would no doubt make venturing out of the car a unique experience. I pulled into the parking area at the Badwater Basin Salt Flats Trail determined to make my way out onto the flat. I drank a full sixteen-ounce bottle of water before I got out of the car and, along with my camera, I took two more bottles with me. The temperature was somewhere in the 125-plus range, but I was not going to let anything stop me now. As I got to the trail, I was surprised to find water at Badwater Basin; an information board explained that it is indeed "bad water." I stepped off of the boardwalk overlooking the Badwater Pool and onto the bright white salt flat itself. The heat was stifling, both baking you from above and reflecting off the flat. When the air temperature is as high as it was that day, the ground temperature can reach 180 to 200 degrees, but it's a dry heat...only blast furnace hot!

Behind me, high up on the rocky mountainside jutting upward from the basin was a sign indicating where sea level was. This was crazy; it gets hot in Tucson, but this was like being in an oven! I was already feeling the effect of the intense heat. The air was still, and under my hat I could feel the hot sun radiating upward off of the white surface of the salt flat. Only minutes ago I had stepped off the boardwalk and now I was already finishing my first bottle of water. This was a half-mile trail and I made it no more than one hundred yards from the car before I decided to turn around to head back. I drank the second bottle of water before I made it back to the parking area. I pulled out my keys and hurried to get into the car so I could start it up and turn on the air conditioning, after which I drank my fourth sixteen-ounce bottle of water; I had only been outside for fifteen minutes!

When I told people at work of my intention to visit Death Valley in the last week of June, everyone said I was crazy. My reply, "Anyone can tour Death Valley in the winter!"

From the heat of Death Valley, I circled around the southern reaches of the Sierra Nevada mountain range and north to the much cooler interior of Sequoia and Kings Canyon National Parks. From there I headed almost straight west to visit the nation's newest national park, Pinnacles. This park was only a national monument when I was planning this trip, so in order to fit it in, I had to move some things around and make it only a short detour. This is a park I would have to dedicate more time to later.

My next stop was in Northern California at Lassen Volcanic National Park. In some ways, this park is a mini-Yellowstone. At its heart is Lassen Peak, the largest active plug dome volcano in the world. At 10,475 feet, it last erupted in 1914 and was only part of a much larger volcano, which was over eight miles wide at its base and over 11,000 feet high.

This is an active volcanic landscape with constantly changing hydrothermal features including bubbling mud pots, steaming fumaroles, and boiling water. The largest of these areas is Bumpass Hell, named after an explorer whose leg was badly scalded and had to be amputated when he fell through the thin crust covering a mud pot.

In addition to all the interesting things about this park it was also very photogenic. Lake Helen, which is a deep blue, sits at the base of Lassen Peak and made for some nice images, as did views of the peak from Upper Kings Creek Meadow. During my visit, snow still filled some of the surfaces of the mountain and at points along some of the trails.

I was captivated by the many windswept and weathered trees and found them to be interesting subjects. When photographing landscapes like these trees I am often able to use some of the same techniques I use when I'm shooting sports, in particular back button focus.

Normally the shutter release button on a camera controls everything: focus, exposure, and the shutter release. Using back button focus allows me to lock the length of the exposure and the focus using two distinct buttons on the back of the camera, separate from the shutter release. For sports this means I can easily refocus on a moving subject almost constantly, while for landscape photography, it allows me to focus on my subject and then recompose the shot by moving the subject away from the center of the frame without losing focus on it. For instance, I can focus on a tree in the middle of the frame and then move it all the way to the side of the image to also show a mountain in the distance.

The exposure button is also a great tool for landscape photography. It allows you to select the exposure for your shot to make the image lighter or darker depending on the length of the exposure, or how much light is let into the camera through the lens. I never use this in sports, but out in the wilderness where you're dealing with contrast issues, it comes in very handy. Both make for nice tools to have at your disposal when shooting landscapes.

The tool I used most often on my vacation was, of course, my car and it was particularly important on these two-week trips where I didn't have a lot of time to spend in any one place. And it could get me into trouble.

I was racing from place to place on the Lassen Volcanic National Park Highway when all of a sudden, I had company. It was a park ranger, and he had his "Christmas tree" all lit up. I pulled over and waited to hear my fate.

"License and registration please sir." Words you never want to hear when driving.

"Sir, do you know why I pulled you over?"

"Yes, I was speeding. I was trying to get to my next location and I just got a little careless," I figured there was no reason to try to get out of anything. We both knew why we were here.

He retreated to his vehicle to call in my information and spent some time back there no doubt writing me a nice long ticket. I watched as he got out of his ranger SUV and came back to my window.

"Sir, you were speeding but I'm going to let you go today because you were very upfront and honest when I asked you why I stopped you. Believe it or not, we don't hear a lot of that in these situations. Slow down and have a good day."

No way, did that just happen? I certainly wasn't going to question it further.

—→

I passed Mount Shasta and a short time later left the state of California, driving into Oregon for my final destination on this road trip, Crater Lake National Park. This is one of a string of active volcanoes in the Cascade Range, including Mount St. Helens and Mount Rainier. The eruption of Mount Mazama 7,700 years ago caused the top of the mountain to collapse in upon itself forming a crater that filled with snow and rain over the centuries.

Today Crater Lake is the deepest lake in the United States at 1,943 feet; it owes its incredible clarity and color to the lack of sediment in the water since there are no streams feeding into the lake. And when I say it has incredible color and clarity, I mean it's like nothing I've ever seen; it's the deepest, most beautiful blue and it's so clear you can see forty feet below the surface!

This park is unbelievably serene and beautiful. You don't have to know anything about photography to get a good picture here; just point the camera toward the lake and shoot!

As with my trip to Glacier National Park in Montana, I knew what I needed to do: get up very early, hope for clear skies and still waters, and if all is just perfect, I could get some nice images of the crater rim reflected in these magnificent waters.

Excited about the prospect, I did everything I needed to do, and the skies were crystal clear. I raced up to the crater hoping the final piece of the puzzle, the absence of a breeze, would also be in place. I had picked out the spot I wanted to shoot from the day before, and when I arrived, I was elated to find it completely calm. It had all come together, the perfect conditions for my shoot.

Then I got out of the car. Mosquitos were everywhere. Thick, almost cloud-like swarms descended on me one after the other as I moved into position to take my photographs. I had no bug spray; I would just have to cope. Focus, frame, shoot, wave arms, slap where I felt a bite. Focus, frame, shoot, wave arms, slap where I felt a bite. Not able to keep up against the relentless attack, I was getting eaten alive.

A couple about my age was there, and the woman, seeing my plight, came flying over to me with a can of bug spray in hand, yelling "Hold still, I got you!" She unleashed a torrent of insect repellant so thick it formed a cloud around me. I hoisted my camera as high into the air as I possibly could to protect it from the onslaught. When the game was over, it would be scored: lady with bug spray, one; mosquitos, nothing. I was free, sort of…

I thanked the kind woman, and she told me her name was Annie and she was here with her husband from Sacramento. Oh, and could I take a picture of them together in front of the lake? Well, sure, it was the least I could do after she rescued me from the clutches of the hordes of mosquitos making a pincushion out of me.

She handed me her camera and ran back to her husband where they sat together on the wall. I snapped a picture and went to hand the camera back to her, but they shifted positions. "Okay, now this," she said. I snapped another picture. They shifted position. I snapped another picture. Again. Again. It became an impromptu studio session…she owned me!

Eventually we exhausted all the possible angles and poses, and the photo shoot ended. Just as importantly, I had gotten my perfect Crater Lake images. Annie from Sacramento had saved my life and in return, taking a few pictures for her was the least I could do.

Twenty

Breckenridge Buds

There was no doubt Atlanta was my home. I missed Tucson, but I enjoyed everything about where I was living. I had a good job again. Alpharetta was one of the best places to be in the metro area and was still growing. It could be a little humid at times, but after living in Houston, the situation here was like heaven.

My neighborhood, Breckenridge, had grown up too. When I first arrived, it was stocked with young couples; now they were having children, and some were moving on to bigger homes. I had cycled through a pair of marriages.

One thing had stayed constant, or maybe two things: Kathy and Beth. The three of us had moved into the subdivision within months of each other as the homes were built in progression down the street. We all played tennis, which is how we became acquainted, playing on the Breckenridge coed Atlanta Lawn Tennis Association (ALTA) team. ALTA had separate men's and women's seasons, which ran at the same time and then alternated with coed seasons in between. I won't belabor the point, but of the three of us, I was the only one to win a city championship and I'm including this fact here for no other reason but to piss off Kathy.

If you put all three of us on a line, Beth is the quiet, religious traditionalist on one end while Kathy is the loud, wild, heathen who always has a glass of wine in her hand on the opposite end. I would fall in the middle, well, maybe more toward Kathy's position. Okay, maybe at the three-quarter point.

By some means the three of us bonded, and although we never agreed on anything, it was somehow workable and always fun when we got together. Beth was continually shocked by the things I said and the things Kathy did; Kathy was amazed at how much of a quiet homebody Beth was and couldn't believe most of what I said, often looking at me and simply saying "What is wrong with you?" Truth be told, I always enjoyed shocking both of them and made it a game to see if I could get Kathy to the point where she would become infuriated and fire her signature question in my direction.

If you wanted a quiet evening and to be home before nine, Beth was the one to call. If you wanted chaos and a possible addition to your rap sheet, Kathy was your woman. When all three of us were together, Beth would temper Kathy, so things would normally not spin out of control; I on the other hand, had no effect over her and quite frankly enjoyed the chaos that often swirled around her.

I MENTIONED TO BOTH Beth and Kathy that I was working with a woman named Crystal who was a singer who had a weekend gig at Six Flags Over Georgia. I'm not a big amusement park fan, but I was going to go to see her performance and lend her my support. Beth wasn't interested, but Kathy perked right up and said she would tag along if we could also take time to ride the Batman roller coaster. I agreed, and the next Saturday we made the forty-minute drive to the park.

Kathy had brought along two cans of Coke because they had ten-dollars-off coupons printed on them, which was great because the park entrance fee was thirty dollars each, and they charge for parking as well. We were arriving early in the day so there wasn't much traffic and the queue to the park ticket booth was empty. In enthusiastic anticipation of her ticket purchase, Kathy had already pulled out her twenty-dollar bill before we even got out of the parking area; it was the last time I would see a smile on her face for some time.

As we reached the booth, cans of Coke in hand, Kathy realized she had lost her cash somewhere along the way. We searched the vicinity to no avail, and she mumbled about how some nearby kids had "probably pocketed the fucking money; the little bastards!" The tide had turned on her attitude and I laughed to myself knowing things would, in the end, be all right as long as I got her on the roller coaster sometime before we headed home. However, it didn't stop me from pointing out she had actually paid twenty dollars more to get into this place than I had, and although she didn't say it, she gave me a "what is wrong with you" look, and I knew this could turn into a very long day.

I wasn't sure exactly where Crystal would be singing, but we had an hour to find her. Looking on the park map, I surmised the theater was the most likely place, so we headed over there. It wasn't the place and when I asked someone inside, they gave us two or three possibilities to check out, which did not make Kathy very happy.

"Oh, for Christ's sake, let's just go ride the roller coaster!"

I reminded her of the reason for our trip and motioned for her to follow me to the next venue.

"Oh, for fuck's sake! Are you trying to sleep with this woman? Is that what this is all about?"

"No, she's married, I'm just here to support her." And we moved on finally finding the outdoor stage where Crystal would be performing, outdoors.

It was overcast but hot and humid. Neither of us were happy about the conditions, but as I sat quietly waiting for the performance to begin, Kathy raged on.

"My hair is frizzing."

"I'm sweating like a pig. You should have to pay for my dry cleaning!"

"This woman better be the second coming of Faith Hill; are you sure you're not just trying to get into her pants?"

"My makeup is a mess. This is all your fault!"

"She should've started five minutes ago. Let's go!"

The show started and went on for almost an hour, as did Kathy.

"Okay, you've seen her, let's go."

"How long is this going to go on?"

"Are you sure you're not just trying to get into her pants?"

As it ended, Kathy hopped up and said "Finally, let's go," but I told her I wanted to go congratulate Crystal before we left. It didn't set well with Kathy, but she followed me up to the stage so I could say hi and tell Crystal how much we enjoyed the show.

Finally, we were on our way to the Batman ride and Kathy's demeanor had noticeably improved. She was still reminding me of how awful a time she was having, but the prospect of the upcoming ride was keeping her as positive as possible under the circumstances. The line was long but manageable, and as we inched our way to the front our excitement was building. We eventually reached the covered area, which we had determined meant we would have to watch only one more group get on before it would be our turn. Then it started to rain, and the operator announced the roller coaster would shut down and not open back up until thirty minutes after it stopped raining.

"Wow, I'm sure glad I didn't pay an extra twenty dollars to get in here," I said, knowing I was probably not going to survive the storm that would soon envelop me.

"Oh, for fuck's sake! Shut up! We're staying! I'm going to ride this thing no matter how long it takes!"

Luckily, we were under the awning so we weren't getting wet, but the rain was slow and constant and after about thirty minutes we agreed we were in a losing battle and headed back to the car.

I sat quietly as the drive home turned into a painful recap of the entire affair as Kathy recounted every disastrous moment in dark and intense detail.

To my dismay, as we approached downtown Atlanta, I had to slow down as traffic ground to a halt because of an accident.

Kathy added this new incident to her ongoing rant, "This is all your fault! What the hell is happening now? Why are we stopping?"

I replied, "It's probably some guy who's had to listen to a woman whine and complain all day, and just to end his own misery drove head long into a bridge abutment!"

It was quiet for a split second and I looked at Kathy expecting the worst; instead, she exploded in laughter and the hilarity of the situation carried us the rest of the way home.

It wasn't the only memorable trip we took together. One Wednesday night I received a call from her saying she had bought a mattress from a coworker and she wanted me to go with her to pick it up. I wasn't happy about an errand like this in the middle of a work week, but I agreed to go on the condition that we would get the mattress and come straight home. Kathy picked me up in her SUV and we went directly to her friend Lisa's apartment where the mattress was located, carried it outside, and tied it to the top of Kathy's vehicle. Easy and quick. Kathy and Lisa then retreated back into the apartment, so I went back inside to see what was happening.

"We're going out for one drink." Kathy exclaimed.

"Kathy, you've got a mattress tied to your car. Let's go home."

"Just one, it'll be okay."

We headed into the nearby Atlanta suburb of Dunwoody to a place called The Fat Lobster, where we would meet Lisa's friend Tootie.

We pulled in and parked, and looking back at the odd scene, I told Kathy and Lisa I wished I was lucky enough to meet a woman at a bar who was so prepared for the evening that she even had a bed strapped on top of her car. For some reason I never meet women quite so "outgoing."

Inside we made our way to a table of about five or six people, all younger than Kathy and me. They had all tossed back a few by the time our first drink was laid before us, so things were already in high party gear.

Lisa, a pretty, petite blonde, was sitting to my left, and at one point several of us somehow got into a conversation about bras, whereupon Lisa proclaimed she was wearing a water bra. I inquired further, never having heard of such a thing, and she explained it was basically a type of pushup bra. Then she took my left hand and slid it up under her crop top to let me feel it…feel her. I tried to remain as cool as a guy possibly could considering I had my hand on the breast of a woman I'd just met. And I thought a bed on top of an SUV would be the highlight of the evening!

One drink turned into Kathy insisting we have one more before we went home, and the makeshift party raged on. Several of the others at the table left over the next thirty minutes, and as we finished our drinks, Lisa declared we needed to go to the Rusty Nail, another local bar that was a bit of a dive. I looked at Kathy, my eyes saying, "let's go home," which she clearly understood but rejected by telling me, "Lighten up. It'll be fun. Anyway, I'm driving."

Back to the bed on wheels we went; Lisa rode with her friend Tootie and we met them at the bar. Somehow, they beat us there; maybe it was because Kathy and I had our arms outside the vehicle and were holding on to the progressively loosening mattress blowing in the wind, but I'm just guessing. As we walked into the bar, the ladies each had a drink and were downing a shot while exclaiming that the two of us needed to hurry if we wanted to catch up. Kathy was all too willing to oblige; I got a drink to sip as a prop because I had already had enough. Then, true to form for this evening, I watched as Lisa, in her short little jean skirt and aforementioned crop top, climbed on top of the bar and started to dance. Immediately, the bartender reached up and put his arms around her waist and yanked her back down to earth. He then pointed at Kathy and me and said, "You need to get her out of here!"

As we reassembled in the parking lot it was obvious the two girls were way beyond drunk; I would drive Tootie's car and Lisa would ride with Kathy so we could get everyone home safely. Luckily, Tootie lived in the same apartment complex as Lisa, so after making sure she got into her apartment I walked back to Lisa's place.

Damned if Lisa and Kathy weren't doing tequila shots as I walked into the kitchen!

"Hey, Jerry's here, let's do another shot for him!" Lisa slurred as she poured me a shot. Again, I shot a cross-eyed look at Kathy, but it didn't faze her earlier and it wasn't fazing her now.

Things seemed to settle down a bit. No more shots were poured, and we all just stood there and talked. Out of nowhere Lisa blurted out, "I bought some cute clothes today. Do you guys want to see?" And with that we all headed upstairs to her bedroom to see what she had purchased.

I sat on the edge of the bed as the two girls began taking items out of several bags, holding them up, and declaring how "cute" or "nice" or "sexy" each one was.

"That is perfect for you," Kathy would say.

"I bet it would look great on you too, Kath," as Lisa held it up against Kathy's chest. "You need to try it on!"

In no time the two women had stripped down to only their panties and were helping each other try on the still tagged items of clothing.

And I thought a bed on an SUV or feeling up a woman I just met would be the highlight of the evening!

As the frenzy wound down, Lisa sat next to me on the bed and suddenly became solemn. "I wish I had big, beautiful breasts like you Kathy, mine are so tiny."

As an independent observer I must say, Kathy's breasts are huge and magnificent; however, Lisa's breasts fit her petite frame very nicely, and in an effort to cheer her up, I told her so.

Unconvinced by my humanitarian effort, Lisa stood up and put her hand on Kathy's breasts and declared, "No, these are amazing, feel them," and took my hand and put it on Kathy's breast.

Again, solely in an attempt to sooth the poor girl's pain, I reached over, and while cupping Kathy's breast with my left hand put my right hand on Lisa's breast and professed how beautiful and perfectly perky her breasts were.

At this point I decided to refrain from declaring anything a highlight of the evening until said evening was actually over; it's better that way!

Lisa smiled at me and jumped onto the bed. Kathy declared she needed a drink and ran downstairs to get something, anything. Still fully dressed, I crawled onto the bed next to Lisa and began to kiss her as Kathy returned with the bottle of tequila, poured herself a shot and then joined us on the bed.

From my prone position I started to undress as Kathy half rolled onto Lisa and they began to kiss.

"Oh, she's out, we better leave her. Let's go." Lisa had passed out.

"Wait, we can wake her up!" The distress I felt as the possibility of having a threesome was ripped from my grasp was intense.

"NO! What is wrong with you?"

There it was, and I wasn't even trying to get her to say it this time.

Kathy got up and started to get dressed as I dejectedly began to rebutton my shirt while lying next to a sexy almost naked blonde woman and assessing whether, being so close to a threesome and failing to reach one of the pinnacles of sexual conquests, this had become the lowest point of my life.

We covered Lisa with a blanket, retreated downstairs toward the bed-covered car and locked the front door behind us.

Kathy froze halfway down the sidewalk. "God damn it! I left my keys in the apartment."

"You've got to be kidding?"

"No."

Luckily earlier in the evening Lisa had mentioned the crazy fact that she never locked her back door, and we were able to get back inside to retrieve the keys.

Holding the sail-like mattress to prevent it from flying away, we finally got back to our subdivision sometime around midnight. Highlight of the evening…finally!

Twenty-One

Odds 'n Ends and the Northeast

I was fully invested in the idea of visiting all the national parks even if I wasn't certain exactly how I was going to pull it off. All I knew for sure was the parks close to my home in Atlanta and those back in Arizona would be easy to visit without taking a lot of extra time off work, they were the proverbial low-hanging fruit of national parks.

Virtually every year I would take a week-long vacation and head back to Tucson for either Thanksgiving or Christmas. In the years Arizona was playing our hated archrivals from Arizona State, the scum devils…I mean Sun Devils, in Tucson, I would go home for Thanksgiving so I could attend the game. Every other year would be a Christmas stopover, and 2013 was one of those years. However, this year would be a little different because I wanted to pick off one of those low-hanging fruits.

I visited Petrified Forest National Park with my parents as a teenager, but I had no pictures, and my goal was not just to visit all the parks, but also to photograph them.

Planning my visit required massaging the logistics of the trip but also convincing my family I still loved them even though I was going to spend some time driving to central Arizona to see a park rather than spend time with them.

I flew into Tucson and picked up my rental car, and even though I was only twenty miles from home, I headed straight up I-10 toward Phoenix as I had no time to waste. Speed was the key to this trip since I also wanted to get back to my family and friends in Tucson.

Over 200 million years ago, a vast floodplain with tall conifer trees lining the banks of its streams occupied this area. Today, as the soft sedimentary rock is worn away by wind and water, what remains of that ancient floodplain is seen throughout the park. Large areas of petrified wood, the vast and colorful badlands known as the Painted Desert, and the remnants of 13,000 years of human occupation make up this fascinating area.

One site stood out for me: "Old Faithful," the most massive and well-known log in the park. I can remember as a kid standing next to this log as my dad took a picture, and now I was standing next to it once again. Obviously, I didn't expect anything would be any different; this log will be virtually unchanged for many centuries to come, but it was a reminder of something my parents gave to me, the love of the road and an appreciation of our national parks.

After the Petrified Forest, I was interested in taking an optional excursion if the weather cooperated. Being it was December in the higher desert of Arizona, snow and ice were always a possibility, but I wanted to see Canyon de Chelly (pronounced "shay") National Monument. National monuments are on a rung below the national parks. They receive less financial support and have slightly weaker environmental protections, but most are no less spectacular. The weather did cooperate and I cautiously headed north.

For my money, Canyon de Chelly National Monument should be a national park. Red and orange canyon walls with stunning sandstone rock formations dotted with ancient cave dwellings and ruins provide vistas for visitors that rival other parks in the system. This park was visited and photographed by Ansel Adams and is located within the Navajo Nation, whose members lead tours into the canyon.

As incredible as the landscapes in this canyon are, one literally stands above all others—the 800-foot-tall Spider Rock. I first viewed it late in the day and it was overcast, so when I got up the next morning and saw the skies were clear I decided to head back out to see it in the early morning. The column of rock was perfect and beautiful as the freestanding spire cast its long shadow into the canyon below.

Now I could head back home for Christmas.

MONTHS LATER I TOOK a long weekend and drove to Great Smoky Mountains National Park. This is the most visited park in the National Park System, and it certainly lived up to its name; even as the clouds lifted, a haze still hung in the air between and over the distant hills and mountains. At one point, as the sun broke through the cloud cover, I could see rays of sunlight painting the landscape.

The weather in the park fluctuated with each passing hour and change in elevation. At Clingmans Dome, the highest spot in the park at 6,643 feet, the views were spectacular until the fog settled in, resulting in eerie silhouettes of the trees in the surrounding area. Elk and wild turkey were abundant, and I saw a black bear send her two young cubs up a tree to protect them from onlookers; she then sat at the base of the tree periodically looking up to keep track of her young.

AFTER RETURNING FROM MY most recent trip, I knew I had my work cut out for me. First, I needed a way to track my park visits, and then I needed to come up with a plan to complete my goal.

Number one was the easy part. I created a national park spreadsheet; how could I call myself a proud corporate employee if I didn't know my way around a good spreadsheet? I listed each park in alphabetical order with its location and year established. Next, I added columns to indicate when I was last there, and whether I had a park brochure and a photograph from the park. The last column was important because there were several parks I had visited when I was young but didn't have a picture to show I was there. After all, the second half of my goal was to photograph each of the parks.

I also added tabs for the national monuments, national historical sites, and a fourth for "other," which could include anything from seashores, wildlife refuges, and battlefields to national landmarks. These are areas I would stop to explore when I was in route to a national park, although some of these, like Canyon de Chelly, could also stand alone as a destination.

Now I had a document I could use to plan future trips. It was easy to select a state and see which parks were there. It also reminded me there were several remote areas that would require extra planning to reach, Hawaii, American Samoa, the Virgin Islands, and Alaska. I knew if I was going to achieve my goal, I would have to get to all of these places, and I'd better start planning to reach them now. I chose to attack the toughest first, Alaska.

With eight national parks, Alaska was not only remote, but also expansive. The parks in the largest state in the union were spread out over thousands of miles of rough terrain, mountain ranges, and ocean waters, and would require special planning to tackle. Of the eight parks only three could be reached by car; to get to the rest you had to fly in, by bush or pontoon plane, or take a boat. I listed the eight parks and started to outline my priorities and how I thought I could achieve them. As I scanned the internet for information, it was clear this would be a daunting task.

At the time I was a member of the American Automobile Association (AAA) so I went to my local office to see if they could help, or at least point me in the right direction. There I sat down with Barbara Diener and laid out my destinations and the issue I was having trying to figure out how to make it all happen. It was clear from the look on her face she knew this was going to be a bit more difficult than the average cruise line vacation. She asked me to give her a day or two so she could process everything and eventually called to tell me she had passed my information on to Knightley Tours in Seattle. They specialized in these kinds of trips, particularly in Alaska, and would work with the two of us to come up with a custom tour itinerary. We would work it out over the phone and through email over the next five months.

MEANWHILE, I HAD ANOTHER trip on my schedule. Of all the places in the United States, the northeast might have well been Siberia to me. Except for a business trip to Boston, I had neglected this area for far too long. But now I had to get to Maine at the very least to visit Acadia National Park.

This trip started in Boston, but only to fly into the airport and rent a car. I headed south to Cape Cod to check out the beaches and more importantly the multitude of lighthouses in the area. Backtracking through Boston and north into Maine, I stopped to see one of the most photogenic places you'll ever see, the Portland Headlight on Cape Elizabeth.

The real reason I was here was still farther north, Acadia National Park. Most of Acadia sits on Mount Desert Island where the park road takes you through lush forests, along the rugged coastline, and to the top of the tallest mountain on the Atlantic coast, Cadillac Mountain, giving you spectacular 360-degree views of the area. I spent most of my time along the coast taking in the sounds of the ocean striking the shore and studying the many picturesque sites from Otter Point to the Bass Harbor Head Lighthouse. This park is both serene and exhilarating.

Early one morning I made my way up to Cadillac Mountain to view the sunrise. Because of the height of the mountain, 1,530 feet, it is the spot where the sun's rays first fall on the continental United States each morning. On this day, sunrise was at 4:51 a.m. Although cloud cover delayed those first rays of light, it was a spectacular experience, nonetheless. And since I was up, I had plenty of time to take in the early morning sunlight along the coast as well.

I was staying in the town of Bar Harbor, which is perched on the edge of the park. It is a quaint fishing town with, as you might expect, a lot of seafood restaurants. I am allergic to fish but can have shellfish; for most people it is the other way around and it is my understanding I am in the minority when it comes to this situation. I have not had fish since the late '80s, but I do enjoy crab legs, shrimp, and lobster whenever possible, but not often since they tend to be expensive. But here I was in the lobster capital of the world, and I wasn't going to pass up an opportunity to have all the freshest lobster I could possibly get! Several times during my tour of Acadia I saw lobster boats hauling in the catch of the day, so it is possible I actually viewed my dinner being caught; so, I mean fresh! I was only here for three days and dined on fresh boiled Maine lobster two nights in a row. Why eat anything else!

It was a long ride to my next destination, and the last time I was at Niagara Falls I got into a lot of trouble. Not at the falls, but because of who I was with at the falls. But that was one wife ago and this time I was alone and here long enough to do a more thorough job of exploring the area. Although I visited both sides of the falls, I stayed on the Canadian side. It was odd being there on the fourth of July weekend and viewing the fireworks displays happening in the United States. Both countries also do a fantastic job of lighting up the falls each night, which is a show unto itself, and taking the boat ride to the base of the falls was a thrill. There's nothing like being under a thundering waterfall.

And here I will take time to call something out that by no means only plagues Niagara Falls. It is the selfie and the selfie stick. Maybe I just noticed it here because there are so many people, but it truly amazes me to see more people taking selfies than pictures of the falls! I have noticed it at other places, but it was more prominent here because it was easier to see all the selfie sticks extended into the air to get that perfect shot. You know, so no one would ever see the "turkey neck" or a shadow under the eyebrows. But let's take this to another level. Why do people think they can improve on something as beautiful as Niagara Falls, or Old Faithful, or the Grand Canyon, or whatever, by sticking their mug in front of it? And I know, you want a picture of yourself at the amazing place. Okay, I understand, but how many do you need? Just check out Facebook to see what people post, multiple pictures of themselves with the attraction all blurry in the background! Let's call it what it is, narcissism. I don't care who you are, you being in a picture is not going to improve on the scenery itself, well, unless you're Beyonce or Sofia Vergara, and if either of you are reading this…call me.

⟶

HEADING SOUTH INTO OHIO, on a line that follows the Cuyahoga River and the old Ohio & Erie Canal, is Cuyahoga Valley National Park. This area has a long history as a primary transportation artery, and it's dotted with old working farmlands surrounded by constantly growing urban areas.

It was at first difficult to believe I was in a national park. I was constantly weaving in and out of neighborhoods questioning where the park began and ended. It wasn't until I found the solitude of Beaver Marsh and the interesting geology of Ritchie Ledges that I felt comfortable with the park and why it was there.

Nestled on the east side of the park are the incredible cliffs and rock formations of Ritchie Ledges. I hiked across a wooded plateau with several open meadows until I came to the cliffs, jagged separations in the ground with exposed earth below. As the trail worked its way deeper into the forest, it went down along the ledges and around the plateau exposing me to the sheer cliffs and a multitude of rugged rock formations. Sunlight was scarce because of the thick growth, giving the area a dark and eerie feeling.

Regardless, it was a truly enjoyable hike that fueled my curiosity and kept me wondering what would be around the next corner.

Near the park's southern entrance lies Beaver Marsh, an area teeming with plants and animals living in a pristine environment. It was a joy to settle in and watch. Amazing as it may seem, this area had been a junk yard until it was cleaned up by the Sierra Club in 1984. Shortly thereafter, beaver dammed and flooded the area to make it what it is today. I spent several hours one evening walking up and down the short boardwalk watching the wildlife. The next day I returned to take it all in again and this time I was lucky enough to see the flowers on the lily pads slowly opening to the early morning sunlight. Families of wood ducks, turtles, birds of all types, and interesting plants were everywhere; however, the majestic Great Blue Herons captured my attention the most. Seeing a four-foot-tall bird in a tree is one thing, but watching a bird with a seven-foot wingspan take flight is quite a treat!

PASSING THROUGH WEST VIRGINIA I pulled into a small town and decided to stop for gas and to get something to drink. It was overcast and as I filled the car, I noticed the smell of rain in the air. By the time the tank was full, the wind began to pick up; I didn't think anything of it until I started to go into the station to get something to drink. The wind was suddenly blowing hard enough to bend nearby trees. I immediately jumped back into the car and took off down the road trying to stay ahead of the storm. Large branches and debris flew through the air and rain and small hail poured from the sky. I was heading away from whatever this was, so as long as I kept moving, I felt like I might be able to outrun it. What choice did I have? Lucky for me there was nothing to slow me down and I was able to avoid the wall of wind as I raced out of town.

My last park visit on this trip was one I had visited before when I followed the crest of the Blue Ridge Mountains for a peaceful 105-mile journey on the Skyline Drive in Shenandoah National Park. Punctuated by thick forest and scenic views of the valley below, the park is alive with animals and flowering plants, all of which can be seen from your car. I took several hikes, the longest and most difficult being the one along the Rose River to Dark Hollow Falls; each hike highlighted the beauty of the park. Unfortunately, the weather presented my biggest obstacle as haze and later thunderstorms made viewing and photographing the park a tough venture.

While driving through the park I had the opportunity to be somewhat of a hero when I narrowly missed a bump on the road that turned out to be a turtle. I slammed on the brakes and pulled to the side of the road and jogged back to get the little guy before someone else came along. I remember hearing somewhere that if you ever found yourself in this situation, you should always take note of which way the turtle is going and move it to that side of the road. The turtle in question was headed for a rather steep and rocky berm; I don't know where he thought he was going, but it was going to require quite a climb, so he was lucky I came along. With turtle in hand, I scaled the rocky mound, placed him on the top and bid him farewell. I hope he got to wherever he was going.

ANOTHER TRIP WAS IN the books. This one held significance because I achieved an interesting milestone along the way: I had now been to all forty-eight contiguous states.

Twenty-Two

Cancer

I'm not a fan of all the poking and prodding, but I go for my yearly physical out of habit more than anything else. Therefore when, not long after returning from my trip to the Northeast, my calendar reminded me of my annual doctor's appointment I naturally just sucked it up and went.

A week later I received the usual call from my doctor's office with the results of all the tests produced from the two vials of blood drawn during my visit. Everything was normal except my PSA levels, which were above the acceptable range. The nurse explained the Prostate-Specific Antigen was an enzyme that when elevated can indicate cancer. She went on to say there may not actually be a problem, but the doctor was suggesting I see a urologist to explore this further.

I dutifully made my appointment, leading to more tests and an assurance from the urologist that we would have our answers within the week. I made yet another appointment with him to come in to discuss the test results and waited, confident everything was going to be just fine.

It wasn't. The urologist explained his testing revealed there were issues but the only way to truly understand what we were dealing with would be to schedule a prostate biopsy. It was clear there was a problem and I had something to be worried about.

The biopsy was an outpatient procedure to remove tissue from the prostate for direct testing and it only took about fifteen minutes. I went home knowing we would have more information in about three days.

I had taken the day off from work to have the biopsy and intended to spend the rest of the day relaxing, but I could not get all the uncertainties of my situation out of my mind. I was uncomfortable and thought a hot shower might help me unwind. It was soothing at first, but I started to become lightheaded and shut the water off; I needed to sit down. Exiting the shower, I moved toward the step at the front of the bathtub and began to lower myself…and then I was out.

I opened my eyes. I was on my back. It seemed like I was in a fog; I was confused. I wiped sweat from my face. My vision cleared somewhat, but without my glasses I still could not see clearly. I looked at my right hand, which seemed blotchy; my left hand was fine, which confused me even more. What was happening? Still not feeling well, I continued to lay there, trying to summon the strength and clarity to do something. I knew I had to move, get to my glasses on the bathroom counter, and then figure out what to do next. I slowly rolled on my right side and pushed myself up, then got onto my knees supporting myself by holding on to the counter. I put on my glasses, looked in the mirror, and saw the blotchiness on my hand was from a bloody cut over my right eye.

Still unsteady, I knew I had to go downstairs to get to the phone. I threw on some clothes and, not trusting my balance, started down the stairs on my butt, one step at a time until I reached the first floor. I stood and unlocked the front door, made my way to the phone, carried it into the living room where I laid down on the floor and dialed 911.

The EMTs arrived and hit me with a wave of questions trying to determine my state of mind as well as what was going on. I told them about the biopsy and the shower. Being cautious they put a neck brace on me which I fought because it made me feel like I was choking. I was loaded on a gurney, wheeled outside, and put into the ambulance.

More questions. They did more stuff, which was a blur. This was new for me. It was my first time in an ambulance, but we weren't going fast. There was no siren. It seemed like we were stopping at traffic lights. I obviously wasn't getting the full ambulance ride experience! I realized if I was thinking like that, I was going to be okay.

I was wheeled into the emergency room and heard a nurse ask, 'traffic accident?' Geez, how bad do I look?

"No, fall," came the answer. I was moved off the gurney and onto a bed where a doctor began to look me over. More questions.

"Okay, we're going to do some tests and while we wait, I'm going to put a few stitches into the cut above your eye."

"Is this going to leave a scar?" I asked.

"No, it shouldn't," he said.

"It's okay if it does," I said, "I could use the street cred," prompting chuckles from everyone in the room.

They drew blood and after I was all stitched up, they wheeled me off to get some x-rays and a CAT scan, after which it was back to the room to wait.

Eventually the doctor came in with more questions and the results of the blood tests that revealed most of my count levels were alarmingly low. There was a definite problem here, and since I had a biopsy earlier in the day, one issue could be abdominal bleeding. He was going to draw more blood to retest everything and ordered an abdominal CAT scan to see if there were any abnormalities. If the second blood tests mirrored the first, I would need an immediate blood transfusion.

Upon returning to my room all I could do was worry. Eventually the doctor came in with the news. Apparently the first blood tests were somehow contaminated, and the second test showed normal levels across the board. The CAT scan also revealed no issues. After a few hours of observation, I was released to go home.

Days later I went back to the urologist to receive the results of my biopsy. I had prostate cancer; we caught it early, but the doctor was recommending surgery. He said if I were over seventy years old, they would probably do nothing and just regularly test and observe to make sure there were no complications since prostate cancer normally grows at such a slow pace. I would be more likely to die of old age than from the cancer. However, I was only fifty-six, and at this stage the cancer could lead to a premature death.

I walked out the door of the clinic with a bag full of booklets outlining my condition and options and climbed into my car where I sat for a moment in shock and then began to cry.

I was finally facing my mortality. This was by no means a death sentence; prostate cancer is one of the more easily treated cancers, but it was a painful awakening. I read my booklets and scanned the internet. I needed to make a decision regarding how I would handle the process.

The doctor suggested surgery, but there would be a four-week recovery period, some of which would require help from someone, and there was no "someone." Although not recommended, I could kick into "watchful waiting" and simply see how the cancer progressed. This was not for me because it would mean having to deal with life knowing there was a possible bomb ready to go off inside of me. I was living with anxiety now with no desire to extend this emotional state. I came to the only conclusion that was workable for me, radiotherapy, or more precisely, Electron Beam Radiation Therapy (EBRT).

EBRT consisted of implanting radioactive marker seeds into the prostate followed by eight weeks of radiation therapy done for approximately eight minutes a day, five days a week. It allowed me to work and go about my life in an almost normal way. Besides the interruption of the daily treatments themselves, there were very few side effects, the most notable being fatigue.

I explained my decision to my urologist and then contacted an oncologist at the Radiotherapy Clinics of Georgia to start the process. First up would be the surgical procedure to implant the seeds into the prostate, and as luck would have it, it was scheduled on my birthday.

As the surgery drew closer, I knew I would have to start opening up to people about what was happening. I told my sisters and let them know I didn't want my parents to know until I was well into the radiation treatments; I didn't want them to worry. I then went to my management at work to lay out the procedure and to Human Resources to fill out the paperwork that would support me throughout the process. I had also told my closest friends, but I waited until the day before I went on leave for my implant procedure to call a meeting of the two teams I was working with to explain my absence and how things would change for the next few months. I explained I would be taking three days off for the surgery and then, after waiting approximately four weeks, would be working six-hour days, taking off early each day for my radiation therapy. Everything had been businesslike up to this point, I had been strong and stoic, but standing in front of this group of people and watching their expressions change as I talked to them was triggering me as I could see my own doubts and fears mirrored in their faces. It took everything I had to get through the moment, listening to their well wishes, seeing their pain for me; tears welled up in my eyes as I walked out of the room and back to my desk.

—⟶

UN-HAPPY BIRTHDAY. MY FRIEND Beth would take me to and from the surgical center for the radioactive seed implant procedure, but because I would have to have a catheter for twenty-four hours, I needed to secure a nurse to stay with me until the next day when it was removed. I had arranged and met a nursing student, Nathan, through a company called Visiting Angels and he would be taking care of me overnight and into the next day.

Once I was knocked out, the procedure was simple; it was waking up to reality again that was hard. Any man will tell you, especially someone who has had a procedure requiring a catheter, the idea alone makes you cringe, shudder, and possibly double over in unreal pain.

Beth took me home where Nathan was waiting for me. He sat me down in the recliner in my living room where I would spend the night, with him sleeping on the couch across from me. In my perpetual state of discomfort, I nodded off for ten to fifteen minutes at a time throughout the night. When daybreak finally came, I only needed to prepare to go to my oncologist to have the catheter removed.

Nathan drove me to the clinic and would be waiting to take me back home. I was moved to an operating room where the nurse told me to lay down and then explained she was going to hold the head of my penis and yank the catheter out with one long pull. Remember, I was out cold when the thing went in; now I was going to be fully awake when it came out.

I asked, "Can I assume this is going to hurt me much more than it will hurt you?"

She smiled and said she had done this a million times and it wasn't going to hurt as much as I thought it would.

She lied!

Listen, she did her job flawlessly, in one long smooth pull she extracted, oh, I'd say about fifteen or twenty feet of tubing from my body. Okay, it was obviously much less but the pain indicated it could have been even more! The good news was I was free of the thing and my instructions were to hang around in the waiting room until I could urinate, at which point I could go home. This step was key because they wanted to make sure there were no obstructions; if there were, the catheter would have to be reapplied.

I waited and waited. I drank water and drank water. Several hours passed and eventually Nathan and I were the only ones left in the waiting room. My anxiety level was through the roof; the last thing in the world I wanted was to have another catheter, and who knows if they would even knock me out this time to put it in! Eventually I squeezed out enough urine to feel comfortable that I was going to be fine, and Nathan drove me home.

I was spent; exhausted. We pulled up to the house and I got out to open the front door and, feeling faint, fell to my knees. Nathan scooped me up and led me into the house where he settled me in my chair. He left only after he was sure I was going to survive. Now I had to wait a month before my radiation therapy could begin.

As MY BODY HEALED from the implant surgery another problem arose out of nowhere. I had developed a half-dollar sized bump on the left side of my abdomen. My general practitioner diagnosed it as an infection, possibly stemming from the surgical procedure a few weeks earlier. It would have to be lanced and cleaned out and they could do the procedure right there in the office. The nurse came in to prepare me and commented how tough it must be for me considering how much I had been through lately. I was honestly just numb. Eventually the doctor came back in and drained and patched the wound. What next?

I STARTED MY RADIATION therapy the week before Thanksgiving. The five-day-a-week grind would be to get to the office at eight in the morning, work for six hours, leave at three o'clock, and then drive approximately thirty minutes to the clinic. On the ride over, I would drink twenty ounces of water, which would act as a buffer to protect my bladder during the treatment. Once at the clinic I would check in and pray there would be no delays because I had to hold said water until after the daily radiation was applied. Too often they were behind schedule, forcing me to try to think nice thoughts while holding on to what was wanting to stream out.

Once on the table, the treatment itself was painless. The nurse would position me under the linear accelerator, which used beams of light focused on the markings put on my body in an earlier "dry run" session. The markings indicated the exact position of my prostate, and the radioactive seeds implanted a month ago.

For eight minutes all I had to do is lie still and listen to my preselected music channel while the accelerator directed high energy beams of radiation into my body, periodically moving as programed to strike the prostate from several different angles. So, when someone tells a woman to stay away from me because I'm radioactive, at least now it's true.

I went through this process for five weeks, and with permission from my oncologist, took a one-week break to head home to Tucson to spend Christmas and New Years with my family. On that trip I was able to sit my parents down to tell them what was going on and why I hadn't told them sooner. Doing it this way was better because they would have me in front of them and see I was doing well and there was nothing to worry about.

Upon returning to Atlanta, I dutifully resumed the last three weeks of my treatments only to find an interesting surprise awaited me. Because my treatment had continued into a new year, the insurance company was again charging me the 3,000-dollar deductible! I had paid the three grand when I started the process; it was the same occurrence, so why should I have to pay again just because the calendar flipped to a new year! This, of course, was a losing proposition because the criminals who run the insurance companies don't give a damn what anyone is going through, or what constitutes fairness, as long as they can get your money. Let's face it, if I had known about this little trick, I would have made sure I had the entire procedure completed within a single calendar year and saved myself 3,000 dollars! Then again, if I knew I was going to have prostate cancer I could've save myself the 800 dollars it cost me to get a vasectomy two years earlier! Ahh, hindsight!

⟶

THE BOTTOM LINE WAS I was going to be all right. Ultimately, this was a life-changing experience. I was rethinking everything. The tried-and-true plan was to work until you're sixty-six and a half, retire, and do whatever you want to do. But what if you're not able to do what you want to do? What if that's too late? You won't know until you get there, and then it may be too late to do anything about it. There's so much I still wanted to do and see. I kept thinking about the Mark Twain quote my former Mirant manager and fellow traveler Greg sent me some time ago:

"Twenty years from now, you will be more disappointed by the things you didn't do than by the ones you did do. So, throw off the bowlines. Sail away from the safe harbor… Explore. Dream. Discover."

Spreadsheet time! I created an accounting of all my assets; my home, my car, everything in my home, cash on hand, IRA, stock accounts, etc. Next, I attempted to determine how much money I would need to live each year on the road, and if what I had would last me as long as I lived considering I also would have Social Security funds when I turned sixty-six and a half. To be clear, I was thinking about divesting myself of everything, downsizing in a massive way, and putting myself in a recreational vehicle (RV) so I could travel throughout the country and see all the things I wanted to see starting now instead of ten years from now.

I had done my homework and it looked doable, but I needed to run the whole plan by someone who could look at it objectively and tell me whether I was crazy or not. So, I sent it all to my financial planner, Richard Lombardi, to let him go over it with the proverbial fine-tooth comb. We discussed my plans at length and my ability to live within my means. Rich indeed declared it doable as long as I stuck to the parameters laid out in my spreadsheets.

Now I had to look at myself objectively. Sure, I could do it, but was the idea itself crazy? I knew I didn't like work or working; I could care less about the corporations I worked for because I knew they didn't care about me. On the other hand, I had a nice house in a nice neighborhood in a nice suburb and I had established a large group of friends in and out of the places I had worked. My life was comfortable and fairly easy, and to top it off I owned a Porsche.

I had nothing to complain about except work and the idea of toiling away at a desk, in a cubicle, in a stuffy building for the next ten years, which was absolutely suffocating. Additionally, when I considered the fickle actions and reactions of the corporations, which tossed individuals out the door merely to readjust their balance sheet so they could increase stock price for the shareholders, it was clear I had nothing to look forward to by sticking around. And if I did stick around and I wasn't among those laid off, then I would be one of the poor souls who were tasked with picking up the slack and taking on the workload of those the corporation threw out. This happened over and over again. And the formula could be applied in all areas in corporate America. Remember the old saying, "Insanity is doing the same thing over and over again and expecting different results"? That's corporate America in a nutshell, and it made the decision easy for me.

Ineptness and continually seeing people promoted into management positions who had no business being there, not because they weren't exceptional at their jobs, but because they had no people skills and no concept of what it took to be a leader, which by the way includes people skills. Promoting these types of individuals cost the corporation money through incompetence, lack of knowledge of employee protections, and a less-than-motivated workforce. Yet throughout my career I worked for people who didn't belong in management.

I left Fiserv in March of 2015; I was retired.

In a book written by John Krakauer called *Into the Wild* (published 1996) comes a quote from a note by Chris (Alex) McCandless to Ron Frank dated April 1992:

So many people live within unhappy circumstances and yet will not take the initiative to change their situation because they are conditioned to a life of security, conformity, and conservatism, all of which may appear to give one peace of mind, but in reality nothing is more damaging to the adventurous spirit within a man than a secure future. The very basic core of a man's living spirit is his passion for adventure. The joy of life comes from our encounters with new experiences, and hence there is no greater joy than to have an endlessly changing horizon, for each day to have a new and different sun.

No truer words have ever been spoken. And for those of you who may know the story already, we'll just put aside the fact that Chris McCandless died in the Alaskan wilderness. However, he died in the Alaskan wilderness chasing his dream, not of old age at a desk, in a cubicle, in a stuffy building.

Now I don't want to leave anyone with the impression my life was totally miserable for thirty years; most of the people I met were incredible and I feel privileged to have known all kinds of people from all walks of life...everyone added a little something along the way and they all made my life better than it was before I met them!

On the other hand, to every college kid looking for a career I offer this observation, if I could do it all over again, I would be a weatherman or an economist because neither one has to be right.

RETIRED AND ON MY own, I now had to make this all work and you guessed it, that meant more spreadsheets. My plan was to move back to Tucson in the fall and have an RV to go on the road in March of 2016. In the meantime, I had to sell most of my possessions, my house, and my car. There would be plenty of time to acquire an RV and plan my first year on the road after I wrapped things up in Atlanta. Ultimately my goal going forward would be to travel and photograph all fifty-nine national parks. I'd already been to many but planned to go back to several to get better park images, and of course, to take more time to explore them.

I still had my Alaska trip scheduled for the summer of 2015, but I needed to take care of one thing before I left the Atlanta area; I needed to visit Virgin Islands National Park.

As one of five island parks I needed to visit, Virgin Islands National Park would be easiest for me to reach by air from the East Coast. I made a snap decision to visit this park now because of the many flights out of Atlanta to the islands. It would be easier to get there from Atlanta than later from on the road in an RV.

The park is on the island of St. John, but I had to fly into Charlotte Amalie on the island of St. Thomas and catch a ferry to Cruz Bay, where I picked up a Jeep to get around on the mostly primitive roads. From Cruz Bay I headed south to Great Cruz Bay and the Westin St. John Resort.

This resort life was just a little more upscale than I was used to, so I thought I might as well enjoy it while I was there. I had a room on the beach and looked directly into the bay, perfect for spending time in the hammock strung between two palm trees just beyond my sliding glass door and the impeccably manicured hedges surrounding my sitting patio. And to top it off, it all faced west so I could take in the sunsets without even moving whether I was on my patio or in a hammock. I haven't spent much time in four-star resorts, but I could definitely get used to it!

In between all the lounging and relaxing I actually got out to visit the park. Deep blue waters, pristine white sand beaches, tropical forests, and an assortment of interesting plants and animals make up Virgin Islands National Park. Covering over fifty percent of the island of St. John, the park, which is primarily known for its beaches, has a long history as a site for sugar and cotton plantations, the ruins of which are part of the park today.

I drove from the popular beaches to the mountainous inland regions with thick tropical forests surrounding narrow, steep, and at times unde-veloped roads. As the islands were once claimed by European settlers you have to remember to drive on the left side of the road making "narrow and steep" the least of your concerns. More than once I met an overloaded truck or a local driver flying at me as I entered a blind hairpin curve.

The views of the sand and water dominate the park landscape, but the rich history and the interesting plant and animal life complete the experience. From a four-foot by two-foot above-ground termite colony to a four-foot-long iguana, there's something new and interesting whenever you venture out. And as much as I like to explore, it was tough for me to leave the hotel compound. Let's face it, it was hard to believe I would find myself living this well in the future; I had a budget to maintain!

Twenty-Three

Alaskan Adventure

I HAD BEEN LOOKING FORWARD TO THIS TRIP FOR OVER A YEAR; THIS was pre-cancer, pre-retirement stuff. My world had changed decidedly since I began planning this trip, but it was coming at the best possible time. I was free to enjoy it unencumbered by ties to work or anything else for that matter.

Months before, I had finalized an itinerary for my trip, prepared by Knightly Tours, a specialty travel company based in Seattle. The end result was a thirty-three-page itinerary covering travel to all eight national parks in Alaska, along with several side trips, over thirty days from June 21 through July 21, 2015. All lodging, transportation, and meals were included for the low, low price of $22,000. A bargain considering the task at hand.

One-fifth the size of the lower 48 states, Alaska is bigger than Texas, California, and Montana combined, yet its population is just under 750,000 with Anchorage, the largest city, having approximately 291,000 residents.

Of the eight national parks I would be visiting, five have no roads into them, so my itinerary included rides on trains, bush and pontoon planes, and boats, from large bus-carrying ferries to a small fishing boat with an outboard motor. This would truly be an adventure of a lifetime.

My JOURNEY STARTED IN relative luxury since I used my Delta SkyMiles to book the trip to Anchorage, going first class all the way. Wide, comfortable seats and a few cocktails had me completely relaxed even as my excitement overflowed in anticipation of what I would do and see over the next thirty days. Upon landing, I checked into a hotel near the airport for my first night and proceeded to their outdoor restaurant overlooking a small lake to grab a snack and watch a band playing under the summer sun; it was ten in the evening and still light out. After downing a plate of BBQ wings, I decided I'd better get some rest because my trip would be kicking into high gear early the next morning. When I got to my room, I realized I had left my camera bag under the table at the restaurant and a wave of panic came over me. I bolted back to the patio area and luckily it was still there, right where I left it. I took a deep breath. It would have been a huge disaster if I had lost my camera equipment on the first day of my trip!

The next morning I flew into Juneau, which would be a staging point before embarking on my national park adventure. There I was able to "warm up" by visiting Mendenhall Glacier in the Tongass National Forest. A fifteen-minute ride from downtown, it gave me my first up-close look at an Alaskan glacier and amplified my level of expectation of what was to come over the next month.

—→

I reached the first of eight primary destinations on this trip, Glacier Bay National Park, via a short flight from Juneau to Gustavus. Even though there was no concourse and we deplaned and picked up our luggage right on the tarmac, I knew this would be considered a five-star accommodation compared to what lay ahead.

I would be staying at the quaint Glacier Bay Lodge, and from there I took a small tour boat to explore the park. Gouged out by a 100-mile-long glacier, the bay is teeming with wildlife including humpback whales, stellar and harbor seals, otters, and puffins, in or around the water. Brown bears and mountain goats roamed the shores, but the majestic glaciers and surrounding mountains stole the show, offering a beautiful vista no matter which way you look.

Sitting below the 21-mile-long Margerie Glacier and looking up at the 350-foot-tall terminus reflected into the waters of the Tarr Inlet is an amazing sight, but then imagine watching ice the size of a house cracking off and calving with a splash into the water below, an unbelievable experience!

Back at the lodge, with the availability of plenty of late-night sunlight, I took several of the many trails in the area to check out some nearby tide pools. At low tide I was able to see all kinds of sea life, including sea stars, urchins, and oysters. I never really connected animals like these with the cold waters this far north. I was discovering new things already and it was only day one of my adventure!

Another trail took me inland through the thick forest to a glacial pool with an erratic boulder in the middle of it. In the distant past, as glaciers receded from this area, they dropped huge rocks like this far from where they were actually picked up and…CRACK, BOOM! I jumped about five feet while throwing my arms over my head. What the hell just happened? I thought I was being attacked, but it turned out to be a large tree cracking and falling to the forest floor. I was just in the right place at the right time to hear this natural occurrence of nature. So, this answers the proverbial question, if a tree falls in the forest and Jerry is the only one there to hear it, does it scare the crap out of him?

THERE ARE NO DIRECT flights to most of the places I would be going over the next four weeks. After leaving Gustavus, I had to go back to Juneau to get to Anchorage and then to Kotzebue so I could catch a flight on Bering Air to the small town of Ambler, my gateway to Kobuk Valley National Park. At the confluence of the Kobuk and Ambler rivers lies this town with a population of approximately 260 people, most of whom speak the Ambler dialect of the native Inupiaq language.

As my flight taxied from the dirt runway to the drop-off point, I noticed the airport was being expanded; they were adding a new cement runway indicating even this little town above the Arctic Circle was growing. As we came to a stop, I noticed something somewhat more troubling. One of the two individuals meeting the plane was covered head-to-toe in mosquito netting, and the other guy was furiously swatting at the air around his head. This was not a good sign and something I was ill prepared to deal with. Sure enough, I was shrouded by a cloud of mosquitos as soon as I stepped off the plane; and they were relentless in their attacks. I shot into the small hanger close by and called for my ride, which arrived a short time later to take me to the Kobuk River Lodge, my home for the next three days.

Run by trail guide Loren and his mother Shirley, the lodge was perched above a small all-purpose store and grille that served the whole town. There were two separate areas in the lodge, the family area and the guest area, which consisted of several bedrooms, a common bathroom with shower, and a common TV room and dining area. The common area looked a little like a hunting lodge and was appointed with several animal heads mounted on the walls, including a bear, elk, antelope, deer, and a very impressive walrus. I was the only guest at the time and Shirley spoiled me with magnificent home cooked meals three times a day including after dinner desserts. It was a good thing I was doing a lot of hiking or I might've grown out of my pants after only three days.

Kobuk Valley National Park, located above the Arctic Circle, is one of the most remote parks in the national parks system, welcoming fewer than 1000 visitors each year; only a fraction of those visitors actually set foot in the park, as most people only travel to the visitor center in Kotzebue. I was here to hike into the park's most recognizable feature, the Great Kobuk Sand Dunes. Unique above the Arctic Circle, these dunes were created thousands of years ago by erosion and more recently by glaciers grinding rocks into dust. About 14,000 years ago, as the climate became warmer, plants began recapturing the area and now only thirty square miles of dunes still exist.

On my first full day, Loren took me out on the river in his boat, a small four-seat fishing boat with a Mercury outboard motor. It was a cool day, maybe in the fifties, and I was wearing a shirt and a hoodie sweatshirt to protect against the cool temperatures. As soon as I boarded the boat Loren unzipped a large travel bag and threw me a heavy down jacket. I felt like this was overkill until we were speeding west along the icy waters of the Kobuk River, when I realized he had saved me from hypothermia! For the next two hours we rode through the park, stopping several times to view wildlife, a shaft of permafrost jutting out from the riverbank, or the remains of a woolly mammoth gradually uncovered by erosion.

Eventually we stopped on a bend in the river and Loren jumped out and started to pull the boat to a flat sandy area. He motioned for me to do the same and I too jumped into the icy waters. Honestly, like the cold, I had not anticipated this; I was expecting a dry land hike to the dunes and back and now my hiking shoes and socks were soaking wet. We reached the shore and Loren secured the boat and grabbed his backpack. He explained that we had a two-mile hike in front of us to get to the dunes and the first quarter mile would be the toughest because we had to go through a bog filled with thick willow brush. He asked if I had any questions, so I inquired whether he had ever run into any bears up here. He told me in the seven years he had been making this trip he had never seen a bear, but he always carried a 45-caliber pistol just in case it was needed. Today it was in his backpack because he forgot his holster, but we had no reason to worry.

I followed Loren into the heavy vegetation to start the hike and immediately we were knee deep in water and fighting our way through willow brush while the mosquitos relentlessly attacked us. They didn't bother us while we were riding in the boat, but now we were on their turf, a thick willow brush bog. We had drowned ourselves in 100 percent DEET as soon as we got off the boat, but this was like a war zone! The swarm was so thick it covered Loren's back like a blanket. As I huffed and puffed my way through the water and parted the thick brush, I couldn't help but to get a few mosquitos in my mouth, spitting them out at first but in the end swallowing a few; I considered it payback for all the times I've been bitten by their relatives!

As we cleared the bog, things became much less intense, and we weaved our way through one-and three-quarter miles of forest and a few small canyons. After two hours of this true wilderness hike, we reached our destination and scaled about two stories of sand to get onto the dunes. It is a spectacular site, especially considering we were in Alaska above the Arctic Circle and not on a beach in Florida!

After a quick lunch and a few pictures, we made our way off the dunes and had begun to work our way back toward the boat when there was a tremendous scuffling in the brush to our left. We froze trying to determine what was happening. I saw a black bear going up a tree, and Loren recognized it as a yearling cub; he knew we could be in trouble as there was sure to be a mother bear close by. He threw off his backpack and went in after his pistol. His hunch was correct, and out from the brush stepped the mother bear less than twenty yards from us. She stood there glaring at us, obviously not happy to see us but also not moving toward us. It's quite possible that in this sparsely populated wilderness, she may have never encountered humans before, and that may be why she never attempted to approach us. I slowly changed lenses on my camera and shot a few images; if I was going to be mauled at least I'd have pictures! Loren whispered to me to begin backing away slowly and once we were out of her range; Loren used his GPS to recalculate our route back to the boat and we continued on our way. I made a point of looking over my shoulder every now and then just for the heck of it, and I mentioned to Loren how trailing behind him made me feel like the "unnamed ensign" in Star Trek who beams down to a planet with the regulars, Kirk, Bones, Scotty, and Spock, only to get shot or eaten buy the planet inhabitants, never to return. Later I would kid him about how he had to dig under our Grandma's cookies and Snickers bar wrappers to get to his pistol and pointed out he would probably never forget this particular hike! Then again, neither would I.

In retrospect, this was a "wilderness" hike in the truest sense of the word. I was nearly carried off by mosquitos while knee-deep in a thick willow brush bog and came face to face with probably the most fearsome animal in the wild, a bear defending her cubs. And I scaled sand dunes above the Arctic Circle. Not bad for a single day.

AFTER LEAVING AMBLER AND Kobuk Valley National Park, my trip took me to Kotzebue, Nome, Anchorage, and finally Fairbanks for one night. The next day, I was to make my way up to Bettles, Alaska, homebase for my trips into Gates of the Arctic National Park.

While waiting for my plane at the Fairbanks airport, I ran into fellow traveler, actor, and director Ricky Schroder, famous for starring in the sitcom *Silver Spoons* as a child, as well as movies like *The Champ* and *Crimson Tide*. He was there with several other people who were traveling to Bettles to take a 10-day wilderness hike through the Arctic. Everyone in the small waiting room was discussing their Alaskan experiences and I made it a point to tell them about the mosquito "war zone" I had encountered on my hike through Kobuk Valley, relating to them how the pests would get into your mouth and how I just began swallowing them because I got tired of spitting them out. A look of concern came over Ricky and his team as they felt prepared for everything except swarms of murderous insects. A woman who identified herself as an Alaskan native just smiled and told them they were in for a unique experience. I agreed, unique indeed!

As with most of the parks in Alaska you cannot simply drive into Gates of the Arctic National Park. The only way to tour the park was by float-plane out of a town called Bettles. Located thirty-five miles north of the Arctic Circle on the Koyukuk River, the town is basically a dirt airfield with a lodge. There is a small national park visitor center and a number of houses for the few hearty souls who call the area home but little else. For such a small town, the Bettles Lodge was very well run, and the staff was incredibly accommodating.

Pilot Kevin took me on my first flight through the rugged mountainous landscape that makes up most of this park, including the namesake "gates," Boreal Mountain and Frigid Crags. We then flew up to the Nunamiut Eskimo village of Anaktuvuk Pass in the northern region of the park. We landed on a small lake near the village and were immediately met by a North Slope Borough police officer. Everyone has their own view of exactly what happened next, but the result was I ended up locked up in the back of the police SUV. I will endlessly declare my innocence, but this event should forever be a warning to anyone who messes with...okay, the truth is the officer wanted to know if we had seen some overdue hikers on our flight and after discussing our route, he offered to give us a ride into town. My guide Kevin hopped into the front seat and I was forced to get into the back, where I was trapped since the doors don't open from the inside, for obvious reasons. Once in town I had to be let out and Kevin apologized for not letting me sit up front. I told him under no circumstances was I going to pay extra for the "prisoner experience," even though I got some cool pictures through the bars from inside the vehicle, and I would be putting the incident on my "rap sheet" to add to my "street cred"!

I was crushed when on my second day, smoke from a nearby forest fire grounded all flights. I was supposed to fly to the Arrigetch Peaks area to take a seven-hour hike that day. Lodge owner Eric instead took me down the Koyukuk River to Old Bettles for an unscheduled tour as pilot Kevin reworked my trip schedule to give me a fighting chance to at least see the peaks if the smoke cleared the next day.

Old Bettles was founded in the late 1800s as a supply depot for prospectors heading north to find gold in the Koyukuk River area. It became a ghost town in the 1940s when its residents moved to the new Navy airfield seven miles upriver where the town of Bettles is located today.

The smoke cleared the next morning and allowed us to fly into the park to the Arrigetch Peaks, a cluster of rugged granite spires in the Endicott Mountains of the central Brooks Range. The name means "fingers of the outstretched hand" in the Inupiat language. Originally this was scheduled as an all-day trip including a hike into the area, but now I would only be able to view the range via flightseeing. But what a view it was! This was the region I had wanted to see from the moment I began my research on this trip. The jagged mountain peaks are incredible and the clouds in the area added to the dramatic views. I was able to get some images from the air; although they are amazing, they do not truly represent the spectacular sights I was lucky enough to see from the plane!

After spending six days above the Arctic Circle, where I experienced twenty-four-hour days of continuous sunlight, I was now heading south into the center of the state to explore the highest mountain in the western hemisphere.

I FLEW INTO FAIRBANKS and spent the night, getting up early the next morning to board an Alaska Railroad GoldStar luxury dome rail car for the four-hour trip to just outside Denali National Park. Alaska's first national park is also the most popular of the state's eight parks. Denali (formerly known as Mount McKinley), is the Athabascan name meaning "the high one." It is the highest mountain in the western hemisphere, and the centerpiece of Denali National Park. At an elevation of 20,320 feet, the massive mountain stands high above the Alaska Range, which slices through the park.

My first full day in the park would be to take the guided bus tour along the Park Road to Kantishna. This ninety-two-mile road, of which only the first sixteen miles are paved, is the only road into this wilderness park. No private transportation is allowed along this road. It is traversed only by the National Park Service buses, which provide tours on a daily basis.

Weather is always a concern in this park and Denali is often shrouded by cloud cover. In fact, upon boarding the bus our driver informed us he had not seen the mountain in the last six days, and on the previous day the fog was so thick throughout the park even navigating the Park Road was challenging. The forecast was for better weather and indeed the clouds were beginning to lift. As the skies cleared, we rounded a corner and there it was, the top of Denali, as clear as can be and in all its glory even though it was still over sixty miles away. Then the bus driver pulled into a rest stop and announced we would leave after everyone had a chance to use the restrooms and walk around a little. I was going crazy knowing how weather affects viewing of the mountain. I kept thinking, "Let's get going before the weather changes and the mountain disappears!" Luckily for all of us the view of the mountain got even better as we made our way along the Park Road to the Eielson Visitor Center, approximately three-quarters of the way to Kantishna. There we were able to get our best views of Denali. True to form however, the clouds began to gather and by the time we reached the end of the road, the mountain was gone and not visible for the rest of the day.

Along with the stunning views of Denali and the Alaskan Range, the bus trip allowed all aboard the opportunity to see a wide array of wildlife including the arctic ground squirrel, elk, hoary marmot, moose, and the massive grizzly bear. The one real surprise was our rare sighting of the not-often-seen lynx, which crossed the road in front of our bus. All-in-all it was quite a day punctuated by actually seeing the mountain itself.

Denali holds the distinction of having the largest vertical rise from bottom to top of any mountain in the world (20,320 feet). It is massive, an incredible sight to behold from the ground, and even more awe-inspiring from the air.

The next day I was in Talkeetna, southeast of the park, to take a K2 Aviation flight to "the high one." I was anticipating an experience that would rock my world. Little did I know I would be rocked even before I boarded the plane. I was moving in to talk to the pilot, who was discussing the passenger load with another K2 employee, when the earth began to move, only for a few seconds, just enough to make me worry. Then it happened again! I looked at the two of them and the employee said to the pilot, "I'm going to say it was a 5.0, how about you?"

He replied, "I'll say 4.8."

"Great," she said, "I'll start the pool sheet."

Apparently, earthquakes happen often enough that everyone here simply bets on the strength of the tremors, winner takes the pool! Turns out the epicenter was only twenty-five miles from Talkeetna. The first tremor was a 4.9, followed by a 5.1. I'm not sure who won the pool, but I simply marked it down as another interesting Alaskan travel experience!

From the beginning of this adventure to Alaska, on most of my flights the co-pilot seat was unoccupied. This presented an opportunity; all I had to do was be early to my flights and figure out a way to make my acquaintance with the pilot. Just a little work and I would be able to literally land a front-row seat to wherever I was going.

This was particularly important on my flight out to "the high one," Denali, the massive mountain and the namesake for this park. Having the mountain in front of me would be key to incredible views and getting great images on our approach. I skillfully executed my plan, found the pilot, struck up a conversation, and when the time was right, I hit him with the question; someone would have to sit there, it might as well be me!

The flight to the mountain was spectacular and I had the best seat in the house! It was beautiful watching Denali get closer, but the real fun began when we started weaving our way around the mountain. It is a completely different experience when you're flying and looking up at peaks and cliffs! Then, as if that was not enough, we landed at the 5,500-foot level on the Ruth Glacier Amphitheater below the famous peak and spent thirty minutes just marveling at the scenery.

On the way back, I relinquished my front-row seat to one of the other passengers and all he got was a view of the muddy Chulitna River and the Talkeetna Airport…hopefully the rookie learned something about flying in Alaska!

I WAS LOOKING FORWARD to getting back to Anchorage because this time I would be picking up a rental car. One of my passions, along with travel and photography, is driving. I love being on the road with the freedom to go where I want and stop where I want. For most of my trip through Alaska so far, I had been locked into a schedule, flights, trains, buses, and tours. Most of it was unavoidable because of the accessibility issues surrounding the parks I was visiting. But now, for eight days, I was free again and would be able to drive along some of the most beautiful highways in Alaska: the Seward and Sterling Highways on the Kenai Peninsula; a ferry from Whittier to Valdez on the Alaska Marine Highway; and the Richardson and Glenn Highways from Valdez back to Anchorage. Sure, I had places to be, but I could get to them on my own schedule.

I was finally heading south from Anchorage driving along the Seward Highway. The view of the mountains over the water was spectacular even though the skies were overcast. The road traveled along the Turnagain Arm, and I stopped at several overviews to take in the sights. Pulling up to one in particular, I noticed several people looking and pointing cameras up high toward the cliffs overhanging the road. They were viewing Dall sheep bouncing from impossible spot to unimaginable position! Watching them was incredible but it wasn't the only opportunity on this leg of the trip where I would get to view exceptional wildlife at work. Later, as I was driving along the Sterling Highway near the Russian River, I would catch a glimpse through the trees of large birds on a sandbar in the Kenai River. I pulled over as soon as possible and made my way across the road and down to the river where I saw ten to twelve bald eagles. I staked them out for two hours, watching and photographing those magnificent birds. I could have stayed there all day, but I had to get to Seward to take a trip into Kenai Fjords National Park.

TOURING THE MAJORITY OF Kenai Fjords National Park requires one to take a boat through the icy waters of the Gulf of Alaska. Within the park, the Harding Icefield spawns many large glaciers, and they were amazing to see especially from the water, but the wildlife stole the show.

We boarded the Orca Song in Seward for our trip into the waters of Kenai Fjords National Park. It was smooth but foggy sailing in Resurrection Bay until we came to the Harding Gateway in the Gulf of Alaska, where we encountered five-foot swells that forced everyone to hold onto something or be thrown about like a rag doll. I felt like I was on an episode of *Deadliest Catch* as we slammed into the walls of water. Luckily, the ocean became calmer as we made our way toward the Aialik Peninsula and on to the waters of Aialik Bay, where we watched the Aialik Glacier calving. Unlike my past glacier experiences, this one included some huge sections of the glacier falling into the bay; the pieces were so large the boat captain had to turn the boat into the swells to keep us from being tossed around!

This trip was also an incredible wildlife show, starting with the sighting of a transient pod of orca, killer whales, off the port side of our vessel, including at least one calf. Next, we saw everything from puffins to harbor seals and large groups of sea otters floating together in the ice-cold waters. It was interesting watching them watch us as we sailed by. We learned otters float on their backs to conserve energy and heat.

Up to this point I had endured all sorts of obstacles on this trip; fires, earthquakes, and even bear encounters, but what happened next was almost the end of me! We were watching a young humpbacked whale play, swimming on its back and smashing its fins against the water, diving down into the water and slapping its tail, or fluking. This went on for some time and I diligently captured each movement. Then he fluked and went under. We waited…and nothing. Thinking he had gone, I turned to shoot a coastal island when I heard the crowd "ooooo" in unison. I turned just in time to see the young whale soar into the air, a beautiful breach! I turned and shot as he splashed into the water. We all looked at our cameras, all I had was a splash. The woman next to me immediately turned to show me the picture she had gotten and yelled "I GOT IT! I GOT IT!" She had. She did. In that moment, and I'm not proud of this, I thought about throwing her overboard, but I didn't because my sense of right and good stopped me…that and the fact her husband was big enough to play linebacker on a college football team! And the shot of that island, it SUCKED! If the two of you are out there, please forgive me for my momentary lapse of judgement and don't worry about the fact I cry myself to sleep each night… because I missed the breach shot!

As magnificent as humpback whales are to watch under any circumstances, on this day we were all treated to an incredible spectacle called bubble net feeding. This is when a pod of twelve to fifteen whales dive deep under a school of fish and create a cylinder of bubbles around them that extends to the surface. The confused fish swim in a circle within the cylinder as the pod of whales dive below and then swim upward together, mouths open, taking in the fish as they come up. The whales then surface to drain the water they've taken in with the fish. The sea gulls, seeing from above what was taking place and wanting to get in on the fishing, always knew exactly when the whales would surface and therefore tipped us off as to where to look. It's an amazing site to witness, and this is another one of those times when I felt as if I was watching a *National Geographic* special! Then we saw it again…five times in all on our seven-hour boat trip!

LEAVING THE KENAI PENINSULA, I made my way to Whittier along the Prince William Sound so I could board a ferry, car and all, to Valdez. The only way to get to Whittier was through the one-lane Anton Anderson tunnel, the longest combined vehicle-railroad tunnel in North America at two and a half miles. I pulled up to the toll booth and asked what the fee was. "Thirteen dollars," the toll attendant said. That seemed a bit much, so I asked the attendant how much it would be one way because, after all, I wasn't coming back through it again anyway.

"Thirteen dollars," she said, "and I'll let you come back through for free whenever you want to." No doubt she had heard this question before; what a deal that was!

The seven-hour journey on the Alaska Marine Highway ferry to Valdez was a pleasant trip along the southern coast of Alaska and included some great views along the Valdez Arm.

From the ferry in Valdez, I continued on to one of the most scenic roads in Alaska, the Richardson Highway. Almost immediately you find yourself in the Chugash Mountains, an area that receives between 600 and 900 inches of fresh snow each year! I made my way up through Thompson Pass, an area surrounded by amazing mountains and glaciers, visiting nearby Worthington Glacier and hiking to its terminus where I had the opportunity to explore a small ice cave and its deep blue ice.

My destination for this leg of the trip was Chitina, a small early 1900s copper ore boom town, where I was staying for one evening before flying into Wrangell-St. Elias National Park the next day.

BOASTING NINE OF THE top sixteen tallest peaks in the United States, Wrangell-St. Elias is the largest national park in the park system. The history of this park includes the discovery of one of the world's richest copper ore bodies, and in 1900, the establishment of the Kennecott mill camp. The camp was closed by 1938 because of dropping ore prices and the limited supply of copper, but the history of the camp has been preserved by the park system.

My priority in exploring Wrangell-St. Elias was to tackle a hike on a glacier. For some reason I always imagined glaciers to be smooth; when I hiked on Root Glacier, I learned the truth. They are not smooth. From Kennecott we trekked approximately two miles out to the glacier and once there, we donned crampons, a set of metal spikes attached to your boots to give you more traction on the snow and ice. We then took off across the ice and I learned very early on that glaciers are not only not smooth, but indeed they were not very good for my knees and ankles. In fact, glaciers are covered with small mounds of hard ice that you have to navigate over and around…constantly! It was a difficult hike but incredibly interesting, revealing a landscape unlike any I had ever seen before. It was a mix of streams, waterfalls, ponds, and rugged formations, all carved out of the ice, a scene like no other! At one point our guide stopped us on the edge of a deep blue pool in a crevasse and carefully scooped water from it, heating it up, and making hot chocolate for us to enjoy as we took a break from our hike. It was yet another event unique to the Alaskan wilderness journey I was experiencing.

For this leg of the trip I was staying in the town of McCarthy, in the interior of the park, which was a unique experience in itself. Like stepping back in time to a little frontier town, main street was a dirt road with potholes and my accommodations at Ma Johnson's Hotel, an authentic old-style establishment, included an eight-by-ten room with a bed and little else. If you needed to use the bathroom or shower it was down the hall and you would simply have to get in line to use it!

One of the great things about road trips like this is meeting people along the way, people from all over the world. A good example of this is a group I met on the Whittier-to-Valdez ferry. They were also on their way to Wrangell-St. Elias and I ran into them again at the Worthington Glacier on the Richardson Highway, in Chitina, and now we were all staying in McCarthy in the middle of the park. I was staying at Ma Johnson's in the "upscale" part of town while they were in a bunkhouse on the other side of town! In fact, I accused them of following me since one or more of them seemed to always be around! The group was from all over. Besides people from the U.S. there were several women from Great Britain, one from Australia, and Anna from South Africa. I made a point to collect her information so we could stay in touch. It's always an added treat to talk with fellow travelers about their experiences and to learn more about where they are from in the process.

—➔

WHEN I SAID I was crisscrossing the state, I wasn't kidding. After taking in all the beautiful mountain and glacier views along the Richardson and Glenn Highways, I pulled into Anchorage to drop off my rental car and checked in at the Copper Whale Inn bed and breakfast, for the third time. This was easily the nicest place I stayed on my trip, an upscale B&B with all the comforts of home. And after "roughing" it in my eight-by-ten room at Ma Johnson's Hotel in McCarthy, it was a welcome change.

Besides the huge suites, there was an expansive common area complete with a small kitchen, fireplace, and several couches where the guests could gather. I would be here for only one night, so I grabbed an iced tea and some snacks and sat down to relax. It wasn't long before I was joined by a couple and their daughter who said they were visiting from North Carolina, and we all talked about how our trips had gone so far. I gave them my business card and said they should feel free to look around as I was working on photographing all the national parks and was also a sports photographer at Georgia Tech. Oddly enough, the mother's first question was, "Have you ever photographed track and field?"

Not knowing where she was going with this, I smiled and said, "Yes, why?" She proceeded to tell me her youngest daughter was a high jumper at the University of Miami, and I had taken a picture of her clearing the bar at a meet in Atlanta; they had seen it on my photo site. We spent the next hour or so exchanging more stories before I headed off to bed. Small world!

The next morning, I had a few hours before my flight to Lake Clark National Park, so I ventured out to get a nice big breakfast. Let's see, eggs, hash browns, toast, and reindeer sausage. I've already had monkey so why not try a little reindeer? For the record, it was very good and after I finished my meal, I texted my sister Vicky and told her she could tell her kids I just ate Rudolph! From her reply I don't think she actually relayed the message to them.

My trip through Alaska continued in the wilderness of Lake Clark National Park, located southwest of Anchorage. Here I experienced the only bad weather during my trip with high winds, drenching rainstorms, and snow as I flew through the park. Even so, from the jagged mountain peaks of the three mountain ranges that converge in the park, the Alaskan, Chigmit, and Aleutian, to the glaciers, lakes, and streams, the breathtaking beauty of this wilderness area was mesmerizing.

Besides the obvious beauty of the Lake Clark area, the park celebrates the story of survival in the wilderness as told through the perseverance of Richard Proenneke, an amateur naturalist and longtime resident of the area. In 1968 he built a cabin in the Twin Lakes region of the park and documented every step of his lifelong journey in a log as well as on film. This record is captured in the book *One Man's Wilderness* as well as in a documentary, which airs periodically on PBS. The story also has a direct tie to my visit to Lake Clark as I stayed at the Farm Lodge in Port Alsworth, an area settled by missionary and bush pilot Babe Alsworth in 1944. Babe was also the person responsible for flying supplies to Dick Proenneke and others in the region on a regular basis, and his family still runs the Farm Lodge to this day. Additionally, the pilot and guide for my trip through the park was Glen Alsworth, Babe's grandson. And to carry on the tradition, Glen's sons and daughters, who all work at the lodge, are in training to also become bush pilots.

The Farm Lodge itself was very nice; I had a cabin to myself, and the food was incredible. In fact, they fed us so much I started requesting half portions because they gave us more than I could eat. Meals were served in a community setting where all guests dined at large tables in a log cabin-style hall overlooking the lake. Each night I would meet new and interesting people, including Ed Hart and his wife from California. Ed took an interest in my travel and photo story because they travel quite a bit themselves and have a son who is into both travel and photography. All in all, everyone at the Farm Lodge was unbelievably accommodating and made my stay there an amazing experience.

Glen took me to see Dick Proenneke's cabin at Twin Lakes and then flew us to a landing on Kenibuna Lake where we hiked to the edge of Shamrock Lake and a great view of Shamrock Glacier. As nice as the view was, it really couldn't beat the view on the way in as we flew down the glacier, top to bottom! The glacier itself is not in Lake Clark National Park, although half of Kenibuna Lake is, and the view over the lake into the park was spectacular. We spent a few hours overlooking Shamrock Lake, where we enjoyed the scenery and our lunch. We were not alone. No less than six black bears were in the vicinity, all feasting on the soapberries, which are in abundance in the area at this time of the year. The bears only had a passing interest in us, periodically stopping to check where we were and then going about the business of the day, their soapberry harvest.

Later when I was sorting through my images for the day, I noticed I had inadvertently caught a picture of a bear relieving himself, the remnants of those bright red soapberries falling to the ground. Now when someone asks, "Does a bear shit in the woods?" I have photographic evidence to prove it!

THE LAST STOP ON my Alaskan National Park adventure was in Katmai National Park on the Alaska Peninsula. Known primarily for its wildlife, the park is also the site of no less than fifteen active volcanos, the last of which, Novarupta, exploded in 1912 in an eruption ten times stronger than Mount St. Helens in 1980, and buried the surrounding forest in up to 700 feet of volcanic deposits or pyroclastic flow. Today this zone is known as the Valley of Ten Thousand Smokes, an area of desolation I was able to view and hike through.

The park is known for its wildlife, particularly the spawning of salmon each year, which in turn leads to the bear feeding frenzy one can easily view at Brooks Falls. This is what the masses come to see and those who do are richly rewarded! There is a deck above the falls to keep humans separated from the bears, and so many people come here during the salmon run a ranger is posted, much like a maître d', at the entrance to the deck to administer a waiting list. You can spend one hour on the deck and then you have to leave. However, you are allowed to put your name on the list again, so the effect is a rotation of everyone in the park on any particular day.

I've often talked about my adventures making me feel like I was watching a *National Geographic* documentary, but there are few places where it was truer than at Brooks Falls in Katmai National Park. This is home to the continent's largest land predators, the brown bear. Larger than their inland cousin the grizzly, a full-grown brown bear can weigh over 900 pounds! But after a long winter of hibernating the brown bears must once again bulk up for the next winter, and for that they come to the Alaskan rivers and streams to feast on fish, particularly the salmon heading back to their spawning grounds. A large salmon can give a bear 4,500 calories worth of protein and fat to help them survive another winter.

The scene at Brooks Falls is fascinating to watch, nature and the cycle of life playing out before your very eyes! There are brown bears scattered throughout this area. Interestingly enough, the more salmon moving upstream, the fewer bears at the falls. This is because the bears are able to get their fill for the day quickly and then move back into the woods. Conversely, if there are few fish, the bears must wait longer to feed which means many more bears looking for food. There is a hierarchy to be followed here; older and larger bears get their choice of where they want to fish, and younger or smaller bears have to yield or are chased out. Some younger bears will not even approach the falls, instead remaining downstream, honing their fishing skills or picking up scraps left by the larger bears.

The costars in this real-life drama are the salmon. Each year almost a million fish move from the ocean to their fresh water spawning grounds, and many of those are forced to navigate over the fifteen- to twenty-foot Brooks Falls. Here they exert an incredible amount of energy propelling themselves into the air in hopes of landing on the top shelf of the falls so they can continue their journey. Not only are bears lying in wait downstream as they approach the falls, but also on and below the falls.

A salmon makes its leap and falls back into the river. A bear at the base of the falls, having watched the fish fall short, collects the fish to eat the richest parts of the salmon and leaves the rest to be grabbed by a smaller bear for the scraps. A bald eagle flies by with the head of a fish left by another of the huge predators. Back at the falls more salmon take their leap. Some are successful, others fall prey to bears sitting on top of the falls where they skillfully judge the trajectory of the jumping fish and grab them out of mid-air. A female bear with her three yearling cubs comes out of the woods. The cubs stay in a pack as their mother surveys the area. She moves into the water and allows her cubs to explore but keeps an eye out for the large male bears, which will attack and eat the cubs if they get too close. Another mother with cubs born this past winter stays far downstream knowing it is too dangerous for them to get anywhere near the falls. A bear catches a fish away from the falls and is immediately chased by a larger bear. The smaller bear eventually gets run down, turns to face the large bear and attacks, dropping its fish into the water. It growls and then roars as it lashes out at its attacker and a violent confrontation ensues. When it's over the larger bears struts off with the stolen fish to eat. What is left is scavenged by a sea gull waiting close by.

Amazing to watch, the scene is repeated in differing variations again and again!

Just when I thought I had seen it all, before my final flight out of Katmai on the last full day of my Alaskan adventure, I experienced a flight delay because there was a bear walking on the beach in front of my floatplane… and as you might have expected, I got the picture!

Twenty-Four

Sell It All

I HAD MADE MY decision; I WOULD LEAVE ATLANTA AND MOVE BACK to Tucson which from then on, would be home base for my travels. Now I just had to get there, which meant I had a lot of work to do in Atlanta. Sell the house, sell most of my belongings, sell the car, sell it all!

Earlier in the year I had contacted a realtor friend, Bob McCormick, to get the ball rolling on the house. He advised me to replace the carpets along with a few other things, which I completed before I left for Alaska. I was shooting to put the house on the market after my trip and hopefully get it sold by the end of September. Everything was on schedule until my master shower started to leak into the kitchen below and I had to go into damage control mode. I arranged and scheduled the repairs to be done while I was away, and Bob really helped out and earned his commission by checking in on the progress while I was wandering through the wilderness of the great white north. I would give him a call whenever I was in cell range to see how things were going, and on one of those calls he mentioned there was someone looking for a house in my neighborhood and he asked if he could show them my place. He did, and several days later I had an offer for 5,000 dollars over my asking price. I told him to go for it as long as I could live in it through the end of September. We didn't even get the thing on the market and it was sold; check one item off the list.

I had also begun to sell off anything of value. Prior to my trip, I threw all the sellable stuff I had into the garage and held a garage sale. It was amazing how much you stash away in closets when you spend twenty-two years in one place; I was literally finding things I had not seen in over twenty years! The sale went well, and I came away with 500 dollars. Anything remaining went to the Salvation Army. Then about a month before my expected departure I had an "Alive in Tucson" party, which is a reference to the television show *The Last Man on Earth*, and how the character spray painted the slogan on a "leaving Utah" sign as he crossed the state line in his RV. It was a well-attended event and since I had put a price tag on each of the big-ticket items in the house, it was also a fairly lucrative affair. I sold all the furniture out of the master and guest bedrooms, the kitchen table and chairs, the patio set, several kitchen appliances, the dart board, and a number of my large, framed photo prints. The place was kind of barren and I had to sleep on the floor for a few weeks, but at least I could check off another box.

Everything was falling into place; the only tasks left to complete were selling the Porsche and driving away with whatever I was actually keeping. Several people had shown interest in the car, but no one followed through so I took it to CarMax to see how much they would give me. Their estimate was 6,000 dollars, which was a little low but understandable considering they figure in all their overhead. Hearing that number, one guy offered me twenty-five dollars more, which offended me and I told him I'd rather give it to CarMax than let him have it. Luckily, a guy in the neighborhood named Paulo, who had been admiring the car, came to the rescue and offered me sixty-five hundred and I sold it to him with one caveat, that whenever I was in town, I could come by to see how the Porsche was doing. He gladly agreed and I sadly turned it over to him the day before I left town on the fifth of October.

I drove out of Alpharetta with a small rental truck filled with all the things I had decided to keep and made the three-day cross-country trip to Tucson. It all seemed surreal. After over twenty-two years of living in Georgia, the longest I had lived anywhere in my entire life, I was moving on. I actually liked Georgia, and along with all my friends I was going to miss Alpharetta, the generally moderate weather, and my Georgia Tech photo work; there really is nothing like standing on the football field on a clear October day in Georgia.

⟶

I ARRIVED IN TUCSON and knew I had my work cut out for me now. First, I had to unload all my worldly possessions into the "shack," my temporary home. The shack is a building on the five acres my parents own just west of the city. On one end is a laundry room, while the rest of the building is set up as a small apartment complete with a kitchenette and bathroom with a shower. This is where I stayed whenever I came to town on Thanksgiving or Christmas vacations, so I was familiar with all the amenities. What was new would be sharing it with all my aforementioned worldly possessions. No matter, this was a temporary home. More immediately I needed to find a towable car and do all the things to complete my move, postal address changes and move all my email accounts to Gmail. Why? Xfinity was dumping all my accounts because I was no longer a customer. I tried to explain I was moving into an RV and they didn't have a cable long enough to keep me connected, but it didn't matter, company policy. For basically the same reason I had to switch my internet access to Verizon so I could connect anywhere I was on the road wirelessly.

In between all the account switching I was also out looking at cars. I had narrowed down my search using a spreadsheet I had developed. You're surprised, I'm sure. I went out to test drive vehicles that were flat-towable behind an RV, with all four wheels on the ground, and that also met my price range of approximately 25,000 dollars. I started out looking at small cars, convertibles, or those equipped with sunroofs, but I quickly moved away from them because they seemed too flimsy or had virtually no ground clearance. The more I looked, the more I realized I needed something that could handle bumpy dirt roads, so it eventually came down to the Jeep Patriot Sport four-by-four and the all-wheel drive Subaru Crosstrek. I didn't necessarily need the four-by-four of the Jeep but it was actually several thousand dollars cheaper, so I started there. Unfortunately, once you added extras like air conditioning and automatic windows, (I didn't even know you could get a car with crank windows in this day and age) the price went up and the several thousand dollars of potential savings evaporated. On the other hand, the Subaru came fully equipped and I was impressed with its turning radius, high clearance, and overall comfort but low stature compared to the Jeep. For just under 25,000 dollars cash, I had myself a Crosstrek.

The truly big-ticket item, the RV, was still hanging out there. This would be my home so it had to be comfortable enough to live in full time; I would have to think about what I needed in it to support my new lifestyle. I started listing my options in a spreadsheet. Now to be fair, this would actually be a new tab on an existing spreadsheet, which you may recall I mentioned some time ago; either way it would guide me in my search. As would my Uncle Merle. He and my Aunt Pat had traveled in an RV for approximately ten years, so I was happy to be able to rely on his knowledge of the subject matter as I picked out my vehicle and future home.

I had set my budget price at approximately 85,000 dollars and we went out to scour the local RV lots for a match. Luckily, Tucson is one of the RV hubs in the United States, along with Colorado and Florida, so there were a lot of places to search through. At the end of October, I landed on a 40-foot-long 2004 Itasca Meridian with approximately 48,000 miles on it, for 69,000 dollars. This was well under my budget, so I had some extra cash to play with, allowing me to upgrade some mechanical workings and put in new carpet, a flat-screen television with DISH satellite antenna, and a computer desk with a flat screen computer monitor. All-in-all, my drive out cost was just a hair under my budget of 85,000 dollars and I was on my way.

I picked up my renovated RV in early December and drove it out to my parent's place where, because my dad had added a full water, sewer, and electrical connection site for my aunt and uncle when they were RVing, I was able to pull in and connect up as if I were in an RV park. The one thing I didn't know was whether I could actually live in this thing. I just assumed I could since it was bigger than my first apartment in college. Only one way to find out, jump in with both feet the first night and see what happens. It was a nonevent as things went smoothly. I spent the next few weeks moving my things from the shack to the RV and making this place my new home. In a little over two months, I would be launching into my new life, but there was one more thing I needed to accomplish before I left Tucson.

MUCH LIKE THE DECISION to go to the Virgin Islands before I left the East Coast and Atlanta, I knew if I was seriously going to pursue visiting all the national parks, I would somehow have to fly my way over and around the Pacific Ocean. I had conquered Alaska's eight parks but there were three, two in Hawaii and one even more isolated in American Samoa, I would have to fly to in order to meet my goal. For a split second I considered ruling out going to American Samoa but I chased the thought out of my mind and declared it crazy. Why even have the goal if you're not willing to complete it? I trudged through a bog above the Arctic Circle, surely a long plane ride to a warm South Pacific Island was doable, even if I had to suffer the inhumanity of economy class!

Once again, I enlisted the talents of Barbara Diener, who was now working out of her own travel company, to get me to Hawaii and then to

American Samoa. And once again she came through. I would spend the last twenty days in January chipping away at the prize.

WITH THREE NATIONAL PARKS on the itinerary and an ocean to traverse, I would get plenty of flight time on this trip. From Tucson to Hawaii would equal 2,883 miles, after which I would tack on another 2,562 miles to get to American Samoa in the South Pacific.

The first stop would be the island of Maui to visit the mountain district of Haleakala National Park, where on my first day on the island I drove directly to the summit for the remarkable views. The centerpiece of this park is the 10,023-foot dormant shield volcano named Haleakala, which means "House of the Sun." This volcano last erupted between 1480 and 1600, leaving a crater 7 miles long by 2 miles wide and 2,720 feet deep. Looking into the crater you would think you were viewing the surface of the moon. Several large cinder cones rise up from the barren basin floor, which is covered with large volcanic rocks and layers of lava flows. The mountain can be surrounded by clouds, and at this altitude, they are often below the summit, so watching clouds roll into the crater below is a particularly interesting sight. This park also holds the distinction of hosting more endangered species than any other national park including the nene, which is the state bird, and the āhinahina or silversword plant.

The next day I had to make my way to the southern district of the park. There are very few roads to this area, but the one I would be taking is quite possibly one of the most well-known roads in the world, the Road to Hana.

I've driven some of the most famous roads in America, the Pacific Coast Highway, the Blue Ridge Parkway, Highway 12 on the Outer Banks of North Carolina, and the Seward Highway in Alaska, and this one beats them all.

With 620 curves and 59 bridges, most of them a single lane, this 68-mile stretch of road through lush tropical forests is heaven to anyone who likes to drive! The road, the view, the ROAD! I left early to avoid the traffic of the middle of the day, so the road was nearly empty. I threw myself into every turn, skillfully guiding my four-cylinder 2016 Nissan Versa through each corner…okay, this wasn't exactly the car I dreamed of having at this moment, on this road, but I still enjoyed the driving… while imagining what it would be like in my old Porsche! It was fun any way you slice it!

One thing about driving the Road to Hana is if you're the driver there's not a lot of time to sightsee, and there are few pull outs. So, I made it to Hana in a little over two hours and moved right along to the coastal and rainforest district, or Kipahulu, of Haleakala National Park.

There I hiked several trails from the coast, where I viewed numerous waterfalls, each cascading into small pools along the 'Ohe'o Gulch, to the rain forest, where I saw Hawaii's tallest waterfall, the 400-foot Waimoku Falls. Along the same trail was one of the most impressive areas I have ever encountered, the Bamboo Forest. It was at least a half mile of nothing but tall bamboo stalks swaying in the wind. The density of the forest was such that the stalks made an almost musical sound as they bumped against each other with each passing breeze. And, as with all of Hawaii, everywhere you looked there was a spectacular sight to see.

Once back on the coast, I decided one drive along the Road to Hana was enough and elected to take another route, the Pi'ilani Highway west along the southern coast of Maui. A lot of this road was dirt or not well maintained but passable, or so I was told by a park ranger. This is an area where the rental car agencies actually forbid renters to take their cars because of the rough patchy roadways, single lane sections, and blind corners. I'm a renegade so I went anyway. There were some places where you had to tread lightly, but there was hardly anything the Versa couldn't handle, especially after spending two hours on the Road to Hana. The wide-open coastal views were beautiful! The sight of the flank of Haleakala sweeping down and into the sea was something I will never forget.

I TOOK A SHORT flight to the Big Island of Hawaii to visit Hawaii Volcanoes National Park, which protects the area hosting two of the world's most active volcanoes, Kilauea and Mauna Loa. Mauna Loa, which is only accessible by trail, is the world's most massive mountain standing 56,000 feet above the sea floor, over 27,000 feet taller than mount Everest!

On the other hand, the Kilauea area can be explored via car and a number of trails. When I visited there was only a small amount of lava running from Kilauea and it was not easy to get to; however, the Halema'uma'u crater in the Kilauea caldera had an active vent and a molten lava lake, which discharged sulfur dioxide gasses high into the air over the crater. It was a spectacular sight in the daytime, even more amazing as the sun went down and the Halema'uma'u crater in the caldera was illuminated by the molten magma lake below.

Several places in the park vent steam from cracks in the earth and the vast lava flows cover this area in a black and brown carpet of lava, frozen in the various shapes where it came to rest when it cooled. I hiked several trails, the most interesting of which was the Napau Trail; it was supposed to be about two and a half miles round trip to the Mauna Ulu crater; somewhere I missed a trail marker and I ended up going to the Makaopuhi crater...a ten-mile round trip! Now honestly, I could have turned around anywhere once I realized my mistake, but every time I thought about it, I would see something interesting in the distance and talk myself into pushing forward. This is the modus operandi of a die-hard explorer...or someone who is about to be lost, never to be heard from again! The mistake paid off in great views, interesting plants, some of which are found nowhere else on earth, and a trip through a field of steam vents. So, at least this time...explorer it is!

Next, I moved on to the most populous island in the chain, Oahu, home to the capital city of Honolulu, the famous North Shore, and the landmark Diamond Head volcano. It is also home to the Pearl Harbor Naval Base, where on December 7, 1941, at 7:55 a.m., the United States was thrust into World War II when it was attacked by the Japanese Naval Air Force. Today the area is set aside in Pearl Harbor as the World War II Valor in The Pacific National Monument. It includes memorials for three battleships, the USS Arizona, Oklahoma, and Utah. Most notably, the USS Arizona Memorial straddles the battleship where it sank on that day in 1941, becoming the resting place for 900 of the 1,177 seamen who perished there. It is, of course, a somber place of reflection allowing visitors to view the battleship, some of which still protrudes above the water. One cannot help but be moved at the site of the ship rusting below and the oil still seeping through the deck bubbling up to the surface of the water, respectfully known as the "Tears of the Arizona."

On my down time while on Oahu, I took several tours to get a better feel for the islands beyond the national parks. One of those tours circled the island with an emphasis on the coastline and particularly the North Shore. The sites were remarkable and helped me gain a better understanding of the islands and their history and culture. For instance, there are only twelve letters in the Hawaiian alphabet (a, e, i, o, u, k, l, m, n, o, p, w), which explains the long names with strings of multiple vowels everywhere!

Besides seeing the beautiful coastline and water, which is incredibly blue no matter where you go, and having fresh pineapple at the Dole Plantation, the highlight of the tour was catching a glimpse of a green sea turtle on a beach in Waimea Bay. At first I thought it was dead, but apparently, they love to crawl up on the beach to bask and sleep in the sun just like so many of the tourists you see in Hawaii! Also like a true tourist, this guy was oblivious to everything around him; we took our pictures and moved on without even the slightest twitch from our subject.

The island of Oahu is probably one of the most diverse places I have ever encountered. From the dramatic North Shore with its pounding surf and the rest of the incredibly beautiful coastline to the tranquility of Pearl Harbor and the rugged inland mountains, there is an interesting assortment of varied sites and scenes. One of the most interesting is a small sliver of land, beach, and sea surrounded by the city of Honolulu called Waikiki Beach.

This is the center of the tourism world of the Hawaiian Islands. Not to take away from any other island or resort, but this is the place everyone wants to visit, and for good reason. There's the beauty of the water, the beach, and the sunsets, all of which you can see on all the islands, but then add the profile of the Diamond Head volcano looming in the background and now you've got something; it's iconic, photogenic, and perfect in every way, a symbol of a vacation paradise known all around the world.

For all those reasons it is the "it" destination for most Americans and the number one vacation spot for people from Japan. The area caters heavily to tourists with upscale hotels and resorts and luxury shops from Gucci to Tiffany's. The area is as crowded as any metropolitan area in the country, but your state of mind is so relaxed and you are so immersed in the beauty of the area that it hardly matters; however, it is most interesting to observe. Probably more than any place I have visited, including Niagara Falls, people here are obsessed with the "selfie" and of course the handheld technology we all possess, the smartphone. Dodging people with selfie sticks in hand could become a sport here as I don't believe I have seen them in such large numbers anywhere else. Now perhaps I should not throw stones at this obsession, since I walk around with a camera and camera bag everywhere I go, and I'm probably the only person ever to come to Hawaii and not get into the water, but since these are my observations, I reserve the right to jot them down here! At least I'm consistent with my rants whether overlooking a famous waterfall or on an island paradise.

As I noted before, none of this detracts from the experience of visiting Waikiki and it may even enhance it by making it even more interesting. The place is truly a thing of beauty from the landscapes to the ritzy shops and the chic and beautiful people everywhere you look. And the heck with Bigfoot or the Loch Ness Monster, I saw two young Japanese women sporting tails and now have photographic proof supporting the existence of mermaids. Waikiki truly has it all!

THE U.S. TERRITORY OF American Samoa sits approximately fifteen degrees south of the equator in the South Pacific Ocean. It wasn't easy to plan a trip to this far-flung set of islands; hotels were limited, rental car reservations were hard to procure, and flights to and from Hawaii were only on Mondays and Fridays. Five days in the middle of the South Pacific, with nothing but time on my hands and palm trees swaying in the ocean breeze…I'm not sensing a lot of sympathy so I shall move on…

After a five-and-a-half-hour flight across the equator we landed at the Pago Pago airport at 11 p.m. and I made my way to an open-air concourse to collect my luggage and find my rental car agency. Both were easily accessible in this small L-shaped strip-mall-like establishment with benches that looked like church pews laid out under a canopy where people would wait for their flight to be called. I was able to pick up my bag right away, but the single door to my rental agency was locked up. Apparently Auto Europe, an Avis Company, was not open. I went to a nearby vendor and asked how I could get in touch with an agent and after jumping on the phone he returned to tell me it would be a few minutes, but they were on the way.

A few minutes turned out to be twenty, but finally a guy showed up and unlocked the door and gave me the necessary paperwork to fill out before I could get my rental car. With everything completed, he handed me a set of keys and pointed toward the parking lot, telling me my blue Toyota Yaris was parked in row four, space two, and "have a nice vacation."

It was only about thirty yards to where the car was parked and I found it right away and threw my bag into the back seat. Then, as I always do with a rental, I walked around the exterior to make sure there was no obvious damage. It was clean, but unfortunately there was a problem; it had a flat tire. I grabbed my bag and hurried back to the rental office where the guy I had talked to was just locking up. I explained the issue and he went to investigate. Realizing there was no spare, he slammed the hatch down and motioned for me to follow him back to the office. After checking some paperwork, he pulled another set of keys out of a drawer and took me back out to the parking lot and pointed at my new vehicle. Apparently, I had been "upgraded" to a Toyota Tacoma, which I suspected might have been someone's personal vehicle. No problem! At least now I had a ride.

By then it was well after midnight and I still had to find my hotel. I had personally made my reservation online for one of the few hotels in the city, the Sadie Thompson Inn, but when I got there the place looked like an old bunk house. I pulled in anyway and got out to walk around to see if I could figure out what was going on, but there was no one around, so I hopped back in the car to drive a little farther. The streets on this small island were "rolled up." There was no one around anywhere. Then again, it was past one in the morning, I had no cell service, and not knowing what to do, I headed back toward the airport. On the way I saw a sign for Sadie's by the Sea, a second Sadie's hotel, which I remember seeing on the internet when I made my reservations. I pulled into the lot, but the office was closed. As I walked back to my car, I actually saw a human being walking among the buildings and tracked him down. At this point the guy could've been a serial killer, I just wanted to talk to someone. Lucky for me, he was a hotel maintenance man and when I explained my situation to him, he chuckled and told me the Sadie Thompson Inn closed some time ago but he could help me. He called someone to come check me in, and my head hit the pillow at a little past two-thirty.

Late night or not, I was up early the next morning to tackle the reason for my trip to American Samoa, to visit the most remote U.S. national park in the park system. The National Park of American Samoa can be found on three of the four primary islands in the territory, with the majority of the park on the largest island of Tutuila. The park protects 9,500 acres of paleotropical (Old World) rainforests and is the only rainforest of its kind in any U.S. national park.

It was incredibly hot and humid, but I took several hikes including the Pola Island Trail. The trail itself was only one-tenth of a mile out to the beach, but the drive to get there was challenging; the instructions specifically stated the need to "take the dirt road on the right and drive by several homes without disturbing them," with an added warning to "avoid the dogs." I've been to a lot of national parks, but I must admit this was a first for me. On the other hand, the Tacoma was made for just this situation. It was definitely worth the trip, as the view of Pola Island from the beach was incredible. And just for the record, the dogs did come out and chase me down the road a bit. I sat there for some time watching the surf pound the rocks and also spent quite a bit of time chasing camera-shy crabs and rippled rockskippers, unusual air breathing creatures which are fish with bulging eyes and long skinny bodies that skip from rock to rock in pools along the shore.

The lush rainforest was full of trees, bushes, and flowers unlike anything I'd ever seen and even bananas ripening on the tree. Birds of all types and sizes, both seen and unseen but heard, were abundant everywhere I explored. The Samoan flying fox fruit bats fascinated me the most. With a three-foot wingspan, they were best viewed hanging from trees during the day and soaring through the air as the sun set. You've got to love a national park with both huge flying fox fruit bats and rippled rockskippers!

Having explored the park and with time to spare, I took off on a driving tour of Tutuila Island and its many small villages. I learned each village was a community unto itself; there was a church and one or more family chiefs, each represented by a fale, which is a covered open-air family meeting place with columns. Also present everywhere were sa bells, a long tube suspended in the air and traditionally rung each evening around dusk to let the people know when to observe a time for prayer. Both men and women wore the traditional sarong, called a lavalava, with the female version having a more elaborate design compared to the plain male form. I was fascinated by the many differently designed buses. Each is a family-owned business with one or more island destinations, the lifeline between the many small villages and Pago Pago, the capital, where jobs ranged from shopkeeper to fishermen to port employee or Starkist plant worker.

Samoa is in the Southern Hemisphere, so it was the late summer, early fall season. Temperatures were in the mid-80s with 90 percent humidity, hot no matter which way you slice it! Beyond any discomfort related to the humidity, getting to know American Samoa and its culture was an incredible experience.

—→

Upon returning to Tucson, I had less than a month to prepare to set out on the road in my new RV. The RV was ready and I was putting the finishing touches on my eight-month-long itinerary. It was an aggressive plan, not only in the West, but all the way to the Florida Keys and beyond.

I'd now taken care of all the hardest places I needed to get to: Alaska, the Virgin Islands, Hawaii, and American Samoa. The goal, and the dream, were easily within my grasp. Not much could stand in my way now. There was an endlessly changing horizon ahead!

Twenty-Five

The First Thirty-Six Hours

I HAD NOT FELT LIKE THIS SINCE MY FIRST DAY OF SCHOOL. EXCITEMENT, anticipation, thoughts of the wonders ahead of me, and a little fear. It was eight in the morning on Monday, February twenty-ninth when I turned over the diesel engine on my RV. It roared to life for the first time with a purpose, signifying the beginning of a long journey. It would not just be the eight months of this year, but the next ten to twelve years, the minimum length of time I expected to be on the road.

I performed my predeparture checks, not only to make sure I had done everything, but also to make sure I had done everything right. To this end I had created an RV checklist outlining all the things that had to be done each time I left an RV park. It listed everything from making sure all loose items were secured on the inside to double checking the electrical power cord had been pulled out of the shore docking station and locked up in the RV. Check, everything was a go.

I pulled forward to the sliding gate in the fence and hooked up the Subaru to the tow bar on the back of the RV, completing the typical final step before leaving. Here at home, though, there would always be an additional step in the process, saying goodbye to the folks. I gave them hugs and told them not to worry, reminding them as I always do that I'm in my middle fifties and I know how to take care of myself. I did one more walk-around of the entire setup making sure everything looked right and then climbed aboard the RV and into the driver's seat, slowly pulling out onto the road and driving off as I watched my dad close the gate through the passenger side mirror.

Today would be smooth and easy, about a five-hour drive on I-10 to El Paso, Texas, where I would pull into my first RV park and set up for the night. The next day would take me south to Big Bend National Park, where I will spend a full week hiking and exploring.

I was again feeling excited as I rolled down the highway. I crossed the border into New Mexico and decided it was time to stop somewhere to have lunch. This is the beauty of RVing, you just pull over and make a meal in your own kitchen, and when you're done, pull back on the road and you're underway again.

I pulled off the highway at an exit where I could see a large parking area, (when you do pull in somewhere, you always need to make sure you have plenty of space to turn around) and positioned myself to easily merge back onto the freeway. I shut down my rig and walked to the kitchen, where I made myself a ham and cheese sandwich. Instead of just sitting there I decided to take my meal and walk around outside. As I walked to the back of the RV, I noticed something dripping from under the engine area. I touched the leaking liquid and discovered it was not simply water but some kind of fluid, most likely antifreeze. I didn't know how bad a problem this was, but I knew it couldn't be good. My excitement turned to anxiety.

Back in the RV, I used my phone to look up the Camping World service store in El Paso. I had seen it passing through town in the past and knew it was on the west side of town. Now I had the exit number. I would stop there to get checked out before I went any further.

A little over an hour later I was at Camping World talking to a service agent who informed me they were so busy they wouldn't be able to get to me today. I told him I couldn't wait and asked if he knew of any other shops in the area who might be able to assist me. He referred me to a place only a few miles further down the road, and armed with the address, I headed in their direction.

Once I exited the highway it was obvious this place was off the beaten path. While looking for the address, I actually saw the sign for the establishment a split second too late and was unable to slow down enough to turn into their entrance. Unfortunately, with a car attached to the back of an RV you can't back up without snapping the towing mechanism, so I had to continue down the road in hopes of finding somewhere to turn around. There were not a lot of options. Finally, I came to a ranch style subdivision with some wide roads so I decided to take a chance and pulled in. I snaked through the neighborhood and finally found a wide area where I thought I might be able to get turned around, but it was just a little too tight. I was forced to stop and unhook the Subaru, turn the RV around, and reattach the Subaru to get going back in the right direction.

Ten minutes later, I was at the repair shop where I told them about my problem and they agreed to take a look, instructing me to drop the car in the parking area and turn the RV around in the grassy field and park it in front of their garage.

I parked car and drove the RV into the open area with short brown grass where I was told to turn around. I didn't know the grass was hiding several potholes, which I hit a little too fast; the RV rocked to the right and then to the left, spilling all the contents of my upper compartments onto the floor. Books, CDs, DVDs, and a lot of other miscellaneous stuff was now laying on the floor in the center of my RV. It looked like a disaster area. While the mechanics worked on the leak, I spent my time picking everything back up and stuffing it all back from whence it came.

The problem turned out to be the antifreeze drain cap that had been fastened too tightly, thus breaking the washer and causing the leak.

Thankfully, it was nothing major but fixing it would entail draining all the fluid into a large tub, replacing the washer, and putting the fluid back into the vehicle. And the last step seemed to be the toughest as I watched three guys lifting the heavy tub and sloshing the anti-freeze back into the cooling system. Since some was spilled, I made sure they topped off the reservoir so I wouldn't run short of fluid. The cost was just over 100 dollars, so I felt like the stop was well worth the effort, well, except for maybe all the carnage inside the vehicle due to my off-road experience.

It was still late afternoon and I knew I had only about twenty minutes of driving to get to my RV park stop in El Paso, which meant I would still have daylight available while I got set up. Almost immediately after I left the repair shop, I began to smell something. I knew it must be all the excess antifreeze burning off the hot engine; there was not much I could do about it now, so I continued to my destination.

I pulled into the RV park, checked in, and proceeded to pull into my assigned space where I would spend the night. I would be leaving early in the morning, so I was only hooking up my electricity and water connections. I would leave the car attached to the rig for an easy and quick getaway. There was only one problem, the acidic smell in the back of the RV, especially the bedroom, was incredibly strong. I opened all the windows and ran the fans and air conditioner, but nothing seemed to work. Because I couldn't breathe in the bedroom, I spent my very first night on the road sleeping on the couch in the front of the vehicle with the window open above me, worried I might be poisoned and die choking in my sleep. Needless to say, it was a restless night. What had I gotten myself into?

I got up early the next morning and prepped the RV for departure. Today I would be making the six-hour drive to Terlingua, Texas, where I would be staying for the next week. As I got underway the smell was still quite strong, but it dissipated as I drove; the fluid was slowly burning off the engine.

The drive went smoothly including a lunchtime stop where I almost didn't go outside for fear I might see something else I didn't want to know about. However, logic prevailed and I actually had a pleasant lunch at a rest stop picnic table.

I drove into Terlingua, an old mining town with a current population of approximately sixty, at around three in the afternoon; there was plenty of time to set up before dark.

I checked in at the RV park office and drove to my site. Since it was a back-in site, I unhooked the car, but when I went to start it up it didn't turn over. It was dead. I left it sitting in the middle of the road with the hood up, luckily the park had very wide dirt roads, and with the assistance of an RV park worker, pulled the RV into my lot. I immediately went back to try to start the car hoping for some sort of miracle but there was no juice and therefore no miracle.

I walked to the park office to see if I could get a jump and to find out if they could point me to the nearest repair shop. The guy behind the counter was in no way helpful, but another RVer who overheard my story told me about the closest gas station and offered to give me a jump. We went out and hooked up the cables and turned over the engine. This guy was a lifesaver.

It was now about half past four, so I didn't even worry about setting up my RV. I was just concerned about finding this gas station before five o'clock to make sure I caught them before they closed. Only a few miles down the road toward the center of town, it was a small station with a two-bay garage and several vehicles in various stages of repair scattered all around the building.

I pulled, nose first, up to one of the bays where there were two younger men covered in grease and oil working on a car. I didn't even shut the engine down in case they couldn't help me, and I got out and approached the mechanics. One of them asked me what they could help me with and

I explained my issue to him. He tested my battery and declared it dead, not even rechargeable. I would need a new battery.

He took me inside the office of the all-white building, where an older guy with a potbelly was sitting behind a long counter. The room, parts scattered everywhere, was crowded with NASCAR racing pictures covering the walls. The old man said, "Hello, what can we do you for?" Then the mechanic explained the situation and went to check their inventory to see if they had the battery I needed. Knowing I had no choice in the matter, I was worried how much a new battery would cost out here in a one gas station town in the middle of nowhere. I struck up a conversation with the old man, complimenting his selection of stock car racing pictures and hoping I might get on his good side, possibly turning a 600-dollar battery into a 300-dollar battery.

The mechanic came back into the office with a new battery singing out "we got it" and explained he would have it installed in no time. I was surprised they had a replacement and followed him out to the car to watch as he removed the old battery and put in the new one.

Once he was done and we successfully started the car, he took me back into the office. I was dreading the moment at hand. The old man wrote up a bill and slid it across the counter to me like a mob boss in an old movie. "How do you want to pay for that?" he asked. I held my breath and looked down at the crumpled piece of paper. One-hundred and twenty-five dollars. I wanted to jump for joy but remained calm. This was, after all, the first pleasant surprise I'd had over the last two days!

By the time I got back to my RV it was almost seven. I completed setting up at a little after eight and sat down to relax.

I WAS EXHAUSTED; COULD it really be this tough all the time? Yesterday I said leaving Tucson felt like my first day of school, but what I failed to mention is I was so afraid of going I actually never got to the building and instead went back home telling my mother I couldn't go to school because I forgot my handkerchief. She took me by the hand and walked me to the front door of the school and watched as I went in, not leaving until the door closed behind me. Somehow the whole school thing worked out, so I imagine this could too.

On the other hand, I left Tucson on February 29, a leap year! Could that have had anything to do with all this?

Twenty-Six

Park to Park

 "Moment 4 Life" with Drake, off the *Pink Friday* album by Nicki Minaj.

And this is what it's all about, truly living. I knew there would be hardships, problems along the way, I just didn't think they would come so soon and happen all at once! No matter, I would just have to make the best of things and get on with the task at hand, exploring the parks. So once the dust settled on all the drama of the first thirty-six hours, I got into my car and headed down the road to Big Bend National Park.

MASSIVE...BIG BEND NATIONAL PARK is larger than the state of Rhode Island, has five visitor centers, and encompasses the entire Chisos Mountain Range. The park is more than fifty miles from one side to the other and sports three distinct ecosystems: the river, desert, and mountains. All areas are amazing, but the Rio Grande River makes this park special and marks the international boundary between the United States and Mexico.

Central to the Park is the Chisos Mountain Range, an oasis rising above the Chihuahuan Desert, where the temperature is cooler than in the rest of the park and the plant and animal life is representative of the higher altitude. The Chisos Basin plays host to not only black bears but also mountain lions, enough of each that trails have multiple warning signs instructing hikers what to do if they come upon one of them.

At the other end of the spectrum is the desert on the eastern side of the park, where the river carves out Boquillas Canyon. This is a beautiful canyon where the cliffs on one side belong to the United States, while the other side is in Mexico and the border is the Rio Grande River. While hiking down the river trails, it was not uncommon to run across an unattended display of Mexican crafts set out for purchase, a sign listing the price of the items displayed and a jar to leave money for anything you might want. Each day Mexican nationals jumped into a boat with their wares and placed them on the trail in hopes a tourist might spend a few dollars on their handy work, and at the end of the day they returned for whatever was left. At one point I was actually serenaded with a Mexican ballad by one of these craftsmen as I passed his display. It was an interesting daily cycle which I'm sure has been playing out for as long as this park has existed.

Among the many interesting sites on the western side of the park and along the Ross Maxwell Scenic Drive, the highlight was the spot where the Rio Grande flows from Santa Elena Canyon. Its sheer 1500-foot limestone cliffs rising straight up from the river demonstrate the power of the water over thousands of years. As with all the terrain along the Rio Grande River, the southern banks reside in Mexico while the northern side of the river belongs to the United States.

LEAVING TERLINGUA AND HEADING to Carlsbad Caverns National Park, I encountered the worst road I have ever driven. Texas Highway 118 and then U.S. 67 all the way to I-10 was clearly a truck route as there were heavy haulers everywhere going both ways. Consequently, the road was shot. Potholes and cracks jolted the RV constantly; not since my off-road adventure in El Paso had I been thrown around as much as this; of course, that was only a week ago. Things got much smoother after I passed under I-10 and headed north into New Mexico.

CARLSBAD CAVERNS NATIONAL PARK is located in a portion of a marine fossil reef that formed over 250 million years ago. As the reef lifted, caverns were formed and water seeping through cracks and faults created the stalagmites, stalactites, and other formations visible throughout the cave. This process began over 500,000 years ago and continues to this day.

Almost every visitor uses the elevator to travel to the most explored area of the cave, the Big Room, but for the last few months before my visit, and into the foreseeable future, the elevator had been out of commission. The lack of funds coming to our parks makes it tough to maintain them, but this is the reality of the situation and nowhere is it more noticeable than here.

So, having planned to hike into the cavern anyway, I began my trek. But because of the aforementioned elevator issue what I had hoped would be a pleasant, peaceful hike became a loud parade of humanity, a one-hour winding line of people a bit like what you would find at an amusement park! And it was clear a lot of the people were not up to a one hour, 755-foot, eight-story descent into a cavern, and more importantly, the march back to the surface! Luckily my plan was to spend the day in the cavern, and by the time I made my way back to the sunlight, the crowds were long gone and I was glad I didn't have to witness the pain and agony of their procession.

Once clear of the masses and after eating lunch 755 feet underground, I joined the guided tour of the Kings Palace which took us to the 829-foot level. In this area there was an array of delicate formations and occasional large stalagmites, almost completely opposite of what I would see on my next hike.

The Big Room is the largest known underground chamber in the Western Hemisphere. It is 1,800 feet long, up to 1,100 feet wide, and 30 stories tall. A dozen football fields could fit inside this awe-inspiring space! I'd been here before, a little over thirty years before, but I always wanted to return to see it again and photograph it. Unfortunately, I am a lazy photographer and I don't like to spend a lot of time setting up or carrying a tripod, which is probably one of the reasons I enjoy shooting sports so much; get the shot and move on! This particular situation stretched my skills to the limit; thank goodness for high ISO and a little understanding of exposure compensation! So, my images are mostly natural light and a pretty good representation of what you can see down there; it is a fantasy land of stalagmites, stalactites, and flowing rock formations unlike anything you would ever see above ground, incredible and a must see for everyone!

IN THIS AREA YOU get two parks for the price of one. Guadalupe Mountains National Park is a mere thirty miles from Carlsbad Caverns National Park; indeed, it is part of the same ancient reef. The section of the reef that rises above the Chihuahuan Desert today includes the highlands and the tallest mountain in Texas, Guadalupe Peak, at 8,751 feet, as well as numerous canyons that act as a transition zone between the two.

I hiked into the Pine Spring Canyon along the Devil's Hall Trail, and to a lesser extent around the McKittrick Canyon area, but one of my favorite views of the Guadalupe escarpment was from the west over the Salt Basin Dunes. This field of gypsum boasts dunes over sixty feet high; although I did not see any animals, the tracks and trails in the sand made it clear the area was teaming with creatures of all kinds. I noted how in some areas plant life grew through the sand, while in others the shifting sands buried the plants. The view of the Guadalupe Mountains, the evidence of animal life, and the struggle of the plants along with the wind patterns in the sand made this my favorite corner of this park.

TO THE NORTH, IN the Tularosa Basin of southern New Mexico, lies the largest gypsum dune field in the world. White Sands National Monument covers over half of these 275 square miles of dunes in the Chihuahuan Desert. Interestingly, the park also sits within the boundaries of Holloman Air Force Base and the White Sands Missile Range, where in 1944, the first atomic bomb was test detonated at the Trinity Site.

It is amazing to walk on the pure white sand glistening in the midday sun, and it's even more spectacular to see it in the glow of a sunrise as I did my first full day here. I stayed on the north side of Alamogordo so I had a forty-minute trip to get to the park, meaning I had to be out the door at 6:15 a.m. The gates opened at seven and I had to get to my viewing spot before the 7:10 sunrise. This is not as easy as it may seem, because the park is used by most visitors as a sledding amusement park; therefore, the dunes closest to the road are marred by sled trails and footprints. Luckily, I had visited the park the previous afternoon and scouted out a more pristine area where I could get the images I wanted; a walk into the amphitheater area would suffice. Sunrise did not disappoint, and the orange hues on the white gypsum sand and the surrounding plants were beautiful. With a little preparation I was able to satisfy my photographic needs. The melding of all my loves, travel, photography, and the national parks, was complete for this day and in this park. It is what I have worked toward in all the parks I have visited and what I will strive to do in every park I visit going forward.

Later in the day I took a hike on the Backcountry Hiking Trail, where the dunes are higher, up to sixty feet tall, and visited by fewer people. There I was able to see and appreciate the different shapes of the dunes and the patterns of the sand, no two alike, in virtual solitude.

That afternoon, I met several people, hardier souls than I, who had camped in the park the night before. One guy with his girlfriend who stopped off to camp as they crossed the country on a move to California to take a new job; one woman who, interestingly enough considering my past ties to the school athletic program, had just graduated as a nuclear engineer from Georgia Tech, where she also played in the marching band; and a gentleman who plays French horn and works with the Seattle Symphony Orchestra and does photography on the side. I'm always amazed by the diversity of the people I meet on the road. Where else can you meet and have a conversation with a professional musician and a nuclear engineer at the same time?

I have visited this park many times, including several times as a child. I suppose it's easy to understand how one might view the white sand dunes differently depending on your stage of life. As a kid it was all about charging up a dune and sliding or rolling down it and then doing it over and over again until your parents order you back into the car. Now older, and supposedly wiser, I avoid the crowds and look for the more pristine areas where I might take in an unspoiled view and catch the light reflecting off of the shimmering gypsum crystals. It's hard to say which approach is more fulfilling, but easy to say if I slid down one of those dunes today, I might not be able to get back up; therefore, photographing the dunes is probably more prudent at this juncture.

MOVING NORTH, I SPENT a week outside of Albuquerque to explore a number of interesting national monuments including the surprisingly beautiful El Moro National Monument with its freestanding monolith rock in the center of a box canyon. Not far down the road, while exploring El Mapais National Monument, I was caught in a blinding snowstorm on a hike across a lava flow. Of course, the snow started to fall at the trail's farthest point from the car just to make my return trip more treacherous, as if walking on a sharp field of hardened lava wasn't tough enough!

While in the area I also visited Old Town Santa Fe. This is a unique area with a large plaza surrounded by old pueblo-style buildings including the Palace of the Governors, where Native American Vendors still sell art and silver and turquoise jewelry to visitors. It's also a great people-watching area where cruising the Plaza in remodeled and souped-up cars is a daily affair.

—

CROSSING INTO THE SOUTHWEST corner of Colorado, my next stop was a small town called Cortez. From here I could reach a plethora of national monuments, all of which protected dwellings and ruins of the ancient peoples who once lived in this area.

One of these places is Yucca House National Monument. Established in 1919, the park has gone totally undeveloped for its entire history. Remember how I lamented getting to the beach along the Pola Island Trail in the National Park of American Samoa? Well, getting to Yucca House was just as interesting!

Once off the main road you drive along dirt roads onto a working ranch and through grazing herds of cattle. These are not just cattle along the sides of the road; at times you are slowly driving through the herd! Finally, you come to a ranch house and turn into its driveway and park next to the barn; this is a working ranch house where people actually live. It felt like I was there to visit some long-lost relatives.

After parking the car, you pass through a "cow catch" in the fence and come to a small sign indicating you have actually reached the park. I don't want to downplay the park itself, because there were interesting ruins with pottery scattered on the ground, sitting exactly where they were left so many years ago, making it a raw and unique experience.

My reason for being in Cortez was to visit Mesa Verde National Park, which protects thousands of archeological sites of the Ancestral Pueblo people along the Chapin and Wetherill Mesas. It includes some of the most spectacular and well-preserved cliff dwellings in the world. People settled in Mesa Verde around AD 550 and started building their dwellings beneath the mesa cliffs around AD 1200.

The weather was beautiful while I was in the park, but because I visited early in the year, the Wetherill Mesa area was closed. Some of the most incredible cliff dwellings reside in the Chapin Mesa area, so I had plenty to explore. However, there was some good news and some bad news. The bad news was because of issues with falling rocks in the cliff dwellings, visitors were not allowed to tour and go into the sites. The good news was because of falling rocks, visitors were not allowed to tour and go into the sites, which meant I could get pictures of the amazing cliff dwellings without people crawling all over them! I'm sure my apparent joy over this development may seem somewhat selfish, but in my defense…okay, I have no defense. I love capturing images of these kinds of places and have many times in the past waited around for people to clear out of an area so I could snap a picture. They, the all-encompassing "they," were in no hurry then, so I don't feel sorry for their loss now!

Going through the park and seeing what was accomplished by the Ancestral Pueblo people so long ago was humbling; they did so much with so little. The largest of the cliff dwellings, Cliff Palace, took almost 20 years to complete, had 150 rooms, and accommodated approximately 100 people.

I visited here almost twenty years ago, but it was a pleasure to have the opportunity to rediscover this remarkable place and this time, and I'm not afraid to say it, in pristine condition absent the masses crawling all over the dwellings. A perfectly remarkable place.

Moab

Anyone who knows me knows I have one, and only one weakness—dark chocolate. I don't smoke, drink, or do drugs, but I can't resist the dark cocoa stuff and always have some on hand. Dove Dark Chocolate Silky Smooth Promises are my fix of choice. They come individually wrapped, which helps me maintain my portion control, two after lunch and four just before eight each evening. If Dove ever just throws them into a bag without wrapping them, they'll be gone in one sitting.

On the road I keep the bag in my refrigerator so they don't melt, and one night while in Cortez, Colorado, I pulled out my evening ration and sat down to relax, chomping down on the first piece. It was a little hard and I was a little impatient, and the combination broke a crown on the left side of my mouth. Damn. It didn't hurt but it was sharp, and I was in Colorado heading to Utah. Now I had to find a dentist on the road.

I pulled up the internet and since I was leaving Cortez, I decided to try to find someone at my next stop, Moab, Utah. There were several close by the RV park where I would be staying, so I picked one and called them the next morning to see if they would have an appointment the following day. They did, at eight, so with an appointment set for the next morning I packed up and took off for Moab.

When I arrived later in the afternoon, the manager of the RV park looked at me in a confused sort of way and let me know my reservation wasn't until the next day. I was so worried about getting to my dental appointment the next morning that I accidentally left Cortez a day early. Luckily, they still had somewhere to put me and all was right with the world. Well, almost.

I slid into my site and began the usual setup process only to notice an unusual smell. It was one of the two engine batteries; it was cooked. Now I had to get someone to come out and take care of this, too. I was broken, now my RV was broken, too. I immediately went back to the park office and they gave me the number of a local RV repair company to call. They were on it and someone would be out in an hour or so. I completed my setup and waited, without electricity, for fear I might damage something further.

A mechanic came out to get the information he needed to find the right battery and left, saying he would be back as soon as he was able to acquire the replacement.

I sat in the dark for the next four hours as the new battery was driven in from out of town. The mechanic dutifully installed the battery and was done by 10 p.m., at which point he took off to finish yet another job. I don't envy guys who do jobs like this, but I certainly do appreciate them! As for me, I was tired and had to get to bed so I could be up early for my appointment.

I walked into the dental office early because I knew they would have forms for me to fill out; they always have forms to fill out! This place was nice, more like a small lodge than an office. Stone walls, fireplace in one corner, and a receptionist behind a nice wooden desk; she could've easily been a concierge. But make no mistake, once in the back it was standard dentist office all the way. I'm not fond of dentists; however, I needed one right now.

He took a look at the damage and did a quick x-ray using a hand-held model, which I prefer over all the cardboard they usually shove in there that literally makes me gag. He proclaimed he would be able to fix me up in no time.

"But how long would it take to get the permanent crown," I asked, letting him know I would only be here for a week.

"Not a problem, we'll map the area right now with a CAD (Computer Aided Design) camera; I'll put a temporary in and we'll have you back this afternoon to fit the permanent crown. I'd do it all right now but I have other patients, so come back at three and we'll fit you in and fix you up."

This was awesome! And new for me; technology is a beautiful thing!

Now I had about four hours on my hands. Instead of sitting around doing nothing, I figured I might as well do some advance work to prepare for the rest of the week. So, call me crazy, but I headed north straight out of town to the Island in the Sky, one of the four districts of Canyonlands National Park. It took about an hour to get out there. I went directly to the visitor center and picked up my maps and brochures, asked my questions of the rangers on duty, took a quick drive on the main road, and had lunch before I headed back to the dentist.

As soon as I walked in the door the receptionist let me know they were running a bit behind, but the big news was my insurance was refusing to pay for the new crown because the broken one was less than three years old. What? She said if I wanted the insurance to pay for the work, I would have to wait forty-two days; otherwise, I would have to foot the bill, although she said it in a much nicer way. This was crazy. It didn't make sense. Are these companies designed to make life more difficult? I already knew the answer, but I also knew I didn't have forty-two days to wait around to get my crown, so out came the credit card.

They immediately teed me up to get the crown, starting by putting a chunk of porcelain into a machine where I watched lasers carve it into the perfect fit for my mouth. About an hour later it was all done and cemented onto my tooth. Now I could get on with the real reason I was here, the two local national parks, Canyonlands and Arches.

CARVED BY TWO GREAT rivers, the Green and Colorado, Canyonlands National Park is a stunning region of canyons and mesas. There are four distinct sections separated by the confluence of the two rivers. The Island in the Sky, which I visited while I waited to get my crown replaced, is the most accessible; as the name implies, it offers sweeping views of all four of the park's sections. The Needles area is full of red and white banded sandstone rock spires created by fracturing and water erosion. The Maze, only accessible via four-wheel drive, consists of canyons of oddly shaped sandstone. The fourth district is the rivers themselves.

Aptly described in the park brochures as the "observation tower" of Canyonlands National Park, The Island in the Sky region primarily overlooks all the canyons, mesas, and rivers below. It provides incredible views in all directions, highlighted by the view of Monument Basin from the Grand View Point Overlook.

I was in this area on a road trip in 2008 and spent less than a day exploring Canyonlands, primarily because I was so enamored with Arches National Park, thirty miles or so to the east. To overlook this park was a big mistake exemplified by my reaction at the time to seeing the sign pointing the way to Mesa Arch. I clearly recall thinking I had just spent the previous two days seeing some of the most incredible arches on the planet, so there's no way a single arch in Canyonlands could top those and I drove on by. Arches is called Arches for a reason, and Canyonlands is called Canyonlands…well, my reasoning was flawed, terribly flawed, and upon seeing pictures of Mesa Arch sometime after returning from that trip I realized the attraction wasn't necessarily the arch itself but the view through the arch. And it is a spectacular view. The long, slender arch actually frames Buck Canyon directly below and to the left several buttes and towers, including the Airport Tower and Washer Woman Arch. As clouds moved over the area casting long shadows, I was able to get an incredible image through the arch of the darkened Airport Tower and Washer Woman Arch silhouetted against a bright background. I always hope for clear days when I'm out exploring, but a little cloud cover at times can certainly add dramatic effect.

I underestimated the entire park the last time I was here, but this time I was resolute to make up for my mistake. I wouldn't get to the Maze, but I was bound and determined to explore the Needles, although quite far from where I was staying, which was definitely reachable.

The Needles is so named because of the great red and white sandstone spires that rise up above the canyons and fields of desert grasses and shrubs. These spires dominate the landscape and can even be seen from The Island in the Sky.

I ventured to this area twice over the next few days, even though it is over seventy miles from where I was camped. First, I came to see what the area was about and then to hike in to explore the interesting terrain. I had decided to take the short six-mile roundtrip hike to the Chesler Park Viewpoint to get an overview of the area, but like before, when I reached my original destination, I decided to go just a little further. Sound familiar? I did virtually the same thing along the Napau Trail in Hawaii Volcanoes National Park, doubling the length of my hike. This time would be different, although "just a little farther" today totaled an eleven-mile primitive trail hike. It was exhausting but exhilarating! Beyond the view of the impressive spires surrounding Chesler Park, the trail wound around the sandstone formations and included a trip through "The Joint," a deep, narrow fracture in the rock at least a quarter mile long.

As with most long treks, it's always the toughest when you're on the tail end of the hike. There are still beautiful sights to see, but you begin to drag a little. Today was no different, only this time just as I was hitting the wall, I was climbing through the rock spires rising from the Chesler Park basin. I was dragging when I came to an area on the trail with several picnic tables under some trees and decided this would be the perfect place to grab a snack and relax. I had just sat down at one of the tables when a woman appeared on the trail, coming from the opposite direction, and walked over to sit down. Now it was almost ninety degrees, but somehow she looked like she had just walked out of a fashion magazine, well dressed in all black, with long pants and a long-sleeved shirt, her makeup and blonde hair all perfectly done. How is it I was such a wreck? I mean, other than the fact I was probably ten years older than she was…okay, twenty-five years older, maybe thirty. She told me her name was Adriana. She was Canadian and worked for a mining company, liked visiting national parks, and just happened to be traveling through the area and decided to stop and go on a hike before moving on to her next destination. I didn't ask her why she looked so fresh and perfect. I'm not sure I really wanted to know, I just accepted it and moved on to finish my hike.

⟶

MUCH CLOSER TO MOAB, Arches National Park protects one of the world's greatest densities of natural arches as well as numerous spires, pinnacles, and balanced rocks. It is one of my favorite parks because of all the odd and interesting rock formations including the arches themselves; no two are alike and each takes on a different appearance depending on your viewpoint. I still remember the last time I was there, taking the long, steep hike to witness the beauty of the sun setting on Delicate Arch and the park below.

On this trip, along with the goals of hiking the Park Avenue Trail and viewing the fragile one-hundred-yard-long Landscape Arch, I was on a mission of sorts, to capture an image of something that no longer existed.

While admiring one of the many arches, I struck up a conversation with a couple who had just arrived in Moab. When I mentioned I had been to Arches before, they asked if the park had changed since my last visit. Normally the answer would be no, but on this occasion, in this park, I sadly had to answer yes. In 2008 I took the trail out to see the arches in the northern part of the park and along the way passed Wall Arch. It was an arch carved out of a fin, a long thin rock formation, which paralleled the trail and was positioned next to another fin making it hard to photograph because I couldn't get far enough away from the arch to get it all in the frame. I backtracked down the trail some to get the shot and moved on.

Back in Atlanta a little over three months later I was paging through *USA Today* when I came across a news story reporting that Wall Arch had collapsed. In an instant on a dark night in August, what had taken thousands of years of wind and water to carve and mold was reduced to rubble by gravity and the very forces that created it. Time and weather had taken its toll and it was gone.

As photographer Henri Cartier-Bresson once said:

"Photographers deal in things which are continually vanishing and when they have vanished there is no contrivance on earth which can make them come back again."

Now, standing below and photographing a blank space where the magnificent stone arch once stood, I felt lucky to have seen Wall Arch, and it made me realize that nothing lasts forever and what I put off seeing today may not be there tomorrow...

Twenty-Eight

Religion of Nature

STRADDLING THE BORDER OF UTAH AND COLORADO, DINOSAUR National Monument is most widely known for its "Wall of Bones," a rock layer that contains over 1,500 dinosaur fossils. Interesting as it is, this is also where you will find yourself in the middle of the throngs of people who visit the park.

For those hardier souls who wish to take the road less traveled, and maybe even dirt instead of paved, there is the canyon area and Echo Park.

Early in the 1950s, more than thirty-five years after Dinosaur became a national monument, this area became a battleground pitting conservationists against politicians in the Western states seeking to use dams to generate cheap hydroelectric power. Dinosaur National Monument had been selected as a site for one of those dams. We had seen it happen in the past. In the early 1900s, the Tuolumne River in Yosemite National Park was dammed, flooding the Hetch Hetchy Valley and swallowing spectacular waterfalls and vistas that rivaled the Yosemite Valley itself. It was here, in Echo Park, that the Sierra Club and the Wilderness Society waged a campaign to stop this type of development in our national parks, arguing if a national monument was not safe from this sort of development, then how could any wilderness area be protected? In the end the conservationists won, and in 1956 the Colorado River Storage Project Act became law establishing "that no dam or reservoir constructed under the Act shall be within any National Park or Monument," setting a precedent for future protection of our national parks.

Weaving my way along the isolated dirt road into the canyon, I already felt the calmness and solitude of the area. It is a spectacular place cut by the Green River and highlighted by the massive feature called Steamboat Rock. Standing in Echo Park was comparatively a religious experience! I spent hours hiking along the Green River surrounded by towering cliffs, through open grassy fields, and along the river's banks. Except for a few other explorers, it was an afternoon of solitude and incredible beauty. Thank goodness for the people with the strength and fortitude to stand up to save it!

Unless you've been to arctic Alaska, Canada, or Siberia you have never experienced anything like the landscape in Rocky Mountain National Park. At altitude you are driving through the tundra, which is a Russian word meaning "land of no trees." Here the winds often exceed 100 miles an hour and temperatures are below freezing for at least five months each year. Still, it is an incredibly beautiful scene, especially if you are as lucky as I was to see it under clear blue skies.

This is the land where the Colorado River is born; here it is merely a stream fed by snowmelt, but downstream it is the force that created Canyonlands and the Grand Canyon! From the great river to the top of its tallest peaks, this park is full of life; valleys of pines, aspens, and spruce give way to alpine plants, which hug the tundra to survive the harsh weather high up in the mountains. Animals too are plentiful, most migrating to the lower altitudes in the winter and returning to graze in the summer; elk, bighorn sheep, moose, and deer are the largest wildlife in the park.

And in this park, I finally captured on film the elusive, at least for me, bighorn sheep ram! There, on the side of a mountain in Horseshoe Park, was the prize. The first time I visited this site there were two, and when I went back a few days later there was a group of five with a baby as a bonus. Because they were in the distance, I had to go to the "big gun" and pull out my 300mm lens with the 1.4x converter to get the shot, but at least I finally had the privilege of seeing them!

AT AN ALTITUDE OF 14,115 feet, Pikes Peak is ranked as the thirty-first tallest peak of Colorado's fifty-four "fourteeners." It is also one of the most easily accessible to anyone by car. The Pikes Peak Highway is a nineteen-mile drive that is both serene and exciting. The ride goes from thickly wooded areas to the desolation of the tundra at the peak with beautiful viewpoints along the way. This is also the home of the Pikes Peak Hill Climb, where cars drive the grueling twelve-mile sprint to the summit that traverses the varied landscapes of the mountain, turning those viewpoints into a blur while also navigating hairpin curves and switchbacks. The road was no match for my Subaru as I crawled up the mountain behind slow tourists who clearly did not appreciate the road itself as much as I did, but I could easily imagine what the drive might be like if I were free to drive it at a "more interesting" pace!

Awaiting my arrival at the top, besides the amazing 360-degree views, were the world-famous Pikes Peak Summit House doughnuts. I had heard about this special high-elevation delicacy long before I made this drive; it wasn't the reason I was here but it was definitely on the agenda of "things to do" on top of Pikes Peak. Because of the altitude, these doughnuts need to be deep fried at lower temperatures, and so the story goes, the recipe must also be tweaked to get the optimum results. So, after racing to the top and taking in the sights I headed inside the Summit House to get a Pikes Peak doughnut and a cup of hot chocolate. The doughnut is indeed unlike any I have ever had; it's crispy through and through and loaded with oil. Not bad mind you, after all I'm not one to shy away from overindulging in things like chocolate, salt, candy, or fried foods, but I'm quite sure this doughnut jammed up some previously free flowing arteries! Just another day on the road…

—➤

The Painted Wall in Colorado's Black Canyon of the Gunnison National Park is a sheer black rock face, marbled with veins of lighter rock, on the north side of the canyon. I was on the south rim as the sun rose bathing the wall with an orange hue as the shadows receded into the abyss.

Abyss, chasm, crevasse, deep, narrow, and steep. Unlike the vastness of the Grand Canyon, this is a "straight down" kind of experience. At one point the canyon is as little as 1,300 feet wide between the north and the south rim at the top, but only forty feet wide at the bottom! The deepest point in the canyon, Warner Point, is 2,772 feet, a respectable depth for sure, but the sheer rock faces of the walls throughout the gorge are mind numbing. As you travel from outlook to outlook, you can walk up to the railing and look straight down to the canyon floor and the Gunnison River. It was not uncommon to see fellow travelers observing the canyon from the end of the trail rather than the railing of the viewing area. I wanted to be on the railing looking straight down into the gorge…it is an awesome view from each and every overlook!

I took the scenic two-and-a-half-hour drive around the canyon itself to take in the views from the north rim, and it was great to get to see things like the Island Peaks formation from a different angle, but since I was staying on the south side of the park, I spent most of my time along the south rim where there were twelve overlooks.

Because of the narrowness and depth of the canyon, it was imperative to visit the various overlooks at different times of the day to view all the areas in the best light; the most spectacular sight of the visit was early morning sun streaming over the canyon walls and illuminating the Painted Wall.

—➤

Farther east and more centered in Colorado lay Great Sand Dunes National Park. Shaped by the combination of prevailing winds from the southwest, storm winds off of the Sangre de Cristo Mountains, and added assistance from two creek systems, these are North America's tallest dunes.

The vast dune field includes two dunes over 699 feet tall and it is one of the few places in the world where one can see "surge flow" on a stream. Surge flow occurs when water flows over sand and small sand dams are created on the creek bed holding the water until the pressure gets too great and the dam breaks, releasing the water in a wave. This event is more pronounced in the spring and early summer, but I was still able to see a scaled down version in Medano Creek during my visit in the typically dry month of July.

Depending on the time of day and weather conditions, the dunes can take on a different appearance from moment to moment. Sunrise, sunset, cloudy, windy, wet, dry; the way the light strikes the dunes reveals interesting views as the shadows crawl across the sand; it is a photographic paradise and I took full advantage of the opportunity.

I also hiked several trails, the most demanding being the hike to the summit of the second tallest dune in the park, High Dune. Normally a two-and-a-half-mile hike with an elevation gain of 699 feet would be considered a moderate hike at best. However, take your basic beach sand and build a 699-foot dune and you add another level of difficulty that will challenge even the most experienced hiker, which I am not. The hike was grueling and I was certainly happy I started early in the morning before the heat of the day could compound the struggle. You couldn't go straight up the thing, so the idea was to follow a set of progressively higher dune ridges until you attained the summit. Walking along the ridgelines was exponentially easier; unfortunately, you had to scramble your way onto each ridge. Either way, you had to climb 699 feet of sand; the ridges just gave you time to recuperate a bit before the next ascent. My climbing technique was to take twenty steps and stop to catch my breath…or what was left of it…then take twenty more and repeat until I made it to the top.

As I approached the summit, I noticed a man standing alone looking out over the dune field toward the mountain range. I normally don't like people in my photos, a fact I believe I've already made abundantly clear, but there are times when having someone in the frame adds scale to an image and this was definitely one of those times so I snapped off a shot. Once I arrived at the top, I learned the man's name was Marcus and he was a schoolteacher, who like me loved to travel and loved the solitude of places like this even more. We agreed on how rewarding it was to scale the dune, how incredible the 360-degree view of the entire dune field was, and on the fact that it was truly "all downhill from here"!

A few weeks after I posted my images, Marcus contacted me to see where I was, and I told him I had a particularly interesting picture of him standing alone at the top of High Dune. I titled it "Lone Visitor on High Dune," and he now uses the picture and the "Lone Visitor" moniker, with my approval, on his own website.

THE GARDEN OF THE GODS is a public park located just west of Colorado Springs; it was donated to the city by an early settler who insisted it always be free to the public. The park is an extraordinary collection of red sandstone rock formations and spires wedged among the sprawl of the surrounding city and subdivisions. It is certainly a testament to the efforts of those who work hard to keep the park in the best shape possible. It is truly a garden, not only of rock, but also open areas filled with forests and animals.

My only objection was the number of people who were allowed to climb all over the beautiful rock formations, whether they were companies with permits to lead rock climbing excursions or children set free by their parents to climb anywhere they wanted, including on the crown jewel of the park, the Cathedral Spires themselves! In a state where people can find an almost unlimited number of places to climb where no one would object, why would it be permissible to climb on these one-of-a-kind formations? And what are we teaching children about protecting wonders like these? It reminds me of being in Arches National Park where I came upon a guy walking on top of Double-O Arch. Signs all over the place forbid people from climbing on the formations, but there he was! I yelled at him to get down, and after I was backed up by others, he relented. I wonder where he got the idea his actions were permissible, probably as an unrestrained child…

IN 1832 THE UNITED States Government, recognizing the importance of the spring water flowing from a particular mountain in Arkansas, declared several large parcels of land in the area a U.S. Reservation. It was the first time such a step was taken to protect a natural resource in the United States. Throughout history, the hot springs in this area have been a source of comfort, whether for medicinal or recreational purposes. In 1921 Hot Springs National Park was created to protect Bathhouse Row as well as the springs themselves.

To call this park unique compared to all the other national parks would be an understatement. Today only Mesa Verde protects more manmade creations and archeological sites. Hot Springs is as much about the businesses developed around the springs as it is about the springs themselves. Early on, the bathhouses touted the benefits of the water including healing diseases of the skin and blood, nervous afflictions, and "various diseases of women."

Today there is a modern spa emphasis by the two existing operational bathhouses and I decided when in Hot Springs, do as the Hot Springers do! So, I walked into the Buckstaff Bathhouse, the only bathhouse which has been in operation continuously since 1912, and I signed up for your basic Mineral Bath.

Inside and out, the facility was much the same as it has been for over a hundred years, and the tubs and fixtures were exactly the same as I had seen in the visitor center museum earlier in the week. The bath house room itself was huge with a high ceiling and a number of tubs surrounded by partitions for the sake of privacy. There were tables cloaked with sheets outside the partitions in front of each bath and several other areas which I could not identify, including one row of sink-like fixtures only about a foot off the ground along one wall. I wasn't exactly sure what I had gotten myself into, but I was a bit uneasy as I was escorted into the hot steam filled room.

I was introduced to my attendant, an older gentleman, who gave me a house coat and instructed me to get undressed and then started to run the water in my tub. Now the spring water comes out of the ground at 143 degrees, so I waited until my attendant had "cooled" my bath to about 100 degrees, after which he instructed me to get in. After I sat in the calming waters for twenty minutes, he came back with a fresh house coat and told me to meet him at the table when I was ready. Turns out I was about to find out what those short little sinks were. He directed me to shed my cover and sit in what was basically a bowl of hot water; it was a sitz bath for the back, or back-side, I'm not really sure what he said but I wasn't asking any questions either. Comfort and modesty went out the window as I was now sitting naked in a sink open to the entire room. Of course, I was not alone as other patrons around me were also experiencing various levels of indignities as they were processed through whatever bath packages they had purchased. Eventually I was instructed to rise out of my butt teacup and cover myself before I was led to the next stage of my treatment, the vapor cabinet. This is literally a metal box with holes poked in it, basically a sweat box. My attendant turned on a shower of water in the corner (remember it's coming out at 143 degrees) and left me there to die, I mean, steam. But really, I thought I was going to die as the air was so thick with steam I could hardly breathe. If I had any impurities in my body, they ran screaming. I was just about ready to pass out when my attendant came back and pulled me out of the "box" and we went back to the table in front of my bath where I laid down to get hot packs applied to "whatever area ails you," which in my case was my knees. Even this was a bit torturous as he slapped two scalding hot towels on me and ran off. Luckily, he had left me with a cool bottle of mineral water to drink, which I guzzled. The last step of the process was a cooling needle shower, after which I dried off, dressed, and walked out on relaxed, wobbly legs. Definitely a unique national park experience!

Now I feel like I've buried the lead a little because the water is the story and the story is quite amazing as the water coming to the surface today, after seeping through rocks and then percolating back to the surface, is actually over 4,000 years old! It's clear, clean, and delicious, and it's free from fountains and spigots all over the city; makes any of those 18-year-old bottles of scotch seem a bit overpriced!

I ZIG-ZAGGED MY WAY through the middle of the country, stopping off in Dallas to see friends; San Antonio to visit missions, including the Alamo, and to do some people watching along the Riverwalk; then to Houston to see more friends and New Orleans for no other reason than to get a "street" daiquiri, some shrimp etouffee, and a coffee with a plate full of Beignets at the Café Du Monde.

Ultimately, I found my way to Atlanta, my longtime home up until just last year, to catch up with everyone I had left behind. However, I was also there to explore one place in particular.

IN THE CENTER OF Atlanta, in the shadow of the downtown district, sits the Martin Luther King Jr. National Historical Site. This area tells the story, birth, life, and death, of perhaps the greatest civil rights leader of our time, Martin Luther King Jr.

Now, on my return trip to the city, I explored the area with my friend Ashli. I had invited to her come along with me to the site a year before only to run out of time as I prepared to move back to Tucson. This was something I had thought about doing for years, twenty-two to be exact, so now I was making good on my invitation to Ashli as well as fulfilling a promise to myself to visit a site which was in my own backyard and therefore easily overlooked for so long.

As an eleven-year-old, Dr. King's assassination was one of the first major historical events to stand out in my memory. I do remember the assassination of President Kennedy, which happened when I was six years old, but five years later, in 1968, the assassinations of Dr. King and two months later of Bobby Kennedy opened my eyes to the real, unsheltered world around me. In fact, the King assassination stood out in my memory because the next day my family left on one of our two-week trips from Chicago to Tucson. I can remember my parents telling my sister and me to get down on the floor of the car and put pillows over our heads as a precaution as we drove on the expressway under bridges, because people were out there lobbing bricks onto the cars below. Later in southern Missouri, I didn't understand what it meant when I heard an older guy in a restaurant talking about the event and saying, "he had it coming."

Now, as we passed Dr. King's birthplace, walking through the Ebenezer Baptist Church where he preached and stood in front of his tomb, it occurred to me that the 1968 versions of Ashli and me might never have been able to interact with each other. You see, Ashli is a Black American and I am a White American. Back then, it didn't matter that we were both American, we would have been segregated from each other by the societal values of the day. Although we have made progress, it is clear we have by no means fully achieved the "dream" Dr. King famously spoke of in Washington in 1963.

Flash back to my early years in Atlanta; there was a fight brewing over the Confederate battle flag being prominently displayed on the Georgia state flag. Some people defended its appearance there as being in a historical context and I wasn't really paying much attention to the politics of it all, so I thought the argument could hold some merit. Then one day I drove out of my subdivision and got stopped at a light near Newtown Park. As I sat there, ten to twelve pickup trucks turned out of the park and onto the road in front of me, each displaying a pair of full-sized Confederate battle flags. It occurred to me none of those pickup truck drivers looked like historians. When I got back home, I did a little research and found out the Confederate flag had been on the Georgia flag in one form or another since it was placed there in 1956 to reinforce segregation efforts, in particular, to protest the 1954 Brown v. Board of Education Supreme Court anti-segregation decision. Eventually the St. Andrew's cross, Confederate battle flag, was removed, but the current flag still holds tightly to the racist past as it closely resembles the First National Flag of the Confederacy.

We still have a long way to go. In my many years in corporate America, I worked alongside men and women of all races, colors, creeds, religions, and sexual orientations and there are several things I know to be true; there is good and bad in all people and I am a better, more understanding person because of the diversity of the individuals who have passed through my life. Dr. King paved the way for that to happen, and the sooner we all accept the fact all men and women are created equal, the better off we will all be.

As Martin Luther King Jr. said in 1963:

"The ultimate measure of a man is not where he stands in moments of comfort and convenience, but where he stands at times of challenge and controversy."

Each of us must reject racism in all forms or the ultimate measure of where we stand will be against human decency and on the wrong side of history.

—→

I HAD ONE MORE major area to travel through before I ended my first year on the road and headed back to Tucson. I would spend two weeks in the Florida Keys exploring South Florida including three national parks: the Everglades, Biscayne, and Dry Tortugas.

Everglades National Park encompasses the entire southern tip of Florida and is bordered to the east by the Miami metropolitan area. This unique park features a slow-moving flow of fresh water from the north through a sawgrass marsh to Florida Bay, where it meets the salt water of the Atlantic Ocean. Unlike the stagnant water in a swamp, the water here moves constantly, lending it the nickname the "River of Grass."

This park is rich with wildlife; alligators and crocodiles are the largest park predators, and birds of all kinds are present with anhinga, egrets, and herons being the most notable. On a 2010 visit to the Anhinga Trail, a short boardwalk over the water, I found myself face to face with dozens of alligators, not only in the distance but in some cases right next to the trail. It was quite a sight to see those ten to twelve-foot prehistoric monsters lounging in the sun or lying in wait for their next meal! Photographically, I captured a manatee and a baby alligator in a pond, as well as an anhinga catching and eating a fish and a vulture eating a snake. Wildlife at its best!

—→

WITHIN VIEW OF THE metropolis of Miami, and twenty-one miles east of the Everglades, sits Biscayne National Park protecting Biscayne Bay and the keys off the coast of Florida.

I visited this park in 2010 but was unable to see much more than the visitor center and a short trail out to Convoy Point. Since most of this park is water, you need to get on a boat to see the keys in the bay. That trip is short but only takes place on the weekends, so this time around I made sure to schedule my visit to the park accordingly. The boat went out past Elliot Key and landed on Boca Chita Key. It was an interesting trip. There's no doubt the bay and its keys are beautiful but it was obvious this key is overused. People who come here don't seem to know, or care, they are in a national park. They come here to picnic, play music, and party, which is fine, but unfortunately, they tend to leave the place without respecting the central tenant of the parks system, and I'm paraphrasing, "leave it like you found it." Regardless of what I witnessed on Boca Chita, the overall "landscape" of the park and the wildlife within are something to see, and if I was a diver I would have certainly seen more.

Dry Tortugas National Park is seventy miles west of Key West in the Florida Keys. Originally named Los Tortugas or "The Turtles," it was renamed to let travelers know there was no fresh water available on these remote keys.

In 1846, the construction of Fort Jefferson was undertaken to protect the shipping lane into the Gulf of Mexico between the Florida Keys and Cuba. That effort went on for thirty years and was never completed; however, the fort was used to house Civil War prisoners as well as individuals implicated in the assassination of President Abraham Lincoln, including Doctor Samuel Mudd, who tended to the wounds of assassin John Wilkes Booth.

Today, along with the fort itself, the park protects the area's coral reefs as well as the nesting places of the endangered green sea turtle and the threatened loggerhead turtle.

It's always special to come to such a unique place, but on this trip I was joined by a fellow traveler. Anna, on a business trip in the U.S., had flown in from Johannesburg, South Africa, to spend time with me in the Florida Keys, which is particularly interesting because of how and where we originally met. In the summer of 2015, we were both traveling through

Alaska touring national parks, Anna with a small tour group and me just winging it on my own. Our paths crossed several times so we got to know each other, kept in touch, and ultimately made plans to do some touring together. We were able to get to Everglades and Biscayne National Parks, but it's interesting to note there are no two spots in the U.S. farther apart than Alaska and the Florida Keys, and we did them both in just over a year!

ANNA AND I EXPLORED the eclectic town of Key West, seeing the shops, bars, and restaurants of Duval Street as well as taking some time to visit the Art Deco buildings of South Beach. After she went back to South Africa, I still had a few days left out on the Keys and was looking for something to do, and I found something alright.

What I didn't expect when I booked this trip was that I would be here for the beginning of the infamous Fantasy Fest, a weeklong erotic celebration culminating on Halloween with the party of all parties. This is Mardi Gras surrounded by emerald waters, sans the beads!

I was leaving the Keys midweek, so my only chance to attend the event would be during its first few tamer days, but I didn't want to miss the opportunity to see it in person and be able to say I went to Fantasy Fest. I could rationalize the trip to the Fest by approaching it as a photographic safari, after all, this could be considered wildlife, a different kind than I normally shot, so therefore it was a way to grow my skills as a photographer...yeah, that's the ticket! Now let's get something straight; don't tell my sisters about this because they would like nothing more than to get me in trouble by running to my parents with wild stories of me swimming in the debauchery of some alcohol-drenched street party replete with painted and topless women. It's not that they would be wrong. It just bugs me that they so enjoy getting me in trouble!

Now I feel it necessary to characterize my experience and provide a few caveats. Again, I was at the Fest early in the week, so I can only imagine things got more interesting the following weekend. Not that it wasn't interesting, it definitely was, after all this wasn't the kind of crowd you saw on an average Monday in most average American cities. There was some nudity. It was an older crowd, and it was not always pretty; however, it was fun and a people–watcher's dream. I even ran into the devil himself… here's to hoping it's the last time we cross paths!

ON THE WAY BACK to Tucson to wrap up my first year on the road, I made an overnight stop in Baton Rouge, Louisiana, and watched the Chicago Cubs beat the Cleveland Indians in extra innings to win game seven of the World Series. I had waited my whole life to see this happen; my grandfather died never seeing it happen. One hundred and eight years. Naturally, to me it was a religious experience.

Twenty-Nine

Everyday Hero

Now back in Tucson, I settled in for my winter "vacation," as I needed time off after all my travels! I know I won't get much sympathy from anyone, especially those of you who have daily jobs, but this is part of my yearly plan; I'll spend four or five months in Tucson relaxing and conserving my financial resources so I can spend what I need when I'm on the road. Besides, it sure is nice to have a place to go where it stays warm in the winter!

The last few months of every year is truly down time for me, as I really don't do much at all besides spend time with family and friends. I always look forward to friends Don and Anne's Christmas party in early December, a quaint affair highlighted by Anne's yearly batch of chili and Don's ever-present over-the-top opinions. Don has sayings for every occasion, and I always like to twist them to fit an opposite reality. For instance, Don likes to refer to himself as a "legend in his own time," whereas I would call him a "legendary old timer." Don would say he's "dull and wants to be duller" and I…well, that one is just true.

Another event I look forward to each year, much bigger than the Christmas party, is Jennifer and Steve's New Year's Scotch party. They hold it on the Saturday before New Year's and it doubles as a birthday party for Steve, who is also the master griller at the event. Others provide the side dishes, but each guest is asked to bring a bottle of their favorite Scotch; basically, the affair becomes a tasting opportunity as everyone goes from bottle to bottle in search of the one finish which best fits their individual palate. It's nice to get the whole New Year's Eve party out of the way early so you don't have to be out on the road with all the amateur drinkers and police.

As much as I enjoy seeing my family and friends, I tend to get bored while I'm home. On the road I'm doing something almost every day: hiking, exploring, learning, photographing, or working on the images I just took while doing all the hiking and exploring. It's nice to settle down a little, but after a while it gets old and I long to be back on the road again.

Things tend to pick up after the new year as I start to prepare for the next campaign. In January I begin to select the places I want to see over the next year and work on my route, schedule my stops, and make RV park reservations. This can take some time, as some of the RV parks in the north and east close for the winter and I have to wait for them to open up in the spring in order to make a reservation.

The other activity I handle at the beginning of the year is maintenance on the vehicles, particularly the RV. I schedule my yearly oil change and tune up in February and normally have a list of smaller items that need attention. This year was a little different because of a little incident back in Waco, Texas, where I backed the RV into a tree, dislodging the lower rear bumper cowling. I used wire bundle ties and duct tape to hold everything in place and continued on all the way to Florida and back to Tucson without a problem; thank goodness for the miracle of duct tape! Now I had to get it fixed for good and have the windshield replaced because of cracking. Lay out the cash, get everything fixed up, and it all culminated in late March as I pulled out for year two on the road.

———➤

THIS WOULD BE ANOTHER cross-country kind of year and if all went to plan, I would achieve my goal of photographing all fifty-nine national parks. It was exciting to think about making that happen, and there were plenty of other thrilling sites to see along the way.

I would begin by heading west to San Diego and then up the coast, visiting several national monuments. My first national park visit would be in Northern California at Redwoods National Park.

Along the West Coast of the U.S., in small pockets with the perfect environment, the world's tallest trees have stood for thousands of years. These pockets of endangered trees are now thriving. In 1994, to better protect the magnificent redwood trees and their environment, Redwood National Park was expanded to incorporate three California Redwoods State Parks: Prairie Creek, Del Norte Coast, and Jedediah Smith.

No matter how much time I spend in this area, I never tire of walking among the redwoods. They are truly spectacular. A redwood can live up to 2,000 years and grow to over 380 feet tall. It's one thing to crane your neck skyward in an attempt to see the top of these trees, but it's another to comprehend their size at eye level, where they can grow up to twenty-two feet in diameter. The brain, knowing what "normal" trees look like, struggles to grasp the reality of these trees' size. You're dwarfed by your surroundings and in a semi-dark environment because the canopy above blocks out most of the sunlight. It is a foreign experience yet an awe-inspiring one.

SEVERAL YEARS AGO, MY friend Greg and his wife bought a used RV and took a seven-month tour of the West, after which he self-published his trip journal. He titled it "Midlife Crisis on the Road," and it is epic to be sure; one thousand plus pages cannot be described any other way; however, it is packed with interesting and humorous tales of his journey through the American West. Since I was embarking on a similar journey, I not only read it, but I also keep it with me to use to map out things I want to do when I get to a park and some of the things I don't want to do as I navigate RV life. If Greg has already made a mistake, there's no use in me also making it! I did learn a few things not to do from the book, but it turns out that freed me up to make mistakes he never even dreamed of. Basically, I was going where no Greg had gone before…

Two of those things actually happened in rapid succession, the first when I pulled into Trinidad, California, to explore Redwoods National Park.

I checked in at the RV office and then drove to my spot where I began my setup process. I hooked up the power, leveled the RV, and then went back outside to finish setting up. As I walked around the vehicle, I realized I left the keys in the RV ignition, so I turned around to go back inside to get them. When I went to open the door, I discovered that it was locked. Locked! And the keys were inside! Now what? I thought about my options and there were few. I couldn't get to my tools because they were locked away in a side compartment, so I stopped a woman outside her RV and borrowed a screwdriver and tried to jimmy the lock, being careful not to break anything; no need to make things worse than they already were. No luck, the lock didn't budge. The windows were all locked too. What now? Then it came to me, I had a roadside assistance plan. They set me up with a local locksmith who showed up and solved all my problems. Well, RV-related problems, anyway. I may still be deemed crazy in the long run, but that's a completely different issue.

Turns out, when I slammed the door, the lower lock, which is a switch-like mechanism (up is open and down is locked) fell into the locked position. Now I know to break up all my keys so I always have the door key with me. I learned a lesson that day; I just wondered what else I don't know…

A little over a week later I was headed to the Columbia River Gorge area to spend a few days photographing the waterfalls I had seen several years ago. I was on U.S. 26 when my GPS decided things were going too easily and insisted I turn off the highway. I believed in her, I trusted her, and therefore I listened to her! She failed me! I ended up on twenty-nine miles of winding roads and hairpin turns, in a forty-foot RV pulling a car.

Another lesson learned. I always map out my route online ahead of time so I know what roads I should be on and never completely trust that bitch again!

OLYMPIC NATIONAL PARK IS unique among national parks as it has it all: spellbinding coastlines, interior old growth rain forests, and dramatic mountain views. Each area would qualify as a national park in its own right, but here on the Olympic Peninsula in Washington state, they are all protected under one umbrella, ninety-five percent of which is wilderness area.

I was here last in the summer of 2006 as part of my trip down the Pacific Coast Highway from Seattle to San Diego. At that time, I had less than two days in the park and literally "passed through," cruising by a fogged in Lake Crescent, getting a glimpse of Ruby Beach, and stopping at Hurricane Ridge, where I saw nothing but clouds where mountains should have been. This time would be different, and after thirty-six straight hours of rain and nearly drowning in my RV as water streamed in through cracks I didn't know existed, I threw away my plans to build an ark and headed into the park when the sun finally came out! Four days of sunshine allowed me to explore all the differing landscapes of Olympic National Park, mountains, interior, and coastline.

My first attempt to finally see Hurricane Ridge yielded the partly cloudy view, but a few days later I returned under clear blue skies to see it as it was meant to be seen, unobstructed by clouds or fog, and it was magnificent! There are some sites which just inspire or leave you with a feeling of awe. Glacier Point in Yosemite, Denali from the Park Road, any point on the edge of the Grand Canyon, the Grand Tetons, the Rocky Mountains from Trail Ridge Road, and Hurricane Ridge! Words can't express the sight of it and pictures can't fully reveal the beauty of it. It must be seen with one's own eyes. The spectacular range, with Mount Olympus as its centerpiece, stretches out before you as viewed from the visitor center along Hurricane Hill Road; thick snow covers the peaks and glaciers, and even when clouds descend over these mountains, it only makes them grander. I could have spent my whole trip hiking in this area, but the rest of the park called.

As with the mountains and the coastline, the interior regions of Olympic National Park are spectacular and unique. Most of this wilderness area is covered in forest; from temperate rain to subalpine forests and in between, there are gems of all kinds.

On this trip I focused on areas I was unable to see when I was here over ten years ago. This meant hiking in to see Sol Duc Falls, visiting the Hoh Rain Forest to view a truly distinctive ecosystem dominated by mosses and ferns of all kinds, and along the way getting to see Lake Crescent put on a show just before sunset where I was able to catch the clouds and surrounding mountains reflected in the calm waters.

A thin band of sand beaches, towering rock formations jutting out from the sea, and wooded wilderness make up the third ecosystem, the Olympic National Park Coastline. There are numerous points to view and hike, all set to the tranquil sound of the waves washing onto sand or rocky beaches, and the ocean breezes blowing inland giving the air its unmistakable salty smell.

I worked my way to two of these serene spots, Ruby and Rialto Beaches. Ruby Beach is one of the more visited beaches because it is right off of U.S. 101, part of the famous Pacific Coast Highway. Rialto Beach, just north of La Push and the Quileute Indian Reservation, takes a little more planning to get to but is still easy to reach. Once there I began to walk toward one of its more well-known features, Split Rock, when I came upon an obstacle, rushing water flowing into the sea. It was either get wet or turn back. As I looked for my best "get wet" option, a hiker named Gary came along and we surveyed the area in front of us. It was clear Gary knew the landscape and had been here before. He was on a mission; he came out here often not only to explore, but also to pick up all the plastics he could and haul them back to the trash bins where they belonged. After telling him my story, he invited me to tag along and he became my personal tour guide, leading us to a trail up and over the Hole-in-the-Wall toward Cape Johnson, a trail I would have never known existed, leading to a view of the beach I would have never seen.

Gary brought back a garbage bag full of plastics and trash of all kinds, earning my respect and strengthening my belief in mankind; in my book he's a true unsung everyday hero. They do exist!

AFTER A QUICK DRIVE through North Cascades National Park, I headed south to a place I had been looking forward to revisiting since I took a hasty drive through it on a whim as I trekked down the Pacific Coast Highway several years earlier. This place is a cathedral among national parks; I was finally headed back to Yosemite.

Thirty

Cool Green Grass

I picked up my socks and shoes and walked over to sit down on the cool green grass. The sky above me was filled with a warm glow and the air was calm and slightly damp. It was like a dream, actually. I started to put on one of my socks and realized there was an ember slowly burning the cloth. I crushed it between my thumb and forefinger.

Fifteen minutes earlier, I was fast asleep; now I was sitting in the grass watching a fully engulfed RV burn…watching *my* RV burn! I'm sure everyone has at least one moment like this in their life. For most it is probably the birth of a child or the death of a loved one, maybe a cancer diagnosis, the shock of your existence taking a turn you may or may not have expected. This was unreal, something that happens to someone else, something you see on the news.

I began to put the burnt sock on my foot when someone grabbed my shoulder. I turned and there was a man crouched over me, "You may want to get your car out of there."

"FUCK!" I jumped up and, still barefoot, ran past the fire to the rear of the RV where my car was connected to the RV tow bar. It was still attached because I was planning a quick getaway in the morning and I had no need to drive it while I was here.

I pulled on the passenger side tow bar pin but it was jammed. This happened from time to time when the angle of the car put pressure on the connecting mechanisms. Normally I would take the time to work it free, but right now, with flames swirling overhead, that was not an option. I once again pulled out my wad of keys and fumbled with them until I found the key to unlock the padlocks connecting the tow crossbar to the car. I unlocked both locks and yanked the crossbar and tow mechanism off of the pins linking the Subaru to the RV and ran around to the driver's side door, unlocking it before I got there. Once inside I backed, the car away from the still burning wreckage and headed back to the patch of grass where all my worldly possessions now sat.

I would guess just about everyone staying there was out watching the inferno, circled around like it was a scout campfire.

I sat down again and was finally able to put on my socks and shoes, and as the police arrived, I picked up my laptop and go bag, filled with things like a copy of my driver's license, an extra set of glasses, and a few days' worth of my prescriptions, and locked them away in the back of my car.

I walked back to the front of the vehicle and suddenly there was a large pop and fire shot out of the passenger side of the RV like a flamethrower in a World War II movie. It was the propane tank releasing the gas. I would later find out it was actually a good thing the tank was full, because when they are half full or less the tanks tend to explode, throwing shrapnel everywhere. However, it was this release that melted the side of the RV parked next to me. Unfortunately, it belonged to an RV park host couple and, in fact, it was the woman who had checked me into the park just hours before. It was lucky this was an RV "resort" and there was thirty to thirty-five feet between each RV. If this had happened in a regular RV park, some of which are so tightly packed that you can stand between the RVs and touch both, five or six RVs may have burned.

Shortly after the extraordinary pyrotechnics, the La Grande Oregon

Rural Fire Department arrived and went to work to put out the fire. It had only been about twenty minutes since my smoke alarm went off.

People were now coming up to me asking if I needed anything, and someone asked if I knew how the fire started. I mumbled "refrigerator" and they told me about some recalls for issues involving shorts and a fire danger. This was the first I heard about it and it was a little late for me. Another person asked how I got out and I said the smoke alarm woke me up. A voice in the crowd quipped, "I guess we'll all be checking our smoke alarms tonight!"

As the fire department continued to put out the fire, an ENT came over and escorted me to an ambulance where he asked if I thought I needed to go to the hospital. I said no, they checked my vital signs, and released me. I asked for some aspirin, but they said they would have to report it to my insurance and it may cost me more than it was worth in the end, so I said forget it and walked back to the park office.

Someone handed me a bottled water and I sat down in an outdoor hallway next to the office. A minute or two later the fire chief came up to me and asked if I had a gun or any ammo in the RV. Apparently there was popping and they didn't want to be in danger. "It's all right if you do," he said, "we just need to know." I told him no. Apparently the popping was aerosol cans exploding.

I went back out to snap a few pictures on my iPhone and watch the firemen do their work. It's not often you get this close to a scene like this. I might as well take advantage of the opportunity, after all I was paying dearly for the right.

The sky was brightening, and this time it was because the sun would soon be coming up over the horizon. One of the park workers came and got me, saying the Red Cross was here and wanted to talk to me, so we headed back to the office. I had a cup of coffee as the woman briefed me on their available services and she gave me a debit card with 295 dollars on it, along with a quilt sewn by a local church group. At first, I turned the quilt down thinking they could give it to someone else more needy, but then I decided to take it just in case I actually turned out to be that more needy person, and I eventually put it in the car with everything else.

I left the office to go back outside and sat down on the bench to tie my shoe when the fire inspector came by to ask some questions, my personal information, how I think the fire started, etc. While we were there a fireman came by to ask if the RV was gas or diesel. I told him diesel and he said they would have to knock a hole in the fuel tank to drain it. This was another plus, as diesel doesn't ignite or explode. He started to leave and I remembered my safe deposit box, asking him if they could dig it out for me from under the floor on the driver's side of the bedroom. He returned several minutes later with the box in hand. I opened it and found all inside was safe, including my two external computer drives, one for sports and the other for travel images, 400 dollars in cash, and my passport. Without my wallet I really needed that now! I removed the money and passport and walked the safe deposit box out to put it in the car.

The sun was now coming up and I looked on as the firemen were combing through the remains of my RV, making sure there were no hot spots, when an older gentleman came by and asked if I would like some of his old clothes, maybe some jeans and a shirt or two. I declined but it struck me how good everyone had been. From the police and fire department to the park workers and guests, everyone just rallied around to do whatever they could.

Someone came up to me and suggested I go into town to get settled. Eventually I got in my car and drove away. The sun had just risen and it had already been a very, very long day!

I DROVE THE TEN miles into La Grande, Oregon, where I stopped at a McDonalds for breakfast, a sausage, egg and cheese muffin, hash browns and an orange juice. I ate and then sat quietly for just a minute or two knowing I would be spending every waking moment from this point on trying to recover from this disaster. I had lost just about everything and my dream of finishing my goal to visit the last of the fifty-nine national parks this year was probably going to end up being a casualty too.

I snapped out of my funk and called my sisters to let them know what happened. I wanted them to be informed first so they knew what was going on before I called my parents.

There was a Super 8 Hotel right behind the McDonalds, so I checked in, having to call my sister Sue back so she could temporarily put the charge on her credit card until I got some new cards sent to me. I had run right by my wallet when I exited the RV, so I lost my driver's license, credit cards, and even my national park pass.

One thing I did save, and it was at this moment worth its weight in gold, was my laptop. It was the tool I would use to fuel my recovery. All my information was there, everything I would need, and whatever wasn't on my drive I could get off of the internet.

Once I was set up in my room, I immediately called the insurance company for my RV and another for my camera equipment, which I had insured at replacement cost. Next I called my bank and credit card companies, who would send replacement cards within the next few days.

I then took a shower and put my smoky smelling clothes back on and headed into town to a JCPenney's, which I heard was having a going-out-of-business sale. At least I'd finally caught a bit of a break! I stocked up on underwear, socks, shorts, golf shirts, t-shirts, and a belt. I then dropped by the local Walmart where I picked up a small suitcase, a computer bag, and an iPhone charger. If I hadn't already had all this stuff less than twelve hours before, it would have felt like Christmas!

Back at the hotel, I washed several loads of my new clothes so I would have something to wear, and then went out to get a late "dinner" at the local DQ…a large Choco Brownie Extreme Blizzard. Don't judge me, I deserved it!

It was almost nineteen hours since my smoke alarm went off. Exhausted, I went to bed and was amazed at how well I slept.

It was Memorial Day, so I washed some more clothes. There was not much else I could do because everything was closed for the holiday. The fire was the headline in the local newspaper, *The Observer*. The rural fire chief said in the article that the smoke detector, "may have saved his life." Newsflash, it did!

Not wanting to waste any time, I decided to do a quick inventory. I had my car, cell phone, laptop, which I needed to find a power cord for, the information and prescriptions in my go bag, my safe deposit box with passport and cash and…that was it. Everything else was gone. Several of the more painful losses included the shot glasses that belonged to each of my grandfathers, a walking stick carved by Dad, the Georgia Tech season photo passes which sported images I had taken, all the national park brochures I had collected from my travels, my 1997 Arizona Basketball Championship floor section, seat cushions and t-shirts, my 1997 ALTA B2 Championship tennis bag tag, the bell my faithful dog Killer used to paw at when he wanted to go out the back door to play in the yard, and "Froggy," a small stuffed frog I found in a second-hand store in Atlanta which reminded me of the much larger version I had as a kid. Of course, this list would become much longer in the days ahead as my insurance company would ask me for a comprehensive list of everything I lost before they would pay out the 10,000-dollar personal items portion of my policy.

After the laundry was done, I drove back out to the RV park to poke around in the ashes and was able to salvage a few small Christmas decorations that had been packed away in the back of the vehicle. Killer's Christmas stocking, a Dr. Seuss "Rein Dog" ornament with one antler slightly melted, and a singed and smoke-damaged Grinch stuffed animal. I also found the pin from the fire extinguisher and put it on the key ring with the RV keys I still had in my pocket.

I stopped by the RV office to say hi and thanks for all the support. The lady at the desk gave me a box of donations they collected from staff and guests. I broke down and cried at the show of generosity; it was the first time I had felt any emotion at all. Back at the hotel I opened it up and there was a little over 400 dollars, including two 100-dollar bills.

OVER THE NEXT FIVE days, while I was waiting for all my credit cards to arrive, I spent time picking up all the odds and ends I needed, everything from a toothbrush to a power cord for my laptop. The Arizona Department of Transportation said I could drive with my passport and registration until they were able to send me a new license, but they were required to send it to my home address, so my parents would eventually have to forward it to me after it arrived. The Red Cross also vouched for me at the Walmart pharmacy so I could get my prescriptions replaced.

Painful as it was, I also made several calls to cancel RV park reservations including Baker, Nevada, where I was to visit Great Basin National Park, and Lee Vining, California, on the east side of Yosemite National Park; sadly, I wouldn't be making it back to the granite valley this year.

Besides working with the insurance company and picking up the little stuff, my main objective had to be answering the question, "what do I do next?" I had to formulate a plan of attack, otherwise the default would be to head back to Tucson and write this year off as a loss. I had a lot of time to think, so it wasn't long before I came up with an idea. I called my sister Sue to ask if she thought it would be okay to ask her brother-in-law Rene to let me stay a while with him in Denver. Rene and his wife Susan and their kids had stayed with me in Atlanta during the Olympics in 1996, and I had visited them a few years ago when passing through the city on one of my trips. We were well acquainted and my sister said it shouldn't be a problem and I should give them a call.

The idea would be to get to Denver and comb through the many RV sales lots to hopefully find a "new" used RV which fit my needs so I could continue my trip. I knew I wouldn't want to overstay my welcome at Rene's, so I limited myself to spending a maximum thirty days there and if nothing happened, I would go back to Tucson. I called and laid out my plan to Rene and he said they had an apartment in the basement that his son lived in before he moved out; they would be happy to let me use it.

I received all my credit cards and used one to transfer the hotel charges off my sister's card. I had stocked up with everything I needed, at least for the short term, and on my sixth day in La Grande, I took one more trip out to the Grande Hot Springs RV Resort to see the shell of my RV one last time. It was still there with orange traffic cones placed at the front and back. The insurance company would eventually arrange to have it hauled away. It was a sad goodbye and as I stood there, I was flooded with fear thinking about all I still had to get done to make it possible to complete my national parks goal this year. I returned to the hotel and packed up what little I had; tomorrow I would leave for Denver.

ONE WEEK AFTER THE fire I was back on the road. It was bizarre driving away from La Grande with absolutely everything I owned packed in my car. Everything! The two-day trip gave me a lot of time to think, about the tasks I had ahead of me and about life in general. It could've all ended in an RV park in La Grande, Oregon, but it didn't, so all I could do was move forward.

I arrived at Rene and Susan's home in Aurora, a suburb of Denver, and they welcomed me with open arms, letting me know I could stay as long as I needed to, and I should make myself at home. Within the first few days of my arrival, they took me to the Greeley Blues Fest, which was a much-needed diversion and a nice relaxing time. I even bought a t-shirt as I continued the process of restocking my wardrobe.

I SPENT MY DAYS working to get things back on track. I cancelled more RV park stops but optimistically made it a point to keep all reservations more than a month out, including a stay in Sundance, Wyoming, to visit Devils Tower National Monument. If I wasn't on my feet a few days before my planned arrival I would deal with it then.

Most importantly, I needed to deal with the insurance company and get my settlement so I could use the money for a replacement RV. This was generally a good experience although it was now clear that putting 15,000 dollars into additions and improvements on my old RV had been a bad idea since it was hard to prove the additions and I would get nothing for the labor costs. In the end I was granted 65,000 dollars for the RV and 10,000 dollars for personal items plus 15,000 dollars for my photographic equipment on a separate policy. I would use 5,000 dollars to buy the camera equipment I needed going forward, I had no need for everything I used when I was shooting sports, and I would put the remaining 10,000 dollars toward the purchase of a new RV.

I WENT FROM RV lot to RV lot in the greater Denver area only to find out there was nothing available that fit my needs. I left my requirements with every salesperson who would listen to me, often showing them a picture of my burning RV to impress my situation and my name into their minds; at this point I was not above trolling for sympathy. I had to venture sixty miles north of Denver to inject some life into my search. Lazydays RV told me they didn't have anything available but they had just gotten a forty-footer in from Florida which was being worked on and would be up for sale when finished. The salesperson went to her manager and got permission to show it to me using the picture of my flaming RV for the sympathy factor and it worked; the RV from Florida was perfect and had all my requirements but the price was 95,000 dollars, quite a bit above my budget. She said she could hold it for me if I put 1,000 dollars down and I initially balked, but after thinking about it overnight I went back and wrote her the check. This RV was exactly what I wanted, was newer, cleaner, and nicer than my old RV, and it was clear my options were limited since I wasn't seeing anything else on the market in the Denver area.

I signed the papers on my "new" 2008 Fleetwood Discovery exactly thirty days after the fire.

Thirty-One

Finish It!

IT WAS A RELIEF TO BE ON THE ROAD AGAIN. I FELT A SENSE OF normality creeping back into my life for the first time since the fire. Even better, I was on my way to Sundance, Wyoming, to visit Devils Tower National Monument. Somehow, I had pulled it off. I was right where I should be at this moment in time; I was back on the schedule I had created almost a year ago.

I pulled into Sundance and checked in at the RV park where I would spend the next week and began my usual setup. Granted, it was all a little new considering I was learning my way around a different RV, but they don't deviate much when it comes to the design of these things, after all there's only so much you can do with a forty-foot chassis manufactured to roll down the road. In fact, about the only thing truly different between this RV and my old one was the bedroom pullouts were on opposite sides; on the old one it was on the driver's side, while on this one it was on the passenger side.

I completed my setup and stepped back to take a few pictures of my new rig, after which I decided to take one more walk around the vehicle to make sure I had completed all my chores. Driver's side connections had all been made; electric, water, and sewer all done. The tow bar had been retracted in the back and was stowed. Now the passenger side looked…

smack! Forehead, meet the corner of your new bedroom pullout! Damn it! I was so trained to be aware of the bedroom pullout on the driver's side of the old RV, I just forgot things had changed. Now I had blood streaming down my face. It was a gusher!

I retreated to the interior of my RV where I used a towel to apply pressure to the wound, which was in the middle of my forehead, right at the hairline. I sat there feeling stupid and cussing under my breath, how could this be happening? Haven't I had enough drama for a while?

Eventually the bleeding slowed to a trickle, allowing me to get a rather large gauze bandage on it, but I could see the damage was bad enough to convince me someone should at least have a look at it. I stumbled outside and crossed the park to talk to a small group of people relaxing under an awning. I was hardly able to get a word out before one lady said, "are you okay?" I explained my situation and asked if they could direct me to the local clinic or hospital. They told me I was just a few minutes away and they would be glad to drive me, but I declined and headed down the road to the Crook County Memorial Hospital.

The place was empty, which I guess is a good thing, and I had to ring a bell to get a nurse to come to the front desk where I once again told my sad story. She led me to an examination room, laid me down, and after looking at my wound, left to get a doctor. Five or ten minutes later, it's a good thing I wasn't actually dying, a young doctor showed up dressed in jeans and a button-down shirt and took a look at my head. "That's going to take a few stitches," he exclaimed as he walked back out of the room. I was alone again, nice bedside manner.

A short time later both the doctor and the nurse returned and I was prepared for my procedure: clean and disinfect the area, a shot to kill the pain, and a cloth-like paper to cover everything except the area to be worked on.

They both left and after a few minutes the doctor came back, washed up, said I should be deadened, and he went to work. I could feel things going on but luckily the area was sufficiently numbed so I happily just laid there and tried to relax. Then the doctor felt compelled to talk to me. It's just like when you go to the dentist and, with your mouth full of fingers and tools, someone asks you a question. Or, my favorite, I once had a dentist and his assistant discuss what they were going to cook for Thanksgiving dinner; I nearly drowned in my own saliva! So, now the doctor was discussing his personal quest to become a medical professional and he uttered the statement, "I didn't become a surgeon because I just don't have the patience for this kind of stuff." Really dude! The guy had a needle in my forehead and now he felt he had to reveal the reason he's not mentally equipped to do what he was doing! Lovely, but I sensed this was not the time to challenge or even discuss the issue, so I just crossed my fingers and let it go!

A few minutes later I had eight stitches and he was done. I promptly asked him if it was going to leave a scar. He said it would not. "Too bad, I could use the street cred!" I know, I've used this line in the past, but unless there is some doctor information network I don't know about, I'm quite sure he hasn't heard it before; and it actually went over well way out here in Sundance, Wyoming.

EVEN WITH MY DEBILITATING injury, actually it wasn't so much debilitating as it was embarrassing, I pressed on, heading east into South Dakota where my next major stop would be underground at Wind Cave National Park.

In 1903 Wind Cave National Park was named the nation's seventh national park, but its explorers like Alvin McDonald, whose mapping and documenting of their findings led to the cave becoming popular. Wind Cave is unlike any other cave in the world; it has few stalactites or stalagmites but many other minerals and formations. This cave is primarily known for the abundance of rare honeycomb-shaped formations called boxwork. The formation is so rare that ninety-five percent of all boxwork in the world is found here!

The cave sits below the South Dakota prairie, a vast grassland on the edge of the Black Hills Forest. After touring the cave, I went off the "beaten path" to explore the parks' above-ground surroundings on a ninety-plus degree day in hopes of seeing some wildlife. Earlier in the day I had seen a coyote, a few scattered bison, and of course prairie dogs, which are everywhere in this part of the country. I headed out of the park and then back in on the Red Valley Road, an unpaved one-lane park road slicing through the rolling grassland. I guess I wasn't surprised at the lack of wildlife considering the heat, but I still crawled along on the dirt road scanning the prairie for something, anything. I eventually looked in my rearview mirror and saw someone on a four-wheeler. I was dusting him pretty good and I felt bad as I pulled over to let him pass. It was a park ranger and he gave me a thumbs up as he raced by me. I continued on my search and about ten minutes later he came back towards me. I again pulled over and he stopped. I immediately apologized for making him ride in my cloud of dust earlier, but he said it wasn't a problem and explained he had to get to a bison which had gotten himself caught in a park fence. Then he smiled as if he knew what I might be looking for and said, "There's a herd of bison up ahead, about 200 of them, just off the road." Two hundred!?! From what I read there are only about 350 in the entire park! I asked him if I would be able to see them from the road and he said, "oh yeah," and then rode off. I wanted to floor it but didn't and eventually crested a hill where I saw below me the unbelievable scene, a large herd of bison! Amazing! I crept up on them and before I knew it, I was driving amongst them. I pulled over, rolled down the windows and began to take pictures of these magnificent animals. They were all around me; several times I had to inch the car forward when one of the more curious beasts would try to rub up against the car. The herd was grazing and moving ever so slowly, going from patch of grass to patch of grass. There were quite a few calves and they were tended to by their mothers, but the large bulls were the most interesting to observe. Several times I watched one of them find a dirt patch and just collapse into it, rolling over and kicking a cloud of dirt into the air around them to ward off the ever-present flies. I sat there for over an hour until the herd started to move away from the road. It's hard to imagine these incredible creatures once blanketed the West, but sitting among such a large herd gives one hope their numbers will grow in protected areas like this. It was an unbelievable thrill!

THE BLACK HILLS OF South Dakota are dotted with interesting things to see, particularly in the southwest corner of the state. Not far from Wind Cave, there is Jewel Cave National Monument, Custer State Park, and Mount Rushmore National Memorial. I had seen the incredible carvings in the past but could not miss the opportunity to see them again, and this time hike the grounds to get images from different angles. One trail looped its way directly below the mountain and I found myself looking straight up into the nostrils of our four most revered presidents.

I had arrived early to get the morning sunlight on the sculptures but realized I would have to stick around for a while if I wanted to see all the faces in direct sunlight; since Teddy Roosevelt was set back from the others he was in the shadows until around noon. I was incredibly lucky as the skies were amazingly clear. It was one of those "not a cloud in the sky" type of days and the temperatures were moderate, especially for a July day.

So, as I waited for the perfect shot of the presidents, I was able to do some people watching. Most interesting were the people positioning themselves so it would look like they had their head next to their favorite president, or hugging them, or even sticking their finger up George Washington's nose as if they had discovered the wonders of angles and perspective; our forefathers would be proud! However, in the category of most disturbing, there was a young woman who was walking around with a backpack with a curious plastic dome sticking out the back. I worried it was some type of medical device she had to carry but it proved to be much more troubling; it was a cat backpack. She was carrying her cat around with her. This was a future scary cat lady; wait, what am I saying, future? She had perfected "scary cat lady" already!

MY TRUE TARGET IN this target rich section of South Dakota was Badlands National Park. This park is an almost otherworldly experience. The strange peaks and valleys cut into the grassland prairie, extend for miles, and seem desolate and uninhabitable. It is a beautiful yet frustrating place as you could take a million pictures one day and come back the next day and take a million more and not one would resemble any previously taken. The scene constantly changes with the movement of the sun across the sky; shadows lengthen and shrink; clouds influence the strength of the light reaching the ground or create new shadows bent over peaks and filling valleys. Then there are the differing colors and hues of sunrise and sunset, or an occasional rainbow combined with what the rain does to the pigment of the landscape. Photographically frustrating yet incredibly fascinating!

This dry, dusty eroded land looks easier to go around than to cross; however, that doesn't mean it is uninhabitable, at least for animals. In fact, I was surprised at the abundance of wildlife. As with a lot of places out West, prairie dogs were everywhere along with the normally abundant deer and coyote. The burrowing owls were a bit of a surprise, and interestingly enough, they prefer to stand on their dens in broad daylight so they can see any predators in the area. Although they are not easy to locate, this made my effort to find them a little simpler.

I drove through another large herd of bison and this time I was treated to two large bulls butting heads in a battle for herd supremacy; you could feel the power behind each crushing blow as the two animals collided, causing the muscles in their large bodies to ripple from the seismic release of energy. It ended after only a few blows and the challenger backed away leaving the victor triumphantly standing his ground. Unfortunately, that "ground" was in front of my car, and having no interest in being the next challenger, I had to simply wait until he was ready to move on, something he did only when he was good and ready.

I always love going to places where the wildlife is plentiful and it's even more fun when I get surprised by an animal I've never before had the chance to photograph. Here I was stunned by the large number of bighorn sheep. First of all, I didn't expect to see them in the grasslands of the northern Midwest, and second, I was floored by how abundant they were. Over the years I have referred to the bighorn sheep as my "white whale," as I've had no luck photographing them. I saw Dall sheep on the mountainsides of Alaska. I waited for hours on a riverbank in Dinosaur National Monument to no avail. I had a close encounter with a group of bighorn sheep in Colorado National Monument that included only females and young, and when I finally caught a glimpse of several bighorn sheep rams on a hillside in Rocky Mountain National Park, they were spectacular but a long way away, yielding only marginal overly blown-up images of them. Now there they were, all over this park and even at close range. Large groups of them move freely from the rough terrain of the Badlands and into the neighboring tall grassland to feed. And they included a number of mature rams with their trademark sweeping arched horns curling to each side of their head. I stopped to get a picture every time I caught a glimpse of one because I wanted to make sure I got a good shot of these magnificent animals.

As if the energy of the world knew it owed me one for my longtime pursuit of this animal, I was finally presented the perfect opportunity. Driving the park road, I came upon a small traffic jam much like you see for bears in Yellowstone National Park or elk in Rocky Mountain National

Park, only this time there were six mature bighorn sheep rams walking on the side of the road. One of the rams was an exquisite specimen unlike any I had ever seen; he was huge and muscular, and his horns not only curled around the sides of his head, but also flared outward at the tips! This had to be the "king" of the desert bighorn sheep! I rolled down the passenger-side window and frantically snapped pictures from inside my car praying he would not turn away from me before I was able to get a decent shot of him. Then it happened; he walked toward me and stopped in the tall grass directly across from me. He turned his magnificent head straight at me, his dark eyes peering directly into my lens. I couldn't have gotten a better pose if I had somehow been able to position him myself, and I ripped off five or six shots before he turned and walked away. Clearly, I was more impressed with him than he was with me! I had gotten the perfect shot of a mature ram staring me straight in the eyes; my hunting expedition was over and I finally had my prize bighorn sheep ram. However, unlike hunting, after I took my shot, the prize walked away unharmed, yet I still have a trophy image to hang on my wall.

WHEN I'M ON THE road I'm either exploring or working on the images from my last exploration. The idea is to get my images sorted, processed, and out on my website within a week of leaving a park. While I was still in the Badlands area, I received an email in reply to my Wind Cave National Park gallery from Holly and Bruce, a couple I met in Katmai National Park on my Alaska trip. It turned out we were going to be in Theodore Roosevelt National Park at the same time, so we arranged to meet for dinner and then take a drive into the park. It is always great seeing a familiar face on the road and even better when meeting up with folks who share your love of the parks. That day we compared notes about our journeys, hiked out on the Wind Canyon Trail, and watched the sunset on the Little Missouri River.

Established in 1947, Theodore Roosevelt National Park, its badlands cut by the Little Missouri River, was for several years in the 1880s home to future president of the United States, Theodore Roosevelt. Here he developed his conservationist vision leading to his signing of the 1906 Antiquities Act, the subsequent establishment of eighteen national monuments, and along with Congress, five national parks. As president, Roosevelt protected over 230 million acres of land.

While driving through the park I was once again thrilled to see large groups of bison. Millions of them once roamed these prairies before they were hunted to near extinction in the West and eliminated from this region altogether. Since being reintroduced into the park in 1956, the bison herds have flourished. Standoffs between cars and bison are common and always culminate with beast winning over man; the bison only move when they are ready to move. I had one such impasse as I approached a herd while driving through the park. Most of the animals were grazing on one side of the road, but two stragglers straddled the dotted yellow line, not interested in moving to accommodate tourists. I was the first of many to approach the roadblock and stopped about twenty feet from them. They stood their ground, staring straight at me. It was interesting to observe them, for a while, and then it just became tedious. Except for the swinging of their tails, they just didn't move an inch. With the line of cars growing behind me, one brave soul moved forward to slowly pass us all on the left, and as if the bison understood the situation, they suddenly moved into the left lane to block him. This freed up the right lane and gave me and the others behind me the opportunity to safely slide by and continue on our way. As for the brave soul who sacrificed himself for the good of his fellow man, I could see in my side mirror he was stuck behind the "bison block" and just assume he was eventually able to continue on his way.

I witnessed several other similar events, but the most amusing standoff of my visit didn't involve a beefy bison at all; instead, it was due to one of the smaller inhabitants of the park. In an area where the road dissects a rather large prairie dog town, I came upon a scene I couldn't have ever imagined: a standoff between a large Chevy crew cab truck and a lone prairie dog! As soon as I saw what was happening, I came to a halt and pulled out my camera to get a picture, otherwise no one would believe the story. It truly looked like the scene in Beijing's Tiananmen Square so many years ago, where a lone individual stopped a column of advancing Red Army tanks. The prairie dog, sitting on its haunches in the middle of the oncoming lane, had stopped this huge truck in its tracks and was not moving. To his credit the driver sat still, peering over the hood of his vehicle, and waited for about five minutes until the tiny animal eventually decided to cross the road. Once again, animal wins over man! As I approached the Chevy driver, I flagged him down. We stopped and laughed about the encounter and I gave him my card and told him to drop me an email so I could send him a picture of the day when he was vanquished by a lone prairie dog!

I went on several long hikes in the South Unit including the Painted Canyon, but the nicest surprise was my trip into the park wilderness area on the North Petrified Forest Trail. Here I passed through a large field of petrified wood highlighted by a small canyon populated with amazingly preserved ancient tree stumps. Most of the stumps sat upright and looked as if their trunks had only recently been cut from above them. I had seen many petrified forest sites in the past but had never seen anything quite like this. Equally interesting was the company I had on my way to the petrified stump canyon. The park is home to a large number of wild horses, and I had seen several during my visit, including a small herd of eleven from the highway bordering the park. So, I wasn't surprised about a mile into my hike when I saw a large black and white male with what looked like a hoof print in his side, possibly from a territorial battle, grazing not far from the trail. As I got closer, it was clear he knew I was there and he was watching me. Eventually I passed by him, and while still keeping his distance, he began to follow me, paralleling the trail from a distance of no more than fifty yards. He stayed with me and escorted me down the prairie trail until I descended into the valley of the petrified wood. Once in the canyon I noticed the horse remained on the rim and didn't move until I came back up the trail over an hour later; he again followed me to the original point where he first saw me. I can't be sure if he was concerned about me or angered by my being there, but he lost interest as I headed back to the trailhead. Perhaps we were there for virtually the same reason; I was there because I was curious about the area, and he was there because he was curious about me.

⟶

I HEADED EAST ACROSS the great prairie of North Dakota and into Minnesota with its great forests and lakes to visit Voyageurs National Park. Situated along the Canadian border on the southern edge of the Boreal Forest, this wilderness park is known for its history of rich beaver hunting and a short-lived gold rush. Except for the roads to each of the park's three visitor centers, the only way to get around inside the park is by boat.

I took two boat tours which ventured out into the wilderness, to Kettle Falls in Kabetogama Lake and to the islands of Rainy Lake. Both tours wound through some of the 500-plus islands in the park and explored the history of the area as a part of a trade route from Montreal to points west. On the water beautiful views abound, bedrock islands covered in lush vegetation with eagles soaring through the air above them.

In search of some land-based wildlife, I took the Echo Bay Trail, which I was told passed by a small pond with an active beaver den. It was obvious this path was sparsely traveled as the "trail" was mostly tamped down tall grasses, and as I went deeper into the woods, I realized forgetting to use bug spray was going to make this trip a little less enjoyable than it could be. This time instead of mosquitos there were pesky little biting flies. Then I caught a branch hidden in the grass and took a face-first dive to the ground, made more painful because of my effort to protect my camera at all costs. It was the kind of incident where as soon as the toe of my hiking boot contacted the branch, everything seemed to happen in slow motion. I lunged forward, rotating my body to raise my right arm and elevate my camera to keep it out of harm's way, crashing to the ground on my left side. It didn't hurt much then, but I definitely felt it a few days later! On I went until I finally made it to the pond and…splaaaash! I froze; something had jumped into the water about ten feet from me. I had no idea what was transpiring, and then it happened again about forty feet away and I realized it was a beaver slapping its tail on the water. I had heard beavers were very curious animals, so I climbed onto a stump at the edge of the pond and waited. Sure enough, the beaver glided back into the area where it first made a splash, and after looking me over, turned around and tried to scare me off with another splash. It came back several times going through the same process, enough to give me ample opportunities to get some solid images and making this hike worth dealing with all the flies and the pain of my impromptu face plant!

NEXT, I HEADED TO Forest Lake Minnesota, outside of Minneapolis, to spend three days parked at my Aunt Pat and Uncle Merle's house, a two-story log cabin with a basement my uncle built, where their entire family came out to celebrate my visit since it had been a while since I had seen all my cousins. This was my last stop prior to setting sail on Lake Superior, the world's largest freshwater lake, to conquer my final national park.

OVER FOUR-HUNDRED AND FIFTY islands make up the wilderness area of Isle Royale National Park; I only needed to get to one of them.

Park number fifty-nine!

This was a special trip for me as it completed my goal of exploring and photographing all fifty-nine national parks. It wasn't the toughest park to reach but there were some challenges along the way. Months before, I had made a reservation on the Sea Hunter II to travel to the main island on Thursday, August 10; however, when I checked weather reports a few days before my departure it was obvious that day would be windy, rainy, and miserable. I scrambled to make another reservation for three days later on Sunday. There were no refunds, so I would have to eat the $75 ticket for Thursday. Indeed, Thursday turned out to be a terrible day and Sunday was about as nice as it could get, so the gamble paid off. Smooth sailing under blue skies and warm temperatures made the boat ride from Grand Portage Bay an enjoyable experience as opposed to the possibility of ending up at the bottom of Lake Superior with the Edmond Fitzgerald! Okay, maybe that's a little overly dramatic but this lake is known for dragging ships into its depths, just ask Gordon Lightfoot!

Safely onshore in Windigo, I unfurled the "59" banner made for me by my aunt just a few days earlier, and had a fellow survivor, rather passenger, take my picture with the Isle Royal National Park sign, only to realize the "59" didn't show up well in the picture. Later that day, after a few hours of hiking, I went to the visitor center to borrow a magic marker to fill in the numbers. We did a successful reshoot before I departed for the mainland.

I received plenty of congratulations and questions from the rangers and my fellow travelers alike, many of whom were in one way or another pursuing the same goal. And even though the trip back to our starting point in Grand Portage Bay was not as smooth as the earlier trip out to the island, I am happy to report all aboard were accounted for and made it back to the mainland without incident.

Thirty-Two

The Ever-Shifting,
Ever-Changing,
Never-Ending Goal

Just six weeks before I set sail on Lake Superior, standing in the warm glow of my burning RV, the least of my worries was completing my goal of visiting all fifty-nine national parks. I was forced to scramble to put my life back together after losing almost everything; I still had my car, laptop, cell phone, and of course my life. Rebuilding wasn't easy, but it was fueled by the will to complete the goal, and the fight to make it happen on schedule became a driving force.

However, my achievement was fleeting. Less than a year after I "completed" my goal in Isle Royale National Park, Congress created park number sixty, Gateway Arch National Park (2018), followed by Indiana Dunes National Park and White Sands National Park in 2019, and New River Gorge National Park in 2020. Sixty-three was now the new number, and after sitting in Tucson for all of 2020 because of Covid-19, I captured number sixty-three in 2022 and once again all was right with the world.

Eventually another national park will be created, which will move my finish line once again. However, it is not simply the pursuit of the goal that drives me. The exploration, learning, and absorbing nature in each of these spectacular distinct locations is my true reward.

With the goal completed I will continue my travels through the many other national monuments, historical sites, seashores, and so on and so forth…until the day the next new national park is created, and I will set sail to explore it …

Epilogue

What is the author trying to say?

There may be a few who are only reading this to get an explanation of how the title of the book ties into the story. What is the author trying to say and why isn't it obvious?

In sports we sometimes celebrate the contestants even though they are not the eventual winners of their event. Someone who came from behind to almost win, or was the only bright spot on a team that lost badly, like the baseball player who has four hits in four at-bats, including two home runs, and makes a play in the field to prevent the other team from scoring yet another run in a 12 to 2 loss.

Remember "Eddie the Eagle," the ski jumper for Great Britain in the 1988 Winter Olympics? He was never a threat to win anything; in fact, he was so out of his league and so ill prepared most people were fearful he might just kill himself. In subsequent Olympics, rules were put in place to prevent individuals without a certain level of experience and competence from competing.

The same was true of the first Jamaican Bobsled team. They went on a "victory" tour after the Olympics, an example of overmatched athletes performing under extraordinary circumstances and capturing the attention of people all around the world.

In 1964, Ken Johnson pitched a no-hitter for the Houston Colt .45s and lost the game when the other team scored a run because of fielding errors. To this day, he is the only Major League Baseball (MLB) pitcher to lose a complete game nine-inning no-hitter.

Chuck Howley, a Dallas Cowboys linebacker, was selected as the Super Bowl V MVP after intercepting two passes and forcing a fumble in a 16–13 loss to the Baltimore Colts. He is the only player from a losing team to ever receive that honor.

All were spectacular in a losing effort.

So, what does it mean in this context? By definition, life is a losing effort. No matter who you are, how rich you are, how successful you are, you are eventually going to die. Life ends and you cannot avoid it.

When I received my cancer diagnosis, even though it was nowhere near a death sentence, it opened my eyes to my mortality. I realized it was all going to end someday, and more importantly I didn't know when someday would be.

I had unrealized goals and dreams I may not have been able to achieve if I didn't immediately act on them. True, if I lived a long life, I may be able to reach them, but simply living a long life didn't guarantee that either. For instance, my knees were bad and getting worse. If I waited until I was sixty-six to retire, eleven years from my cancer diagnosis, would I be able to hike to a waterfall in Hawaii or to a remote sand dune in Alaska, or to a far-flung freestanding stone arch in Utah?

I didn't know, and that was my dilemma. So, I retired early to set out to do all of those things while I knew I still could. I wanted to do and see all of the remarkable things I was dreaming about before it was too late for me. Using my own standards, I wanted to make my life spectacular so I had no regrets at the end; whether the end was simply not having the will, means, or health to go on, or it was the ultimate end…death.

Author Bio

JERRY F. PILLARELLI WAS born in Chicago, Illinois, served four years in the U.S. Army, graduated from the University of Arizona, and escaped almost thirty years in corporate America by retiring early. He is currently a full-time RVer based in Tucson, Arizona. With a love of photography and the national parks, this book is a compilation of his lifelong experiences as a traveler, whether interesting, poignant, embarrassing or simply too amusing not to share. Although he is an experienced and published sports photographer, and he has designs on developing travel and sports photo books in the future, this is his first written book.

See Jerry's travel and sports images at:
www.pbase.com/jfp_photo

www.ingramcontent.com/pod-product-compliance
Lightning Source LLC
Chambersburg PA
CBHW060520160726
47991CB00001B/117